My
Samsung Galaxy S®5
for Seniors

Elna Tymes

800 East 96th Street,
Indianapolis, Indiana 46240 USA

Real Possibilities

My Samsung Galaxy S®5 for Seniors

ISBN-13: 978-0-7897-5402-8
ISBN-10: 0-7897-5402-9

Library of Congress Control Number: 2014946219

Printed in the United States of America

First Printing: October 2014

Trademarks

All terms mentioned in this book that are known to be trademarks or service marks have been appropriately capitalized. Que Publishing cannot attest to the accuracy of this information. Use of a term in this book should not be regarded as affecting the validity of any trademark or service mark.

Warning and Disclaimer

Every effort has been made to make this book as complete and as accurate as possible, but no warranty or fitness is implied. The information provided is on an "as is" basis. The author, AARP, and the publisher shall have neither liability nor responsibility to any person or entity with respect to any loss or damages arising from the information contained in this book.

Special Sales

For information about buying this title in bulk quantities, or for special sales opportunities (which may include electronic versions; custom cover designs; and content particular to your business, training goals, marketing focus, or branding interests), please contact our corporate sales department at corpsales@pearsoned.com or (800) 382-3419.

For government sales inquiries, please contact governmentsales@pearsoned.com.

For questions about sales outside the U.S., please contact international@pearsoned.com.

Editor-in-Chief
Greg Weigand

Acquisitions Editor
Michelle Newcomb

Development Editor
Charlotte Kughen,
The Wordsmithery LLC

Marketing
Dan Powell

Director, AARP Books
Jodi Lipson

Managing Editor
Kristy Hart

Senior Project Editor
Lori Lyons

Senior Indexer
Cheryl Lenser

Proofreader
Kathy Ruiz

Technical Editor
Patrick McAsey

Editorial Assistant
Cindy Teeters

Cover Designer
Mark Shirar

Compositor
Bronkella
Publishing LLC

Contents at a Glance

Table of Contents

18 Shooting, Editing, and Sharing Photos   397

19 Travel and Driving Applications   437

About the Author

Elna Tymes has been writing books and manuals about computers and software since the late 1960s; she's probably written enough to fill a small storage shed. She and her writing partner, Charles Prael, have written a large number of books about Windows and Apple products, as well as telecommunications and networking software. Elna has been a consultant with a variety of large and small Silicon Valley companies since before the term "Silicon Valley" came into use. She is working on a PhD and is very active in senior policy-making in Santa Clara County, CA.

About AARP and AARP TEK

AARP is a nonprofit, nonpartisan organization, with a membership of nearly 38 million, that helps people turn their goals and dreams into *real possibilities*™, strengthens communities, and fights for the issues that matter most to families such as healthcare, employment and income security, retirement planning, affordable utilities, and protection from financial abuse. Learn more at aarp.org.

The AARP TEK (Technology Education & Knowledge) program aims to accelerate AARP's mission of turning dreams into *real possibilities*™ by providing step-by-step lessons in a variety of formats to accommodate different learning styles, levels of experience, and interests. Expertly guided hands-on workshops delivered in communities nationwide help instill confidence and enrich lives of the 50+ by equipping them with skills for staying connected to the people and passions in their lives. Lessons are taught on touchscreen tablets and smartphones—common tools for connection, education, entertainment, and productivity. For self-paced lessons, videos, articles, and other resources, visit aarptek.org.

Dedication

To Adrian, Charlie, and Kelly: Thanks for dinners, tech support, sufferance, and listening. There is room in my life for flowers, sunshine, and cats.

Acknowledgments

Special thanks to the following:

- Carole Jelen of Waterside Productions, who kept trying to find me a book contract related to seniors

- Steve Schwartz, whose chapters provided the templates for this book and were a godsend

- The well-oiled editorial and production team at Que, including Michelle Newcomb, Todd Brakke, Charlotte Kughen, Patrick McAsey, Lori Lyons, Cheryl Lenser, and Tricia Bronkella

---

For More Advanced Reading

After working through this book, you can find more detailed information about using and configuring the Galaxy S5 in our more advanced title: *My Samsung Galaxy S5* by Steve Schwartz. For example, you can learn how to transfer files between your computer and phone, synchronize your data, convert DVD videos for playback on the phone, use advanced camera and video recording options, power other devices, and troubleshoot any problems that arise.

Note: Most of the individuals pictured throughout this book are the authors themselves, as well as friends and relatives (and sometimes dogs) of the authors. Some names and personal information are fictitious.

We Want to Hear from You!

As the reader of this book, *you* are our most important critic and commentator. We value your opinion and want to know what we're doing right, what we could do better, what areas you'd like to see us publish in, and any other words of wisdom you're willing to pass our way.

We welcome your comments. You can email or write to let us know what you did or didn't like about this book—as well as what we can do to make our books better.

Please note that we cannot help you with technical problems related to the topic of this book.

When you write, please be sure to include this book's title and author as well as your name and email address. We will carefully review your comments and share them with the author and editors who worked on the book.

Email: feedback@quepublishing.com

Mail: Que Publishing
ATTN: Reader Feedback
800 East 96th Street
Indianapolis, IN 46240 USA

Reader Services

Visit our website and register this book at quepublishing.com/register for convenient access to any updates, downloads, or errata that might be available for this book.

Status or Notification Bar

Widget

Google
Search

App
shortcuts

Home screen
page indicator

Primary
shortcuts

In this chapter, you become familiar with the basics of setting up and operating your new phone. Topics include the following:

→ Familiarizing yourself with the phone hardware, operating system, interface, and customization options
→ Adjusting the display and volume
→ Using a headset or headphones

Getting Started

This book is written primarily for people 50 and older and covers the sorts of activities in which they are interested. Because most people 50+ will purchase the Galaxy S5 with options already loaded, this book does not cover some of the hardware options, such as the add-ons that can be purchased separately.

What is a smartphone? If you're upgrading from a cell phone that is five or more years old, you're dealing with a new phone that looks and feels different, has far more features and options, and operates more like a small computer than your previous phone. This book explains how your new Galaxy S5 works, how you can use it, and the kinds of information you can get with it.

Which carrier should you use? When buying a smartphone, you need to pick a telephone carrier, just as you need a carrier for your land-based phone or your previous cell phone. You can use your Galaxy S5 with plans offered by AT&T, Sprint, T-Mobile, Verizon Wireless, U.S. Cellular, and others. You can find a full list at http://www.samsung.com/us/mobile/cell-phones/all-products.

No Signal?

You may have problems receiving a cellular signal with your Galaxy S5 if you live in one of your carrier's "dead zones," such as areas that are remote or simply aren't covered by your carrier. You need to contact your carrier about coverage problems.

About the Galaxy S5

As the latest entrant in Samsung's all-star lineup of Galaxy S-series phones, the Galaxy S5 is a fast, feature-laden smartphone. This chapter discusses the phone hardware, the Android operating system, using the touchscreen, what's on the screen, charging the battery, powering on and off, adjusting the volume, and using a headset with your phone.

In this chapter and Chapter 2, "Understanding the Galaxy S5 Interface," you become familiar with the fundamentals of operating and interacting with your new Android-based phone. In Chapter 3, "Running the Setup Wizard," you learn how to customize your phone to make it look and work the way that you prefer.

The Hardware

To create a powerful, flexible smartphone, Samsung equipped the Galaxy S5 as follows:

- 2.5GHz quad-core processor, running the Android 4.4.2 operating system
- HD 1080-pixel, 432 ppi, 5.1" touchscreen display
- 2.0-megapixel front-facing camera; 16-megapixel rear-facing camera with UHD (4K) and HD video recording
- 16 or 32GB internal memory; 2GB RAM; and support for up to 128GB of additional memory with a microSDHC card
- 4G/LTE network support
- Wi-Fi (802.11 a/b/g/n/ac) on 2.4 or 5 GHz, USB 3.0, Bluetooth 4.0, and NFC connectivity

- GPS (global positioning system)

- Accelerometer, gyro, proximity, compass, barometer, Hall sensor, RGB ambient light, gesture, fingerprint scanner, and heart rate sensor

- IR (infrared) remote; MHL 2.1;

- Dust- and water-resistant

The following are the key hardware components of the Galaxy S5:

Power/Lock button. Press the Power button for a few seconds to turn the phone on or off and to manually darken (lock) or restore the screen.

Volume control. Press this button to raise (top part) or lower (bottom part) the volume of the current activity, such as conducting a call or playing music.

Microphones. Speak into the bottom microphone when participating in a call, giving voice commands, or using the phone's speech-to-text feature. The top microphone is used for noise cancellation and stereo recording.

Earpiece/receiver. When you're not using a headset, call audio is transmitted through this front speaker. The external speaker on the back of the phone is used to play music, ringtones, and other audio.

Headset jack. Port for connecting a compatible 3.5mm wired headset or headphones; enables stereo sound when playing media.

Front-facing camera. Low-resolution (2-megapixel), front-facing camera for taking self-portraits and participating in video chats.

Rear-facing camera. High-resolution (16-megapixel), rear-facing camera for taking pictures and high-definition movies.

Flash. Illuminates photos shot with the rear-facing camera (unless you've disabled it for the shot).

Heart rate sensor. Used in conjunction with health apps (such as S Health) to measure your pulse.

Touchscreen. Touch-sensitive screen; displays information and enables you to interact with the phone.

Recent Apps, Home, and Back keys. Press these hardware keys to interact with the operating system and installed applications. (Note that these keys dim in about 5 seconds if they aren't used.)

USB charger/accessory connector. Enables the phone to be connected with the supplied USB cable to a computer for file transfers or to the charger head and a wall outlet to charge the phone's battery.

Don't Lose Power

Keeping your cell phone charged is important so that its services will be available when you need them. Make sure to use the USB cable or wall plug to keep your phone charged. See the "Charging the Battery" section later in this chapter.

LED status or indicator light. Displays a flashing or steady light to indicate that the phone is performing its startup sequence, denoting notifications (such as newly received email or text messages), or showing the charging status.

Ambient light, proximity, and gesture sensors. The ambient light sensor enables the screen's brightness to adjust to current lighting conditions. The proximity and gesture sensors detect how close an object is to the phone and whether particular gestures are occurring. During calls, the proximity sensor determines when your face is pressed to the screen and locks the keypad to prevent accidental key presses.

Infrared transmitter. With the appropriate apps, enables you to control infrared devices, such as flat-screen televisions, DVRs, and set-top boxes.

Adding a Memory Card

In addition to using the Galaxy S5's built-in memory for storing email, photos, music, apps (applications or programs), and other material, you can purchase a memory card (up to 128GB) to increase the phone's available storage—much like adding a second hard disk to your computer. For information on installing, formatting, or removing a memory card, see the Troubleshooting page at www.samsung.com/us/mobile/cell-phones/SM-G900VZKAVZW.

The Android Operating System and TouchWiz

Just like a computer, every smartphone has an *operating system* that controls virtually every important activity that the phone can perform, as well as the ways in which you interact with it. On the Galaxy S5, the operating system is Android 4.4.2 (KitKat).

Like many of the other major cell phone manufacturers, Samsung has customized the Android operating system to differentiate its phones from those of competitors. Samsung's TouchWiz interface is that operating system customization. Although phones from other manufacturers run Android 4.4.x, TouchWiz ensures that Galaxy S5 phones operate in a similar—but never identical—fashion to those phones.

Note that operating system updates are periodically made available to phones through the carriers, and some carriers might add different apps and programs.

The Touchscreen

The Galaxy S5 is equipped with a screen that is responsive to your touch. In fact, you do a lot of interacting with the phone simply by touching the screen in different ways. Briefly, here are some of the things you can do by touching the screen:

- On the Home screen page, tap the Apps icon, and then tap Settings.

- Because there are now so many icons in Settings, you can elect to display them in several different ways. To change their display, open Settings, tap the menu icon, and choose Grid View, List View, or Tab View.

- Open the Notification panel by dragging the status bar downward, and then tap the Settings icon.

Settings icon

- The top of the Notification panel also contains a row of scrolling icons called Quick Settings. Tap any of these icons to quickly enable or disable important features, such as Wi-Fi and Bluetooth. For information about using and customizing the Quick Settings, see "Respond to Notifications" in Chapter 2.

- You can also tap the icon with the three vertical dots at the right end of the Notification bar—sometimes called the Menu icon.

Smartphone Lingo

Most older telephones and cell phones still have buttons. Typewriters and keyboards have keys. With the arrival of touchscreens, such as on the Galaxy S5, instead of buttons or keys you see icons or symbols that you're supposed to tap. In this book, the terms "button," "key," and "icon" are used interchangeably—and, with few exceptions, they mean the same thing.

The Interface

Much of what you do with the phone involves using its touchscreen. The Home screen consists of a series of customizable pages that you can optionally expand to seven. On these pages, you can place shortcuts to the applications (*apps*) that you use most often, as well as small applications called widgets that run directly on the Home screen. To interact with the touchscreen, you tap app icons to launch programs, flick up or down to scroll through lists, pinch and spread your fingers to change the current magnification, and so on. Chapter 2 explains in detail how to work with the touchscreen interface.

Easy or Standard Mode

If you're new to cell phones (or just to Android phones), you can elect to use a Home screen variant called Easy mode. Although the material in this book is based on Standard mode, you may want to use Easy mode until you're comfortable with the phone. See "Set the Home Screen Mode" in Chapter 2 for instructions and information about switching modes.

Charging the Battery

The Galaxy S5 includes a two-piece wall charger that consists of a special USB 3.0 cable and a charger head. You charge the phone's battery by connecting the assembled wall charger to the phone and a standard wall outlet. It's recommended that you fully charge the phone before its first use.

Note that it isn't necessary to wait until the battery is almost fully discharged before charging. In fact, the phone's manual recommends that you *not* wait because repeatedly letting the battery completely drain can reduce its capability to store a charge.

Connecting to a Computer

The battery also charges while the phone is connected to a computer by the USB cable. The included cable is compatible with computers with USB 3.0 or 2.0 ports. If you have an older computer with USB 2.0 ports, you don't need a different cable to connect the phone to your computer—for any USB task, such as charging the battery or transferring data. See the following steps for instructions on making the phone-to-computer connection.

(1) Gently flip open the USB lever cover on the bottom of the phone.

(2) Plug the end of the USB cable with the single rectangular connector into the right side of the phone opening you just uncovered. Make sure the plug and the receptacle match—the metal on the actual plug is smaller on one side than the other.

(3) Plug the other end of the cable (the one with the symbol like that shown) into the charger head.

(4) Plug the charger head into a wall outlet. The LED indicator light on the front of the phone glows while the phone charges.

(5) When the LED changes color to green, the phone is fully charged. Disconnect the USB cable from the wall outlet and phone. Replace the USB cover on the bottom of the phone.

Charging While the Phone Is On

If you need to complete a call or use apps when the battery is almost drained, you can continue to use the phone while it charges.

Adjusting the Volume

You can press the volume control on the left side of the phone to adjust voice volume during a call, media playback volume, or ringer volume (when you're neither playing media nor participating in a call). The volume control is context-sensitive instead of being a general volume control; in other words, what is affected when you press the control depends on what you're doing.

① To change the volume, press the volume control on the left side of the phone. A context-sensitive control appears.

② To raise or lower the volume, drag the slider. You can also press the top part of the hardware volume control to raise the volume or press the bottom part to lower the volume.

Same Settings, Different Presentation

You can also open Settings to adjust the various volumes. From the Home screen, tap Apps, Settings, Sound, and Volume. Adjust the volume sliders by dragging and tap OK.

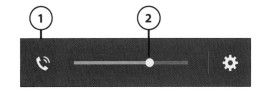

Volume settings

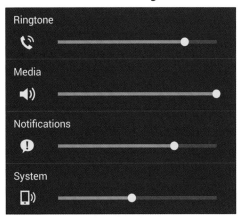

Volume dialog box

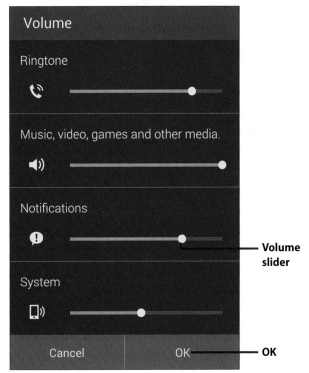

Volume slider

OK

Using a Headset or Headphones

By connecting the headset that's included with the Galaxy S5 (or any other compatible 3.5mm wired headset or headphones), you can improve the phone's audio quality. For example, the Music app supports 5.1 channel sound when a headset is connected. And a wired or a wireless (Bluetooth) headset is great for making hands-free calls.

Connect a Wired Headset or Headphones

(1) Plug any compatible headset or headphones into the jack at the top of the phone.

(2) Adjust the volume for whatever you're currently doing (taking a call, playing media, and so on) using the phone's or the headset's volume control. For instructions on the former, see "Adjusting the Volume," earlier in this chapter.

Learn More About Headsets

For further information about using a headset, see Chapter 4.

>>>Go Further

A COUPLE OF HARDWARE WARNINGS

Get a spare battery. You never know when you're going to be in a situation where your battery's charge is depleted and you aren't near a power source (such as when you're travelling). Spare batteries for the Galaxy S5 are relatively inexpensive—I found some on Amazon.com at a price of three for $20—and they're easy to replace. On the back of the Galaxy S5, find the small indentation on the upper left between the back cover and the phone, and then use a fingernail to pry off the back. Lift the bottom of the battery and replace it with the new one. Then pop the back in place again.

Ensure that the SIM card lock is off. The Subscriber Identity Module (SIM) card is a small square item underneath the battery, used to back up your Contacts records. After you lift off the battery, you can see the white edge of the SIM card. Printed below it are the words "microSD SIM." If you have accidentally typed the wrong password 10 times, your Galaxy S5 prompts you to enter a PUK code to unlock it. Call your Verizon office in order to get the PUK number.

If you can't do that, you can remove and re-insert the SIM card by gently pressing it into its slot. If it doesn't pop out, attach a small piece of adhesive tape to the bottom part of the SIM card and gently pull out the card. To re-insert the card, slide it into the slot—notch first, gold contacts down—until you hear it click into place. Then replace the battery and the back cover of the phone. This should unlock the SIM card.

You will want to confirm that the SIM card lock is off by tapping the Settings icon, scrolling down to the Personal section, tapping Security, and checking the Set Up SIM Card Lock section to confirm that the SIM card lock is off.

For more specific instructions on setting various kinds of security options, please see Chapter 14, "Securing Your Cell Phone."

Recorded text

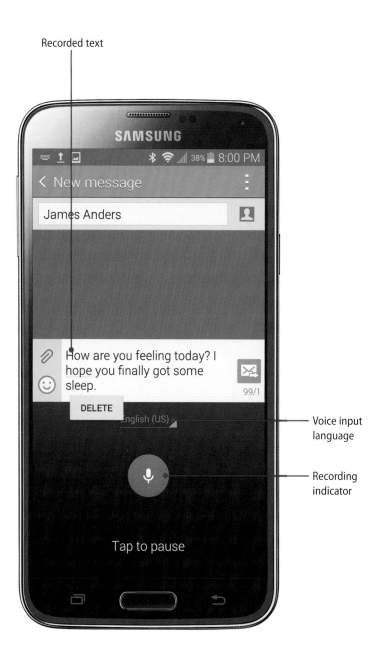

Voice input language

Recording indicator

In this chapter, you become familiar with the Samsung Galaxy S5 interface and how to interact with it. Topics include the following:

→ Understanding the Home screen and its components
→ Working with the Notification bar
→ Using the three hardware icons below the touchscreen
→ Tapping and interacting with icons and other touchscreen elements
→ Using the onscreen keyboard and voice input to enter and edit text
→ Searching for material on the phone

Understanding the Galaxy S5 Interface

The Galaxy S5 has a touch-sensitive screen (or *touchscreen*) that can detect location, pressure, and motion on its surface. The system determines how the phone and its apps react to various touches. Even if you've previously owned an Android phone or another touch-sensitive device, such as an iPod touch or a tablet, you need to be familiar with the information in this chapter. Read on for the essential methods of interacting with the touchscreen and the hardware keys below the screen, techniques for entering and editing text, and methods of conducting searches for material on the phone.

The Home Screen

Go to the Home Screen by pushing the Home button once or twice if necessary after you turn on the power to your Galaxy S5. The Home screen is Command Central for your phone. You launch *apps* from this screen, view the latest information presented on widgets (such as the local weather from AccuWeather.com), and initiate phone calls and messaging sessions.

The important parts of the Home screen include the status or Notification bar, the main area (equivalent to a PC or Mac desktop), Home screen indicator, and icons for five primary shortcuts.

The Status or Notification Bar

The status or Notification bar at the top of the screen serves two functions. First, icons and other information on the right side of the bar show the active communication features (such as Wi-Fi, 4G, Bluetooth, and GPS) and display status information (such as the current battery charge and Wi-Fi signal strength). Second, the left side of the bar displays notification icons for important events, such as new email, new text messages, missed calls, and downloaded or uploaded items.

Although it might be tempting to do so, you can't interact with the bar; tapping its icons does nothing. To change the active features or respond to notifications, use the Notification panel.

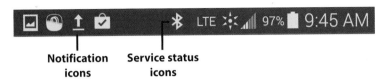

Notification   Service status
icons   icons

Respond to Notifications

When new notifications appear in the Notification bar announcing received email, text messages, software updates, and the like, you can display the Notification panel and optionally respond to or clear the notifications.

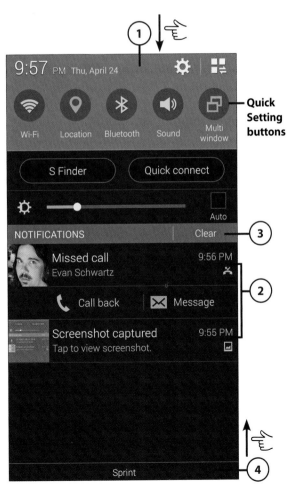

(1) Open the Notification panel on the Home screen or within most apps by touching the status bar and dragging downward.

(2) Tap a notification to respond to or interact with it. For example, tapping a New Email notification launches Email and displays the Inbox. When you respond to a notification, it's removed from the Notification panel.

(3) To remove a notification without responding to it, drag it off the screen to the left or right. To simultaneously remove *all* notifications, tap the Clear button.

(4) To close the Notification panel, touch the gray bar or carrier designation at the bottom of the screen and drag upward. Pressing the Back key also closes the panel.

>>>Go Further

QUICK SETTING BUTTONS

At the top of the Notification panel is a horizontally scrolling string of icons called *Quick Setting buttons*. By tapping these icons, you can quickly enable or disable system features, such as Bluetooth, GPS, or Wi-Fi. When a feature is enabled, its icon is bright green. Swipe left or right to scroll through the icons until you find the one you need, and then tap the icon to toggle the feature's state. If you need to *configure* a feature (connecting to a new Wi-Fi network, for example), press and hold its Quick Setting button to open its section in Settings. To display all the icons as an array, tap the grid icon.

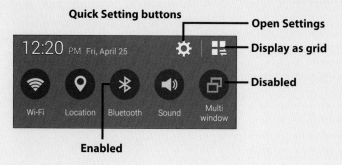

Main Area

The Home screen is yours to embellish as you like. As you can see, you can place widgets and shortcuts wherever you want, as well as choose a custom background (*wallpaper*) for it, as explained in Chapter 13, "Customizing Your Screen."

— Widgets

— Wallpaper

— Folder

— App shortcuts

— My Magazine

— Active Home
screen page

— Main Home
screen page

Extended Home Screen

The Home screen can consist of up to seven different screens or pages, each represented by a Home screen indicator—plus square dots for other pages. As with the main Home screen page, you can add different widgets and shortcuts to each page. To get from one page to another, do any of the following:

- Press the Home key to go directly to the main Home screen page (indicated by the house icon).

- Tap the Home screen indicator of the page that you want to view.
- Swipe left or right to move to the desired page.

- Drag a Home screen indicator to the left or right to see a visual and numeric representation of each Home screen page.

Dragging an indicator

Home screen
page number

Other Screen Indicators

The indicator dots in Apps and Widgets work in the same manner as they do on the Home screen pages. Each dot represents a screen or page of icons. The lit dot indicates the screen or page that you're viewing.

>>>Go Further

EASY MODE

To make it easier for new smartphone (or Android smartphone) users to become comfortable with their Galaxy S5, the Home screen can be changed from Standard mode (which is the focus of this book) to the simpler Easy mode. Easy mode provides

- Three simple Home screen layouts with larger icons and text
- Large, easy-to-read text in important apps, such as Contacts, Calendar, and Phone
- Fixed shortcuts to 12 essential apps and the option to add 3 more of your choosing
- Three fixed widgets (time, date, and temperature)
- Access to additional apps as a scrolling alphabetical list

Main Home screen (Easy mode)

Set the Home Screen Mode

You can switch between Standard and Easy mode whenever you like. Customizations that you've made to the Home screen pages in either mode are restored when you return to that mode.

1. On the Home screen, tap the Apps icon, and then tap Settings.

2. In the Personalize section of Settings, tap Easy Mode.

3. Select Easy Mode, select up to 12 important apps that you want to display as Home screen shortcuts, and then tap Done.

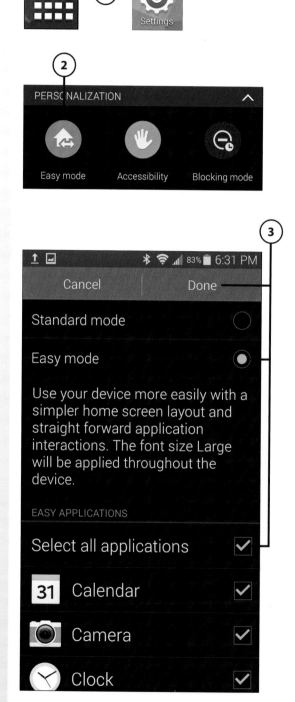

4 On the first Home screen page, you can add contact icons for people that you frequently call or text. Tap a placeholder, and select a person from Contacts or create a new record from scratch. To later call or text the person, tap his or her icon.

5 To add or edit your Home screen app shortcuts, do either of the following:

- *Adding app shortcuts.* You can add app shortcuts to the second or third Home screen page—as long as there are empty spots marked with plus (+) placeholders. Tap a placeholder and select an app from the list of all installed apps.

- *Removing app shortcuts.* Display the Home screen page from which you want to remove one or more app shortcuts, tap the three dots in the upper-right corner, and choose Edit. To remove an app shortcut, tap its icon. (App shortcuts that can be removed are marked with a minus (–) symbol.)

Restoring Standard Mode

If you later decide that you're ready to try Standard mode, tap the Easy Settings icon (or open Settings by another means). Tap the Easy Mode icon, select Standard Mode, and tap Done.

Adding an app

Removing an app

>>>Go Further

KIDS MODE

In addition to Standard and Easy modes, the Galaxy S5 has yet another mode. When you want to entrust your $650 smartphone to a young child or grandchild, you can enable Kids Mode. To install Kids Mode, add the Kids Mode widget to any Home screen page (see "Adding Shortcuts and Widgets" in Chapter 13), tap the widget, and follow the instructions. To later enable Kids Mode or exit from it, you must enter a PIN. Be sure to remember the PIN or write it down and store it in a safe place.

Managing Passwords

Having trouble remembering all those passwords? Some people keep track of their passwords in a separate file on their computer. The file lists the device, directory, password, and the date it was set. If you change a password, you have to remember to change the listing in your password file. But at least it's there when you forget it.

Primary and Other App Shortcuts

Beneath the indicator dots on every Home screen page are icons for Phone, Contacts, Messages, Internet (or Chrome), and Apps. These are known as the *primary shortcuts*. With the exception of the Apps shortcut, you can remove, reorder, or replace the first four. If, for example, you seldom use Messages, you can replace its shortcut with one for Email, Settings, or another app that you constantly use, such as Angry Birds or Facebook. See "Repositioning and Removing Home Screen Items" in Chapter 13 for instructions.

Depending on your carrier, you may see additional app shortcuts above the indicator dots on some Home screen pages. Like the primary shortcuts—as well as other shortcuts that you add to any Home screen page—you can freely remove, reorder, or replace these shortcuts.

Primary shortcuts

Using the Icons

There are three hardware icons located directly below the touchscreen but invisible until you touch the screen: Recent Apps on the left, Home in the middle, and Back on the right. When pressed, each key performs a function related to the operating system (when you're viewing the Home screen) or the app you're currently using.

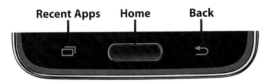

Recent Apps Key

When you press the Recent Apps key, a list of recently run and active apps appears. Tap any app thumbnail picture to launch or switch to that app. To remove an app from the list, swipe it horizontally off-screen. To remove all items from the list, tap the Clear All icon. Tap the Task Manager icon if you want to force stop one or more running apps.

Recent Apps

Task Manager   Clear All

The Missing Menu Key

In previous iterations of the Galaxy S, the first hardware key was the Menu key. To display an app or Home screen's menu on the Galaxy S5 (if there is one), tap the three stacked dots—frequently found in the upper-right corner of the screen. This is the icon denoting an Android menu. (Note that you can also use the Recent Apps key to open certain menus by pressing and holding the key.)

Home Key

The Home key has multiple functions, depending on whether you're on the Home screen or using an app. You can also use it in combination with the Power button to take screen shots (as described shortly).

Within an app. Press the Home key to exit the app and return to the most recently viewed Home screen page.

On the Home screen. When you press the Home key while viewing any Home screen page, it displays the main Home screen page—the one marked with the house icon. If you quickly double-press the Home key, S Voice is activated (see Chapter 9, "Using Voice Services," for information about using S Voice). Finally, with some carriers, pressing and holding the Home key launches a Google app, such as Google Now.

Within an app or on the Home screen. If you simultaneously press and hold the Home button and Power button, the phone performs a screen capture, creating a graphic image of the screen. All captures are saved in the Screenshots folder and can be viewed in Gallery. You can also perform a screen capture by dragging the side of your hand across the screen. With either method, you might have to wait a second or two until you hear the click (like a shutter closing) or until the border flashes briefly.

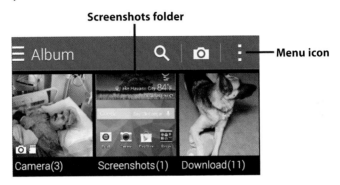

Screenshots folder

Menu icon

Back Key

You use the Back key within apps to return to the previous screen or—if on the app's initial screen—to exit to the Home screen.

Within an app. Press the Back key to return to the previous screen. If you press it on the app's initial screen, you exit the app and return to the most recently viewed Home screen page.

Within Internet and Chrome. Press Back to display the previous web page. The Back key has the same function as pressing Backspace (Windows) or Delete (Mac) when using a web browser.

Within a dialog box or an options menu. Similar to pressing the Escape key in many computer programs, you can press Back to exit a dialog box or options menu without making a choice.

When typing. Press Back to dismiss the onscreen keyboard.

Within the Notification panel. Press Back to close the panel.

Interacting with the Touchscreen

Your phone has a touch-sensitive screen that you interact with by tapping, touching, and making other motions with your fingers or hand. In addition, within many apps, the phone can optionally recognize and respond to the angle at which it's being held or its proximity to nearby objects.

Using Your Fingers

You can interact with the touchscreen by doing any of the following:

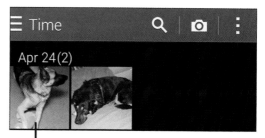

Tap a thumbnail to view a photo (Gallery)

- *Tap.* To launch an app, open a document, choose a menu command, select an item in a list, activate an icon, or type characters on the onscreen keyboard, tap the item lightly with your fingertip. (A tap is equivalent to a mouse click on a computer.)

- *Touch and hold, press and hold, or long-press.* You can interact with some items by touching and holding them. The result depends on the particular item or active app. For example, you can use touch and hold to move or delete a Home screen item, select a word in a text message that you're composing, or select an item in a list. Long-pressing a few items, such as a link on a web page, causes a contextual menu to appear.

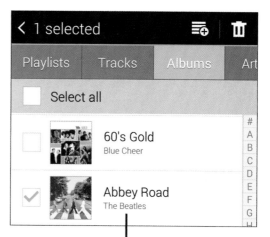

Touch and hold an album in
Music to select the album

- *Flick.* Scroll up or down through a lengthy menu, a vertical list of items (such as a message list in Email), or a long web page by making light, quick vertical strokes, such as flicking a crumb from the table.

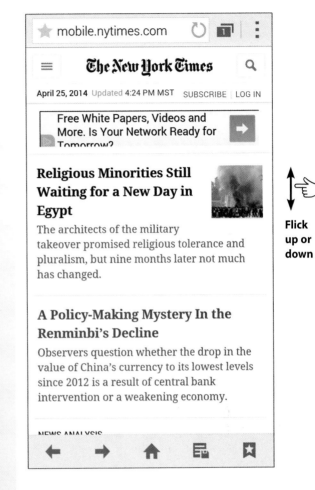

Flick up or down

- *Swipe.* A swipe is the horizontal equivalent of a flick. Swipe to flip through images in a Gallery folder, view different Home screen pages, or move through the Apps and Widgets screen pages.

- *Drag.* To move an item (such as a widget or app icon on the Home screen), press and hold the item, and then drag. Don't release it until it's in the desired position—on the current screen page or a different one.

- *Spread/pinch.* To zoom in or out (increasing or decreasing the magnification) when viewing a photo or web page, place two fingers on the screen and spread them apart or pinch them together, respectively.

Try a Double-Tap

In certain apps (Gallery, Internet, and Chrome, for example), you can also double-tap the screen to zoom in or out. Spreading and pinching, however, provides more precise control over the amount of magnification.

Current image

Swipe left or right
(Gallery)

Drag a Home screen item to change its position

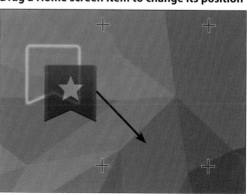

It's Not All Good

Inconsistent Touch and Hold Behavior

In most—*but not all*—Galaxy S5 core apps, touching and holding (also known as long-pressing) the same item types now causes the pressed item to be selected, allowing you to select additional items within the list so you can simultaneously move or delete them all, for instance. Long-pressing is now a shortcut to choosing the Select command from the app's menu, while marking the pressed item as your first selection.

In addition to causing you to make additional, less convenient taps to perform an action, touch and hold behavior is now inconsistent between apps. Sometimes it results in selecting the item, whereas a contextual menu appears in other apps. You'll have to experiment to see which behavior occurs in which situations.

Rotating the Screen

In many apps, you can rotate the screen to change from portrait to landscape orientation and vice versa. It's extremely useful when viewing photos in Gallery, when reading web pages, and when using the onscreen keyboard, for example.

Portrait **Landscape**

When screen rotation is enabled—its default state—the Galaxy S5 automatically rotates the screen when you rotate the phone. To enable or disable Screen Rotation, tap its button in the Quick Setting buttons or in Settings, Display.

>>>*Go Further*

USING MOTIONS AND GESTURES

In addition to tapping, flicking, swiping, and pinching, you can perform certain activities using other actions. For example, when Motions and Gestures Settings are enabled, tilting the phone or waving your hand over it are treated as commands. After mastering the basics of controlling the phone and apps via touch, you should explore motion, air-based, and other options in Settings (see "Using Motions and Gestures," "Enabling Air View," and "One-Handed Operation" in Chapter 5, "Using the Keys and Gestures") and decide which ones, if any, you find helpful and want to enable.

Entering Text

In addition to simply viewing and listening to content on your phone, much of what you do involves entering text. You can enter text by using the onscreen keyboard or by speaking into the phone.

Using the onscreen keyboard requires only that you tap letter, number, and punctuation keys as you would on a computer keyboard or typewriter.

Keyboard Variations

Depending on the current app, you may notice some minor differences among the keyboards. For example, the Internet app's keyboard has additional keys in its bottom row that make it easier to type URLs.

Use the Keyboard: Tapping

(1) Tap to select a text field or box, such as the Internet address box, a password field, or the message area of a text message. The onscreen keyboard appears. A blinking text insertion mark shows where the next typed character will appear.

(2) Tap keys to type.

Entering Non-Alphabetic Characters

Tap the SYM key. The key above it is now labeled 1/2, and the layout displays numbers, currency symbols, and common punctuation. Tap this key (1/2) to cycle to the symbol (2/2) layout. To return to the alphabetic layout, tap the ABC key.

(3) To dismiss or hide the keyboard, perform the action necessary to complete your typing (such as tapping Send) or press the Back key. To make the keyboard reappear after pressing Back, tap in the text box or field again.

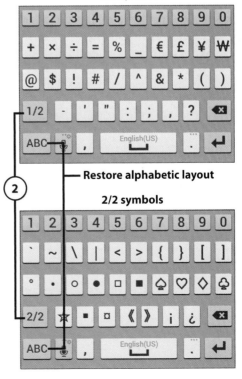

Capitalization

When you begin entering text into a field or are starting a new sentence, the first character is typically capitalized automatically. Subsequent capitalization is determined by the state of the Shift key. Tap the Shift key to toggle it among its three states: lowercase, capitalize next letter only, and capitalize all letters.

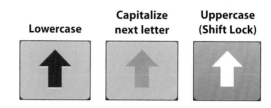

| | Capitalize | Uppercase |
| Lowercase | next letter | (Shift Lock) |

>>>Go Further

TYPING TIPS

Although the basics of typing are straightforward, the following tips can help you fine-tune this sometimes difficult process.

- *Try landscape mode.* To use a larger version of the keyboard, simply rotate the phone to land-scape orientation. (For this to work, the phone's auto-rotate feature must be enabled. Open Settings, tap Display, and ensure that Rotate Screen is enabled. Unless you've changed the default Quick Setting buttons, you can enable or disable Rotate Screen there, too.)

Landscape keyboard (Internet)

- *Multiple languages.* When typing in Samsung Keyboard mode, the active language is shown on the spacebar. If you have more than one language enabled, swipe across the spacebar to switch languages.

- *Change the input method.* The phone supports typed and voice input (Google Voice Typing). To switch input methods while entering text, open the Notification panel, tap Choose Input Method, and select an alternative method in the dialog box that appears.

Current input method —

- *Explore the Language and Input settings.* By tapping the settings icons in Settings, Personal, Language and Input, you can configure each of the input methods. In the Samsung Keyboard settings, for instance, you can specify whether to display predictive text and enable the insertion of boilerplate text (My Shortcuts) when you long-press an assigned number key. By tapping Default, you can change the default input method. You can view onscreen help for typing by tapping the Samsung Keyboard settings icon, opening the menu, and choosing Help.

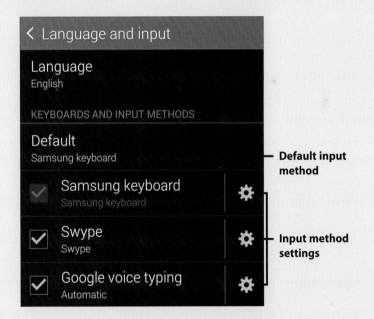

- *Change the language.* If English isn't your native or preferred input language, you can select a different one. In the Language and Input settings, tap the Samsung Keyboard settings icon, followed by Select Input Languages. Select a language from the Downloaded Languages list. If the desired language isn't shown, tap the menu icon, choose Update List, and then download the desired language by tapping its name in the Available Languages list.

- *Use Predictive Text*. As you type or trace, the phone presents a scrolling list of suggestions (predictive text) for the word it thinks you're typing. If you see the correct one, tap it to use it as a replacement for the current word. You can also tap the arrow icon—when it's presented—to view additional replacement words.

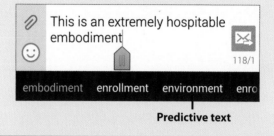

Predictive text

Fine-Tuning Predictive Text

You can improve the predictive text suggestions by allowing your Galaxy S5 to study what you type in Facebook, Gmail, Twitter, Messages, and Contacts. In Settings, Language and Input, tap Predictive Text and review the options. If you don't find predictive text helpful, you can disable it by dragging its slider to the Off position.

- *Character preview*. You can type secondary characters (such as the symbols above some letter keys) without leaving the main alphabetic keyboard. If you press and hold any key, its secondary characters, if any, appear. If there's only one secondary character, release the key to insert the character into your text. Pressing and holding other keys results in a pop-up menu of characters, numbers, and/or symbols for the key. Slide your fingertip onto the one that you want to insert or do nothing to insert the currently highlighted character.

Secondary characters for t

Press and hold

Use Voice Input

If you hate typing, or you're abysmal at using the onscreen keyboard and are unwilling to take the time to master it, voice input (also called *voice typing*) might be more to your liking. You speak or dictate what you want to type, and it's translated into text.

(1) To enable voice input, press and hold the multi-mode key and select voice input—the microphone. If the key already displays the microphone, simply tap it.

Switch Using the Notification Panel

When the keyboard is visible, you can also switch input methods by opening the Notification panel, tapping Choose Input Method, and selecting Google Voice Typing in the dialog box that appears.

(2) A recording indicator appears. Speak the text, saying punctuation (such as comma, period, question mark, and exclamation point) where it's needed. The text is transcribed as you speak.

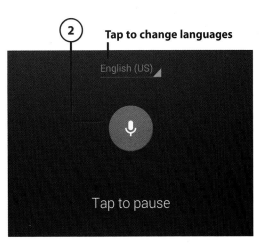

Voice input

Tap to change languages

(3) When you finish recording, tap the recording icon and then tap the keyboard icon. (After a sufficiently long pause, recording ends automatically.)

Poor Results
If a transcription is unacceptable, you can reject it by tapping Delete.

(4) Any instance of questionable transcription is marked with a faint gray underline. If the underlined text is incorrect, tap it to review possible corrections. You can select a replacement from the suggestions, tap Delete to remove the entire word or text phrase, or dismiss the suggestions by pressing the Back key and then manually edit the text.

Getting Better All the Time
Voice input is great for converting straightforward, common speech to text and every update includes improvements. However, the need for some after-the-fact editing isn't unusual. To determine if voice input will work for you, test it. Say some normal text and try reading a few sentences from a book or magazine. Whether it's a winner for you will be determined by how accurate it is and the amount of cleanup you typically need to do.

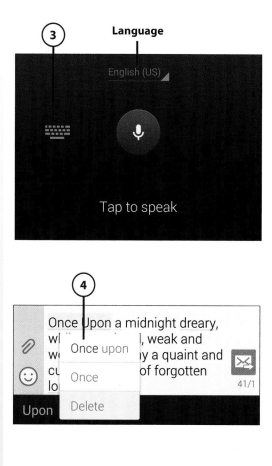

>>>*Go Further*

CHANGE THE VOICE INPUT LANGUAGE

You can configure the keyboard for other languages, and you can configure Voice Input to type in languages other than English.

1. Tap the language indicator above the recording icon and select a language. If the desired language isn't shown, go to Step 2.

2. Choose Add More Languages.

3. Remove the check mark from Automatic, select the language(s), and press the Back key to return to Step 1. (If you ever want to revert to the original language for voice input, check Automatic again.)

Editing Text

Typos, incorrect capitalization, missing punctuation, and bad guesses in voice input are common in entered text. Instead of just tapping Send and hoping your message recipient will *know* what you mean, you can edit the text by doing any of the following:

- At the blinking text insertion mark, you can type or paste new text or press the Delete key to delete the character to the left.

- To reposition the text insertion mark for editing, tap in the text. If the text insertion mark isn't positioned correctly, carefully drag the blue marker to the desired spot.

- To select a single word for deletion or replacement, double-tap or long-press the word. To delete it, tap the Delete key; to replace it, type over it.

- To select a specific text string (a word, sentence, or paragraph, for instance), start by selecting (or double-tapping) a word at the beginning or end of the text that you want to select. Drag the selection handles to highlight the desired text. Then select a command from the pop-up menu above the selection (to cut or copy it to the Clipboard, for example), press the Delete key, or overtype the selected text. (Note that the command icons, their appearance, and whether they're labeled can vary from one app to another. If there are more icons than can be shown at once, they scroll horizontally.)

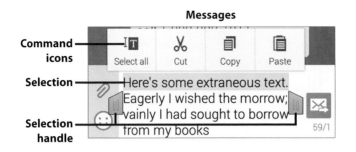

- To paste the most recently copied or cut text into a text box, set the text insertion mark, tap the blue marker, and then tap Paste in the pop-up that appears.

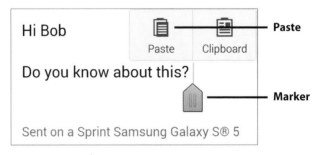

- When entering and editing text in Email (but not Gmail), you can tap icons on the formatting toolbar above the message area to insert images, apply character and paragraph formatting, or undo the most recent change.

Copying Text from a Web Page

You can also use editing techniques to copy text from a web page. Press to select the first word, and then drag the handles to select the material to copy. In the toolbar that appears, tap Copy to copy the material so that you can paste it elsewhere or tap Share Via to copy the material directly into a new email, text message, or Google+ post, for example.

Selection

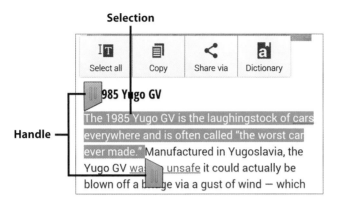

Handle

Searching for Items on the Phone

Rather than relying on your memory or a lengthy series of taps to find buried Settings, launch apps, open contact records, and so on, you can use the Galaxy S5 search features to quickly locate material of interest.

Use S Finder

As you type, paste, or speak a search word or phrase, S Finder displays a scrolling list of potential matches arranged by category, such as email messages, contacts, phone calls, and Settings names or sections. Matches can be the names of items or text contained somewhere within the item—in a text message, email, or Word document, for example. And if you know even part of an app's name, S Finder can double as a program launcher.

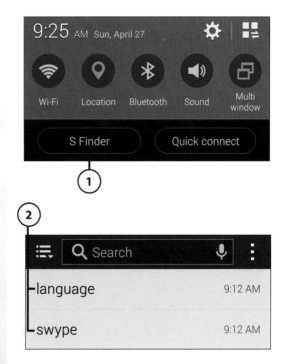

1. Pull down the Notification panel and tap the four squares in the upper right; then tap the S Finder icon.

2. A scrolling list of recent searches is shown. To repeat a search, tap its entry and go to Step 4; otherwise, continue with Step 3.

(**3**) Enter a search term or phrase in the text box. As you type, a suggestion list appears. Tap one of the suggestions or continue typing.

Precision Counts

Potential matches must include your search term or phrase (or a simple variation of it). Searching for *privacy*, for example, will not consider references to the lock screen to be matches—unless *privacy* is used as a word in the description or help text.

(**4**) Scroll through the various match categories until you find the correct item, and then tap its entry.

Search the Web

To perform a web search for the term or phrase, scroll to the Web Search section of matches and tap the Search icon.

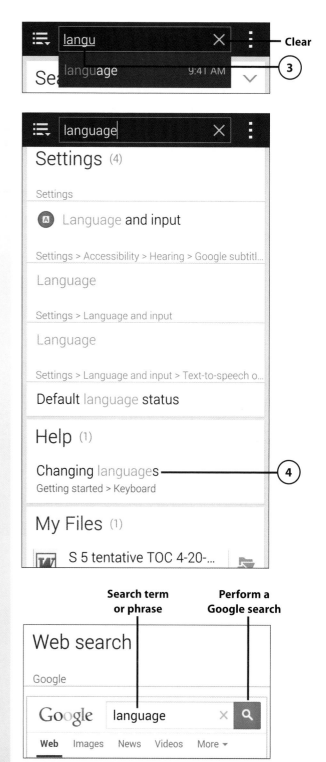

Clear

Search term or phrase

Perform a Google search

Search in Settings

Settings categories and options seem to grow exponentially with every major Android release. When you're searching for a particular setting or option, you can restrict the search to Settings only.

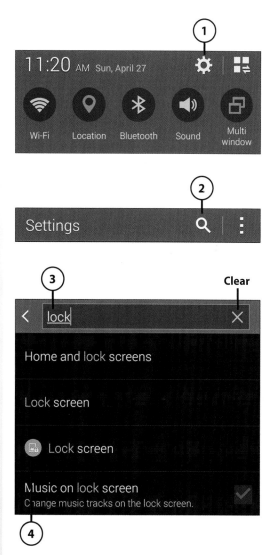

1. Open Settings by tapping its icon in the Notification panel or using one of the other methods discussed in Chapter 1.

2. Type the search icon at the top of the opening Settings screen.

3. Enter your Settings search term or phrase in the text box. Matches are displayed as you type. (Only Settings or options that contain the search term/phrase in their name or description are considered matches.)

4. When you see the desired setting or option, tap its entry to go directly to that Settings screen.

Starting Over

If a search fails, you can try again by tapping the Clear icon (X) and entering new search text.

In this chapter, you learn how to set up your Samsung Galaxy S5. Topics include the following:

→ Running the Setup Wizard
→ Darkening and restoring the display
→ Setting a screen timeout interval

Running the Setup Wizard

The first time the phone is turned on (and after a Factory Data Reset), the setup wizard automatically launches and displays its Welcome screen. You can respond to its prompts to set up some essential services, such as creating or signing in to a Google account and Samsung account, configuring your Wi-Fi settings, and adding an email account.

Now or Later?

It doesn't matter whether you use the setup wizard to immediately set up the phone or configure it manually when it's more convenient. For instance, if a salesperson sells you the phone and runs the wizard, you won't be able to select your particular Wi-Fi network until you go back home or to work. All important options in the wizard can be manually reconfigured whenever—and as often as—you like.

Run the Setup Wizard

The pages referenced in this task explain how to establish these basic settings manually—without the wizard's assistance.

(1) On the wizard's opening screen, select a default language. (See the "Changing the Default Language" in Chapter 10 to manually choose a new default language.)

(2) *Optional*: If you have hearing, vision, or dexterity issues, tap Accessibility to review or modify Accessibility settings, such as the size of the display font. To manually configure these settings, tap Settings, Accessibility.

(3) Tap Start (on the opening screen) or Next (on the Accessibility screen) to continue.

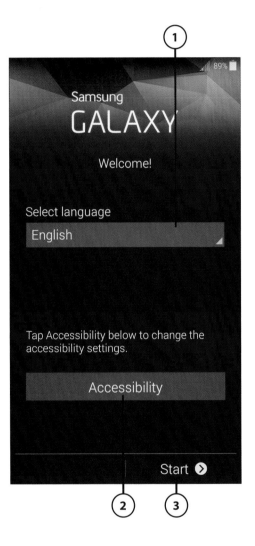

(4) If you have a Wi-Fi (wireless) home or business network, ensure that the Wi-Fi slider is On, select the network's name, enter your network password (if any), and tap Connect. Tap Next to continue. (See "Connect to a New Wi-Fi Network," in Chapter 8, for details.)

Where's My Network?

If your wireless network doesn't appear in the list, ensure that it's active (by checking your router or modem's lights) and that you're reasonably close to it. Tap Scan to refresh the list of nearby networks.

(5) Read the End User License Agreement (EULA), and tap the I Understand… box.

(6) Read the Consent to Provide Diagnostic and Usage Data information, select Yes or No Thanks, and tap Next.

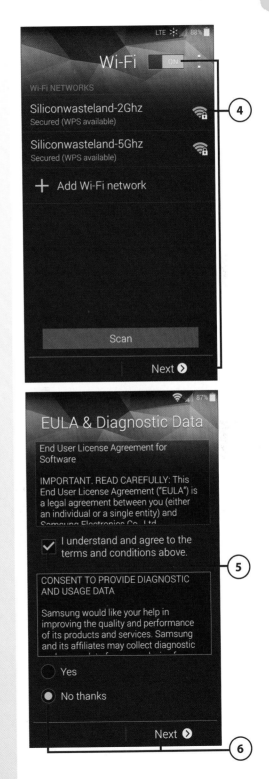

7 A Google/Gmail account is essential for accessing a variety of Android services and apps with the Galaxy S5. Do one of the following:

- If you already have a Google/Gmail account and you'd like to register now, tap Yes and enter your account information (see "Registering Your Gmail Account," in Chapter 7 for instructions).

- If you'd like to create an account or would rather register an existing account later, tap No. Then tap Get an Account (see "Setting Up a Gmail Account," in Chapter 7 for instructions) or Not Now, respectively.

8 Set Google location preferences by tapping check boxes. Tap Next.

Concerned About Being Tracked?

There are pluses and minuses about letting yourself be tracked. Tracking your location lets various apps know where you are so they can notify you of nearby places you might want to visit, such as a branch of your bank, the post office, or some local coffee shops. On the other hand, you might not care for these notifications. If you are more concerned about privacy than convenience, do not check the boxes.

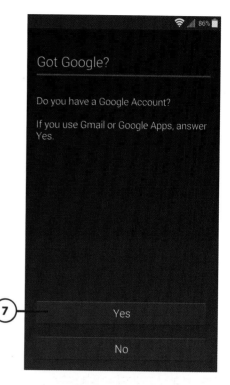

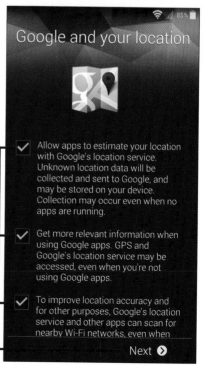

9 Personalize your phone by entering your name. Continue by tapping the right arrow icon at the bottom of the screen.

10 Certain Samsung apps require a free Samsung account. Do one of the following:

- Tap Sign In if you already have a Samsung account that you'd like to register now. Enter the email address that you associated with the account and your Samsung password.

- Tap Create Account if you'd like to create a Samsung account (see "Setting Up a Samsung Account," in Chapter 7 for additional details).

- Tap Skip to ignore this option.

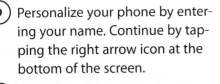

(11) *Optional*: Edit the name that will be used to identify the phone.

(12) *Optional*: If you're new to Android phones, you might want to enable Easy mode to present a simpler interface for your Galaxy S5 (see "Set the Home Screen Mode" in Chapter 2). Note, however, that instructions presented in this book assume that you're using Standard mode rather than Easy mode.

Easy Versus Standard Mode

When you're ready to experience the Android operating system and TouchWiz interface in its full glory, you can restore Standard mode by tapping Apps, Settings, Easy Mode.

(13) Tap Finish to dismiss the wizard. Depending on your carrier, additional options and dialog boxes may appear as the wizard configures your phone for initial use.

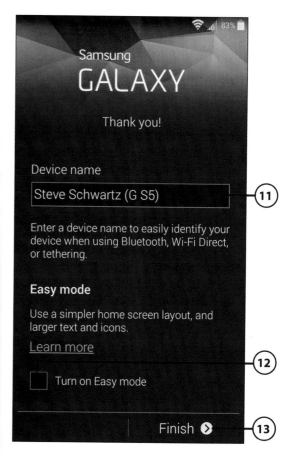

>>>Go Further

SAMSUNG SMART SWITCH

If the Galaxy S5 isn't your first cell phone, you may be able to ease the transition from your old phone by visiting www.samsungsmartswitch.com and downloading the free content-transfer program. In addition to various iPhones and Samsung Galaxy devices, support is provided for transferring data from an LG, HTC, Sony, BlackBerry, or Huawei phone to your new Galaxy S5. (Click the FAQs link for the current list of supported phones and devices.)

When you run Smart Switch, selected content is backed up from the old phone to your computer and then transferred to the S5. If you're an iPhone user, Smart Switch can even transfer your iTunes music, videos, and podcasts, as well as recommend Android apps that are similar to the iOS apps installed on your iPhone.

Darkening and Restoring the Display

Depending on your screen timeout setting, the display automatically turns off during periods of inactivity. In addition to waiting for this timeout to occur, you can manually darken the display to conserve the battery or maintain privacy by pressing the Power button on the right side of the phone.

Restore a Dark Display

(1) Press the Power button on the right side of the phone to make the lock screen appear. (The lock screen also appears when you turn on the phone.)

Dimmed, Not Dark

The display momentarily dims for a brief period before it turns black. To restore a dimmed display, tap any blank spot on the touchscreen.

(2) Swipe in any direction to dismiss the lock screen.

Working with a Locked Phone

You can secure the phone by other methods, such as assigning a password, to require more than a simple swipe to dismiss the lock screen. See Chapter 14, "Securing Your Cell Phone," for instructions.

Lock screen

Set the Screen Timeout Interval

(1) On the Home screen, tap Apps, followed by Settings.

(**2**) In the Device section of Settings, tap the Display icon.

(**3**) Tap Screen Timeout.

(**4**) In the Screen Timeout dialog box, select a new timeout interval or tap the Cancel button to retain the current setting.

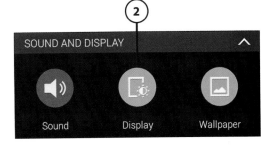

It's All About Trade-Offs

Substantial juice is needed to power the phone's gorgeous display, so the sooner it dims during idle periods, the longer the current charge will last. The key is to select a screen timeout that enables the phone to sit idle as long as possible before dimming and still have sufficient charge to meet your daily calling and app requirements.

To avoid timeouts when you're reading or viewing material onscreen, enable the Smart Stay setting. (In Settings, tap Display and ensure that Smart Stay is checked.) If the front-facing camera detects that you're looking at the screen, it prevents the normal timeout from occurring. Smart Stay works best when you hold the phone upright, the lighting is adequate, and you aren't wearing glasses (which can make it more difficult for the camera to detect that you're looking at the phone).

In this chapter, you learn to use the phone to place and receive calls. Topics include the following:

→ Making and receiving calls
→ Accessing the call log
→ Setting up and checking voicemail
→ Using a Bluetooth headset
→ Getting help with emergency calling
→ Using speed dialing
→ Setting up three-way conference calling
→ Using call waiting and call forwarding
→ Using in-call options, such as the speakerphone
→ Configuring call settings

Using the Phone

With all the functionality that your smartphone provides, it's easy to forget that you can also use it to make and receive calls. But smartphone power comes at a price. To optimize your use of the phone as a phone, you should learn the various calling procedures and the different options for performing each one.

Making a Call

The Galaxy S5 provides many convenient ways for you to make calls. You can manually enter numbers, dial a number from a contact record, use the call logs to return missed calls and redial numbers, call embedded numbers in text and email messages, create and use speed dial entries, and make three-way and emergency calls.

With or Without the 1

When dialing a number, you need to add the dialing prefix/country code only when you're calling a country that uses a *different* code. As a result, most numbers that you dial manually, as well as ones stored in Contacts, can either omit or include the dialing prefix in your cell phone number area code. Similarly, local numbers (in the phone's area code) can usually omit the area code, too.

Manual Dialing

You can use the Phone app's keypad to manually dial numbers. The procedure differs slightly if the number you're dialing is also associated with a record in Contacts.

The Phone/Contacts Relationship

Although you'll generally launch Phone to make calls, Phone and Contacts are essentially two parts of the same app. Within Contacts, you can make a manual call by selecting the Keypad tab. Within Phone, you can select the Contacts tab, and then select a contact record. Thus, it doesn't matter which app you run when you're ready to call someone.

Call Someone Without a Contacts Record

 Tap the Phone icon at the bottom of the Home screen.

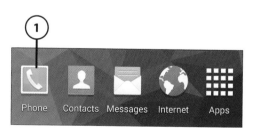

(2) Select the Keypad tab if the keypad isn't displayed. Then tap the digits in the phone number.

Dialing International Numbers

To make an international call, press and hold **0**. A plus symbol appears as the first character in the number. Enter the country code, followed by the phone number.

Mistakes Happen

If you make a mistake, you can press the Delete key to delete the last digit entered. To remove the entire number and start over, press and hold Delete. You can also use normal editing techniques to position the text insertion mark within the number and make changes, such as inserting the area code.

(3) *Optional:* To create a new contact record for this number or add the number to an existing contact record, tap Add to Contacts and then select an option.

Keypad tab (3)   (2)

Voicemail   Delete

Voicemail speed dial   (3)

Create contact   Update existing

④ Tap the green phone icon to dial the call. Tap the red End Call icon to disconnect when you finish talking.

Call Someone with a Contacts Record

① Tap the Phone icon at the bottom of the Home screen.

2 Tap the Keypad tab if it isn't automatically selected. Then type any of the phone number's digits. You can start at the beginning or with any consecutive string of digits that you remember. As you enter digits, potential matches from Contacts and from numbers you've previously dialed are shown.

Dial by Name

If you can't remember a person's number but are sure he has a Contacts record, use the keypad to spell part of the person's name, company, or any other information that you know.

3 Do one of the following:

- Select the main suggestion by tapping the person's or company's name.

- View additional matches by tapping the numbered down arrow and selecting someone from the Search Result list.

- Continue entering digits until the correct match is suggested, and then tap the person's or company's name.

4 Tap the green phone icon to dial the call. Tap the red End Call icon to disconnect when you finish talking.

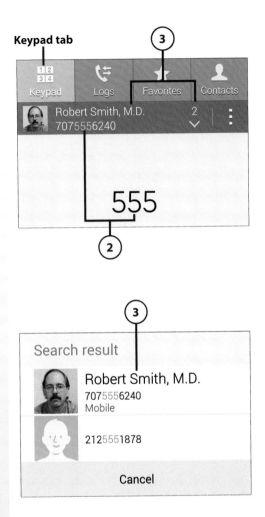

Call from a Contact Record

Many of your outgoing calls will be to people and companies that have a record in Contacts. Rather than typing part of their name or number, it is often faster to find them in Contacts.

Contacts tab

1. Open Contacts by tapping its icon at the bottom of the Home screen, tapping the Phone icon on the Home screen and then selecting the Contacts tab, or accessing Contacts from another app, such as Messages.

2. Tap the Contacts tab if it isn't already selected. Find the record by scrolling or searching, and then tap the entry to view the full record.

3. Tap a listed phone number or its green telephone icon to dial that number.

4. Tap the red End Call icon to disconnect when you finish talking.

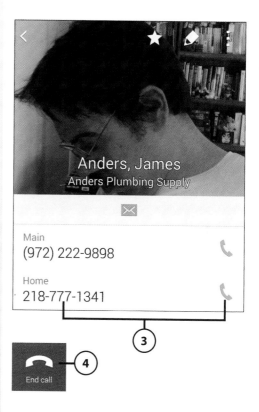

Calling from the Call Logs

Every incoming and outgoing call is automatically recorded in the Logs section of Phone and Contacts. By viewing the logs, you can determine which calls need to be returned, as well as initiate the calls.

Return and Redial Calls

By selecting a particular log, you can see whom you've called and who has called you. You can then dial any log entry.

(**1**) On the Home screen, tap the Phone icon.

(**2**) Tap the Logs tab (on some phones this will say Recent) at the top of the screen.

(**3**) Select a log to view by tapping All Calls above the log and choosing an option. (If you don't select a log, the last one viewed appears.)

(**4**) To call a person without leaving the Logs screen, swipe your finger across his entry to the right. The displayed number is automatically dialed.

(**5**) To text a person, swipe the log entry to the left. A new message window in Messages appears.

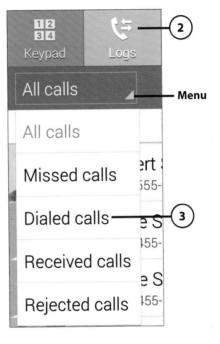

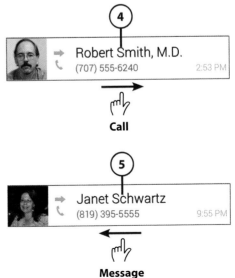

Call

Message

Tap Versus Swipe

If you don't like swiping or you want more control over what happens, tap the log entry. On the screen that appears, you can call the person by tapping the phone icon. To send a text or multimedia message to the person, tap the message icon.

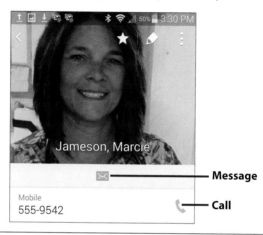

Message

Call

PHONE LOG ICONS

In each log entry, icons provide information about the call (see Table 4.1). The icon beside each person, company, and number shows the type of call, as well as whether it was incoming or outgoing.

Table 4.1   Phone Log Icons

Icon	Meaning	Icon	Meaning
	Incoming call		Rejected incoming call
	Outgoing call		Auto-rejected incoming call
	Missed incoming call		

>>>Go Further

OTHER PHONE LOG OPTIONS

Using the logs to return calls is often more convenient than dialing manually or searching for the person's contact record. Here are some other actions you can take when viewing a log:

- Press and hold a log entry to select it. You can tap the Delete icon to delete this single entry or select additional entries prior to tapping Delete.

- With a log item selected, open the menu and choose a command. *View Contact* displays the individual's record, *Copy to Dialing Screen* enters the person's phone number on the dialing screen, *Send Number* embeds the person's name and phone number in a new text message, and *Add to Reject List* causes any future calls from this number to be automatically sent to voicemail.

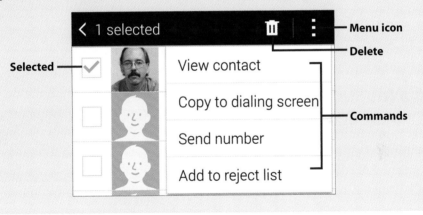

- Another way to delete old, duplicate, and unwanted entries is to choose an appropriate log from the left-hand menu, tap the menu icon (on the right), and choose Delete. Select all log entries that you want to remove (or tap Select All), tap Done, and then tap OK in the confirmation dialog box.

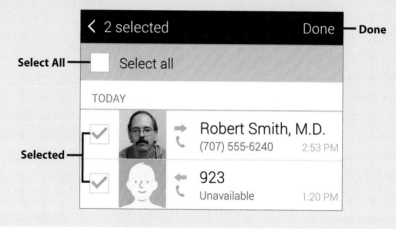

Dialing a Number in a Text or Email Message

A phone number in an email or text message acts as a *link* that, when tapped, can dial the number.

Text Message Links

1. In Messages, display the received or sent message that contains the phone number, and then tap the number.

2. Tap Call in the dialog box that appears. Phone launches and dials the number.

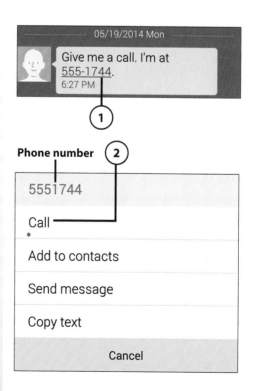

Email Message Links

1. In Email, display the received or sent email message that contains the phone number, and then tap the number.

2. The number appears in the Keypad section of Phone. If necessary, you can edit it (adding or removing the area code, for example) using normal editing techniques.

3. Tap the green phone icon to dial the number.

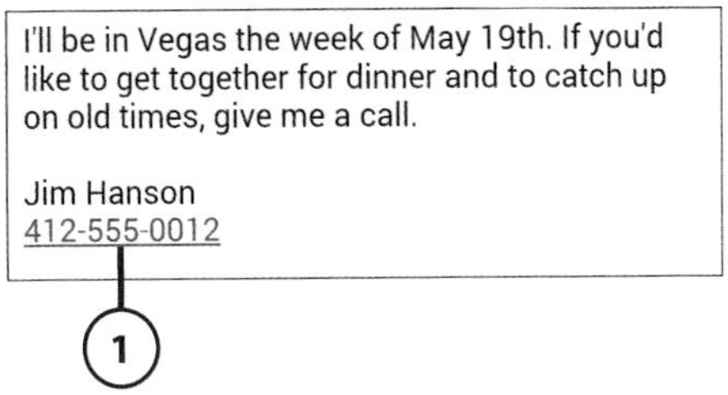

> I'll be in Vegas the week of May 19th. If you'd like to get together for dinner and to catch up on old times, give me a call.
>
> Jim Hanson
> 412-555-0012

1

2

| Keypad | Logs | Favorites | Contacts |

+ Add to Contacts

PA

(412) 555-0012

1 ⌒	2 ABC	3 DEF
4 GHI	5 JKL	6 MNO
7 PQRS	8 TUV	9 WXYZ
✳ P	0 +	#

3

>>>*Go Further*

QUICK DIALING TECHNIQUES

For people and companies with a record in Contacts, you can also call them using a voice command, such as "Call Janice Gunderson." For information about using voice apps, see Chapter 9, "Using Voice Services."

You can also quickly call anyone whose name appears in the Contacts, Logs, or Favorites list of Phone/Contacts or with whom you've recently exchanged messages in Messages. Locate the person or company in the Contacts, Logs, or Messages conversations list and swipe your finger across the item to the right. The Phone screen appears, and the person or company's number is automatically dialed.

Setting Up Voicemail

After your phone is activated, one of the first things you should do is set up voicemail. Doing so identifies the phone number as yours and ensures that callers have an opportunity to leave a message when you're unavailable.

(1) On any Home screen page, tap the Phone icon.

(2) On the Phone keypad, press and hold 1 (the speed dial number reserved for voicemail) or tap the Voicemail icon.

(3) When prompted, record your name, enter a password, and select or record a greeting. When you finish reviewing voicemail options, tap the End Call icon.

Bluetooth Headset

Although a few Bluetooth headsets support stereo (making them suitable for listening to music), most are mono devices intended primarily for hands-free phone calls. With a maximum range of 30 feet, using a Bluetooth headset enables you to place the phone nearby and conduct a conversation. Unlike using a speakerphone, the audio is routed directly to your ear and the headset's microphone won't pick up as much ambient noise.

Working with a Bluetooth headset involves two steps: pairing the headset and phone (a one-time procedure) and using the headset for calls. The procedures for pairing and answering calls are specific to your headset and are explained in the headset's instructions. As an example, the following tasks illustrate how to use a Jabra EasyGo Bluetooth headset with the Galaxy S5.

Pair the Headset with the Phone

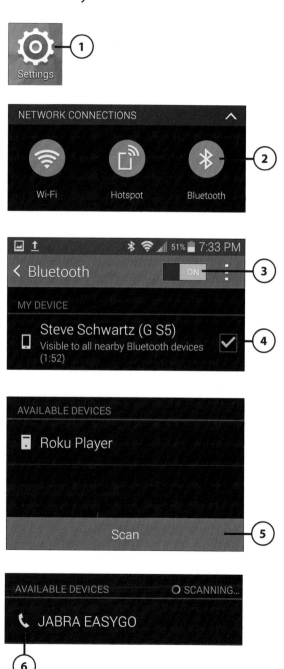

(1) On the Home screen, tap Apps, followed by Settings.

(2) Tap Bluetooth in the Network Connections section of Settings.

(3) Enable Bluetooth by dragging the slider to the On position.

(4) Make the phone visible to the headset by ensuring that the check box is selected. Turn the Bluetooth headset on.

Check Your Headset's Manual

Your Bluetooth headset may require more than simply turning it on to enter pairing mode. The Jabra EasyGo, for example, can be paired with two devices. You must hold down the Answer button for 5 seconds to initiate the second pairing. Similarly, if your headset is already paired with one or more phones, it may be necessary to manually release the pairings to initiate this new pairing.

(5) *Optional*: Tap the Scan button if the headset doesn't appear in the Available Devices list.

(6) Tap the headset's name in the Available Devices list to pair it with the phone.

(7) A confirmation appears when pairing is successful.

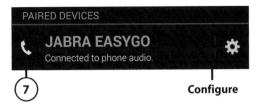

Configure

Future Headset Sessions

When you later use your headset for making and receiving calls, the Bluetooth Settings screen will list the headset as a paired device. You can tap the Settings icon to the right of the headset's name to configure or unpair it from your Galaxy S5.

Use the Headset for Calls

(1) Turn on the headset and place it in your ear. If Bluetooth isn't currently enabled, open the Notification panel by dragging the status bar downward. In the Quick Setting buttons, tap the Bluetooth icon to enable it.

When the Headset Won't Connect

If a previously paired Bluetooth headset refuses to connect to the phone, open the Notification panel, and then disable and re-enable Bluetooth.

(2) To place a call, dial using any of the methods supported by the phone (see "Making a Call," earlier in this chapter).

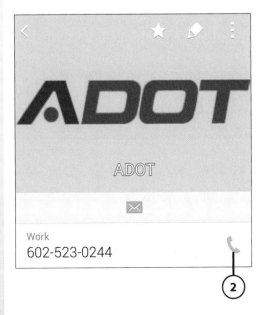

3 To receive an incoming call, tap the headset's Answer/End button or drag the green Accept Call icon to the right.

Adjusting the Volume

You can adjust the volume by pressing the volume control on the left side of the phone or on the headset.

4 Tap the headset's Answer/End button or tap the End Call icon on the phone to end the call.

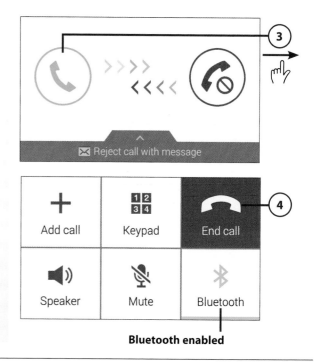

Bluetooth enabled

Conserve Power

Turn off Bluetooth when not in use to save battery power.

In-Call Options

During a call, you can freely disable or enable the headset by tapping the Bluetooth icon. In addition, your headset may support a variety of in-call options. For example, you can also use the Jabra EasyGo to reject incoming calls, redial the last number, mute the microphone, and place the current call on hold to switch between two conversations (if you have call waiting). Refer to your headset manual for instructions.

Emergency Calling

Where available, the Galaxy S5 supports *e911* (Enhanced 911), enabling it to connect to a nearby emergency dispatch center regardless of where in the United States or Canada you happen to be. (The equivalent emergency number is different in other countries. In the United Kingdom, for example, it's 999.) When you place a 911 call, your position can usually be determined by the phone's GPS or by triangulating your position using nearby cell sites.

Call 911

① Do one of the following:

- Tap the Phone icon on the Home screen.

- If the lock screen is displayed and the phone is protected with a pattern, password, PIN, or fingerprint scan, you can go directly to Phone by tapping the Emergency Call text.

② On the normal Phone or the Emergency Dialer screen, respectively, enter **911** (or your country's equivalent number) and tap the green phone icon to dial the number.

911 if Locked

As a safety feature, you can even call 911 from a locked phone.

Lock screen (bottom)

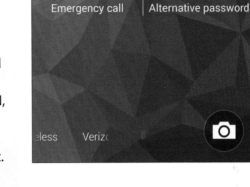

Emergency Calling Tips

Keep the following in mind when seeking emergency assistance:

- Even if you've disabled the phone's location/GPS functions for all other uses, these features remain available for 911 use.

- Not all emergency dispatch centers support e911. Instead of assuming they've determined where you are based on GPS or triangulation, be prepared to state your location.

- Some emergency dispatch centers use an automated voice menu that prompts you to enter numbers. According to Sprint, for example, "If you encounter a prerecorded message instead of a live operator, wait for the appropriate prompt and say 'EMERGENCY' instead of pressing 1. Not all wireless phones transmit number tones during a 911 call."

Other Outgoing Call Options

The Galaxy S5 also supports some additional outgoing call options: speed dialing, blocking your caller ID information, three-way calling, and inserting pause and wait commands.

Speed Dialing

To make it easy to dial your most important numbers, you can assign a *speed dial number* to anyone with a record in Contacts. The digits 2–100 are available as speed dial numbers; 1 is reserved for voicemail.

Access the Speed Dial Screen

(1) Launch Phone or Contacts by tapping an icon at the bottom of the Home screen.

2 Display the Speed Dial screen by selecting the Keypad or Contacts tab, tapping the menu icon, and choosing Speed Dial.

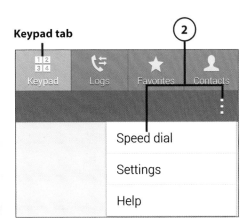

Keypad tab

What Next?

When you reach the Speed Dial screen, jump ahead to the section that describes the task you want to perform.

Assign a Speed Dial Number

1 On the Speed Dial screen, tap + Add Contact next to a currently unassigned number.

2 Tap the name of the person or company with which to associate this speed dial number. (You can do this quickly by tapping the first letter of the person's or company's name or tapping the search box and entering the name.)

3 If the contact record contains only one phone number, that number is automatically used. If the record contains multiple numbers, select the number to use.

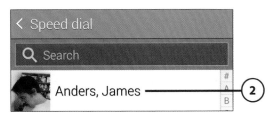

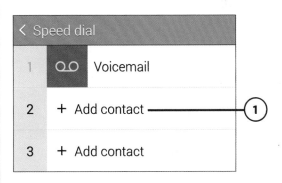

4 The contact's phone number is assigned to the speed dial number.

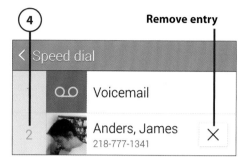

Remove entry

Removing Speed Dial Entries

An X appears beside each assigned speed dial entry. To remove an entry, tap the X. The speed dial number is now unassigned and labeled Add Contact.

Dial a Speed Dial Number

1 Launch Phone by tapping its icon at the bottom of the Home screen.

2 With the Keypad tab selected, enter the speed dial number. Press and hold the final digit.

3 The phone dials the person or company associated with the speed dial number. Tap the red End Call icon to disconnect when you finish talking.

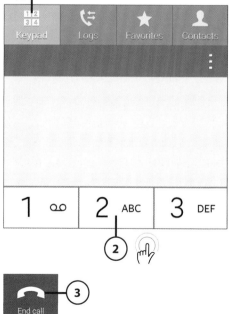

Keypad tab

Dialing from the Speed Dial Screen

If you can't remember a particular speed dial number, you can initiate a call or message from the Speed Dial screen. Scroll to find the person or company's entry, tap the person's picture or placeholder, and then tap the Call or Message icon in the dialog box that appears. (If the person or company has multiple numbers, flick up or down in the list to find the number you want to call.)

Temporarily Blocking Your Caller ID Information

If you want to prevent your caller ID information from displaying on an outgoing call, precede the number with *67, such as *675591234 for a local call or *672145591234 for a long-distance call. The recipient's phone should display Private Number rather than your name, city, or number. Note that *67 is the correct prefix in the United States and Canada only; other countries have a different prefix.

If you want to prevent your caller ID information from displaying on *every* call, contact your service provider for assistance. If your phone number is blocked, you can unblock it by adding *82 to the end of the number you dial.

Three-Way Calling

By making a three-way call, you can talk to two people at the same time. (If you don't have an unlimited minutes plan, check with your service provider to determine how three-way calls are billed.)

(1) Launch Phone and dial the first number.

(2) When the first person answers, tell him to wait while you call the second person. Tap the Add Call icon and dial the second number. The first person is automatically placed on hold.

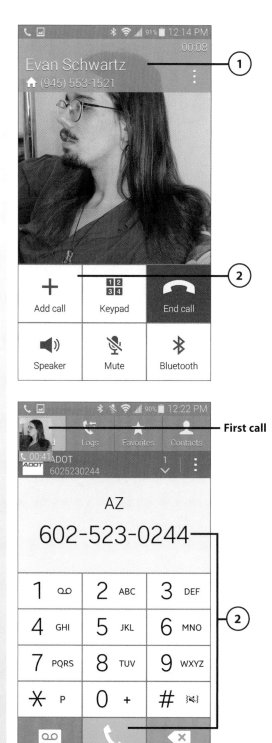

— First call

(3) When the second person answers, tap the Merge icon.

(4) The display shows that you're all connected to a conference call. When the call is completed, tap End Call. Any person who is still connected will be disconnected.

Second call

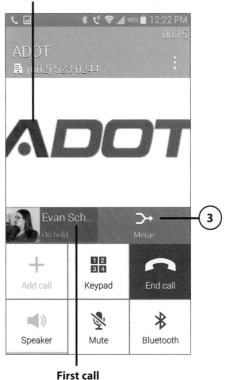

First call

>>>*Go Further*

WI-FI CALLING (T-MOBILE AND METRO PCS)

T-Mobile and Metro PCS customers can optionally make calls over a Wi-Fi network rather than using their normal cellular service. This can be very useful when you live or work in a place that has a weak cell signal and, hence, poor call quality. Note that Wi-Fi calling doesn't cost extra, but it does use plan minutes. And if you want to make out-of-country calls, you still must have an international plan.

To turn on Wi-Fi calling, ensure that Wi-Fi is enabled and that you're connected to an available network. Then open Settings, tap More Networks, and move the Wi-Fi Calling slider to the On position. If you want to set calling preferences, tap Connection Preferences and make a selection (such as Wi-Fi Preferred).

Receiving Calls

The other half of the phone call equation is that of receiving and responding to incoming calls.

Respond to an Incoming Call

1. When a call comes in, the caller is identified by name and number (if he has a Contacts record), by number (if there's no matching Contacts record), or by Private Number (if he has blocked his caller ID).

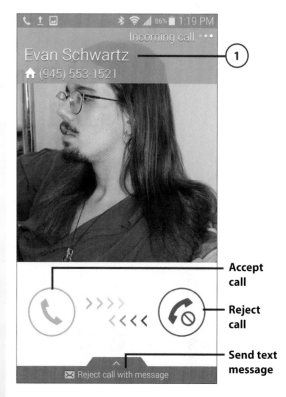

Accept call

Reject call

Send text message

(**2**) You can respond in any of the following ways:

- *Accept call.* Drag the green phone icon in any direction.

- *Reject call.* Drag the red phone icon in any direction, sending the caller to voice-mail.

- *Ignore call.* Do nothing; let the phone ring. After a number of rings, the caller is transferred to voicemail.

- *Reject with explanation.* Drag Reject Call with Message upward and select a text message to transmit to the caller. (Note that if the caller doesn't have a messaging plan or is calling from a landline, the text message might not be delivered.)

(**3**) Tap the red End Call icon to disconnect when you finish talking.

(**2**)

			📶 86% 🔋 1:26 PM

✉ Reject call with message

＋ Compose new message

Sorry, I'm busy. Call back later.

I'm in a meeting.

I'm driving.

 (**3**)

>>>Go Further
MORE WAYS TO ACCEPT AND END CALLS

In addition to the normal methods described in this chapter, the Answering and Ending Calls settings provide novel ways to accept and end calls. To view or change these settings, launch Phone, press the menu key, choose Settings, and tap Call, Answering and Ending Calls. Options include the following:

- *Pressing the Home key.* Press the Home key to answer an incoming call. This can be more convenient than dragging the green Accept icon, especially in the dark or when driving.

- *Voice control.* Incoming calls are announced by caller name or number. You can say "Answer" to accept the call or "Reject" to send the caller to voicemail.

- *Waving hand over device.* Wave your hand back and forth over the phone to accept a call.

- *Pressing the power key.* You can press the Power key to end a call.

‹ Answering and ending calls

ANSWER CALLS BY

Pressing the Home key ✓

Voice control ✓
Answer calls with voice commands.

Waving hand over device ✓

END CALLS BY

Pressing the power key ✓

Call Waiting

Call waiting enables you to answer an incoming call when you're already on a call.

(1) Answer the new call by sliding the green phone icon in any direction.

(2) The initial call is automatically placed on hold while you speak to the new caller. To switch between callers, tap the Swap icon. The active call is always shown in green at the top of the screen.

(3) Tap the End Call icon to end the active call. The other call becomes active, ringing your phone if necessary.

Incoming caller's info

Active call

On hold

Call Forwarding

Depending on your carrier, you can have all or only particular kinds of calls that your cell phone would normally receive automatically forwarded to another number. Forwarding works even when the Galaxy S5 is turned off. To restore normal calling, deactivate call forwarding when you're finished. (Check with your service provider or review your plan to determine the cost of using call forwarding.)

Before starting Call Forwarding, be sure you know the number (such as your home phone) to which you want the calls forwarded.

The following are two of the simplest implementations of call forwarding: Sprint and Verizon. Enabling and disabling call forwarding with other carriers is often handled by tapping Phone's menu icon, choosing Settings, and then tapping Call, Additional Settings, Call Forwarding. Consult your carrier's website for specific instructions.

- *Sprint.* To activate call forwarding, launch Phone and dial *72, followed by the number to which calls should be forwarded. When you're ready to deactivate forwarding, dial *720. When activating or deactivating call forwarding, a tone signifies that the change has been accepted.

- *Verizon.* Launch Phone, tap the menu icon, and choose Settings. To enable or disable call forwarding, tap Call, Call Forwarding, and then choose Turn On Call Forwarding or Turn Off Call Forwarding, respectively.

In-Call Options

While on a call, you can access common in-call options by tapping icons and choosing menu commands. Additional options are available via hardware controls and the Notification panel.

Menu commands. Tap the menu icon and choose one of these commands:

- *Contacts, Memo, or Messages.* View information in Contacts, take notes in Memo during the call, or send a text message to the other party.

- *Personalize Call Sound.* Choose an audio equalizer setting for the current call. Before you can use this feature, you must set it up as described in the "Personalize Call Sound" sidebar later in this chapter.

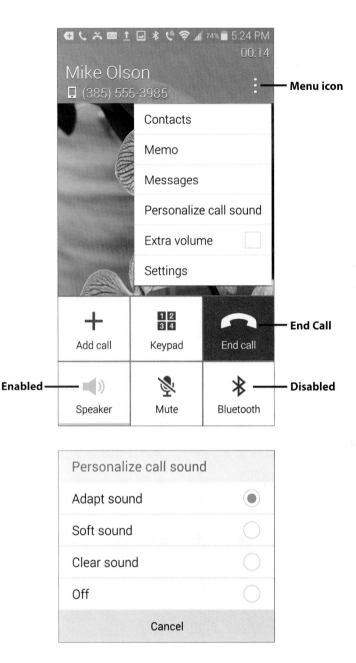

- *Extra Volume.* You can boost in-call volume above the normal maximum when this command is checked. Tap it a second time to disable the volume boost.

Onscreen icons. You can tap the following icons during a call. When an icon-based option is enabled or active, it is green.

- *Keypad.* If you need to enter an extension or information to respond to a voice prompt, tap the Keypad icon to display the dialing keypad. The icon's label changes to Hide. To dismiss the keypad, tap the Hide icon or press the Back key.

- *Speaker.* Tap the Speaker icon to toggle between normal and speakerphone modes.

- *Mute.* To temporarily turn off the phone's microphone so that the other party can't hear you, tap the Mute icon.

- *Bluetooth.* To use a Bluetooth headset on the current call, tap the Bluetooth icon. To resume using the built-in earpiece, tap the icon again.

- *End Call.* Tap End Call to "hang up," disconnecting from the other party.

Other options. Two other important options are available during calls that aren't represented by icons.

- *Volume adjustment.* To change the volume, press the hardware Volume control on the left side of the phone. An onscreen volume indicator appears. Press the top half of the hardware Volume control to raise the volume; press the lower half to lower the volume. You can also adjust the volume by dragging the onscreen slider.

- *Notification panel controls.* You can drag down the Notification panel to access the Speaker, Mute, and End options. This is especially useful if you exit the Phone screen during the call in order to run other apps.

Notification panel in-call controls

Phone Call Multitasking

You can indeed run other apps while on a call. Return to the Home screen by pressing the Home key and then launch the apps. You can also open Phone's menu to launch Contacts, Memo, or Messages. To indicate that you're still on a call, the status bar turns neon green, a phone icon is added to the status bar, and a call progress icon is displayed. You can drag the call progress icon to a new location if it's in your way.

If you want to return to Phone, tap the call progress icon, tap the picture or place-holder icon in the Notification panel, or launch Phone. When you're ready to end the call, launch Phone or tap the End icon in the Notification panel.

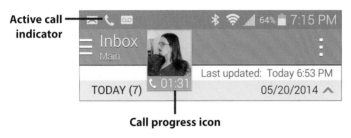

Call progress icon

Checking Voicemail

Using your service provider's voicemail, people can leave messages for you when you're unavailable or the phone is turned off. When voicemail is waiting, a voicemail icon appears in the status bar and an entry is added to the Notification panel.

Voicemail Password

If you set up voicemail to require a password, you'll be asked to enter it each time you contact voicemail. When prompted, tap each digit in the password and end by tapping the pound sign (#)—or follow whatever instructions your carrier provides. Refer to the "Setting Up Voicemail" section earlier in this chapter for more information.

You can check your voicemail in two or more ways:

(1) Connect to your carrier's voice-mail service by doing one of the following:

- Drag down the Notification panel and tap a voicemail entry. The carrier's voicemail is automatically dialed or its voicemail app launches (if one is provided).

- Launch the Voicemail app by tapping the icon on the main Apps page. Press and hold 1 (the speed dial number assigned to voicemail). The Phone app dials the carrier's voicemail.

- Launch your carrier's voice-mail app (if one is provided).

NOTIFICATIONS

Evan Schwartz   7:10 PM

(1)

Voicemail indicator

(**2**) You connect to the carrier's voicemail system. Because the voicemail menus require you to enter numbers to choose options, tap the Keypad icon to reveal the keypad (if it's currently hidden). Listen to the menu options and tap numbers to indicate your choices.

(**3**) Tap the End Call icon when you finish using voicemail.

Changing Voicemail Settings

You can change your voicemail settings (such as your greeting, password, and notification methods) whenever you want. Connect with voicemail and respond to the prompts.

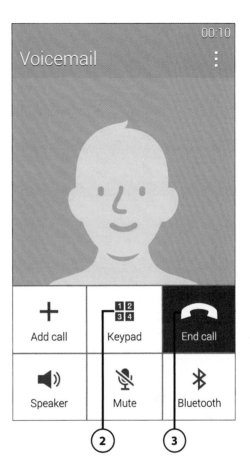

Enabling Mute, Vibrate, or Airplane Mode

Your phone has three special settings that you'll occasionally find useful: Mute, Vibrate, and Airplane mode. Enable Mute when your phone *must* remain silent, such as when you're in a meeting or place of worship. Vibrate also silences notifications, but denotes them by vibrating the phone. Enable Airplane mode during flights to quickly make your phone compliant with government and airline regulations by disabling the ability to place or receive calls, as well as transmit data.

Mute and Vibrate

When Mute is enabled, all sounds except media playback and alarms are disabled. Incoming calls cause the Phone app to launch—even when the screen is dark—but no sound or vibration occurs. Vibration has the same silencing effect as Mute, but important events are signaled by vibration.

(1) To enable muting or vibration, do one of the following:

- Press and hold the Power button until the Device Options menu appears, and then tap the Mute or Vibrate icon.

- On the Home screen, press and hold the Volume down key until the onscreen volume control shows that Mute or Vibrate is enabled. (Lower the volume all the way to enable Mute. When the Mute icon is shown, you can quickly switch to Vibrate by tapping the Volume up key once.)

- Open the Notification panel. Repeatedly tap the Sound button to toggle between its three states: Mute, Vibrate, and Sound.

(2) When Vibrate or Mute is active, a matching indicator displays in the status bar.

(3) Restore normal sound by selecting Sound in the Device Options menu, enabling Sound in the Notification panel, or increasing the volume.

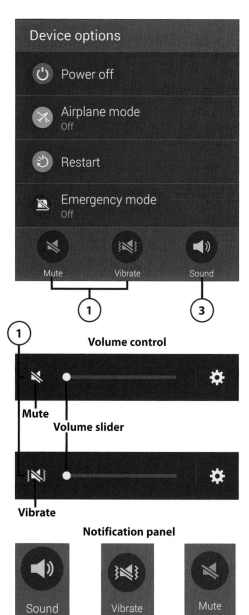

Airplane Mode

When flying, you can quickly set your phone to Airplane mode, disabling its ability to place or receive calls and to send or receive data. Other functions operate normally.

(1) To quickly enable Airplane mode, do one of the following:

- Press and hold the Power button until the Device Options menu appears. Tap Airplane Mode.

- Open the Notification panel, scroll the Quick Setting buttons to the right, and tap Airplane Mode. When enabled, the button is green. (If the button isn't visible, tap the Grid View icon and *then* tap the Airplane Mode button.)

- Open Settings, tap the Airplane Mode icon (in Network Connections), and move its slider to the On position.

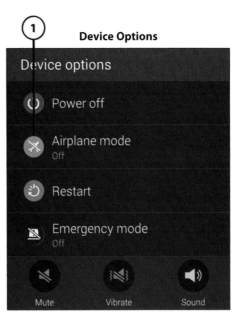

Device Options

Notification panel   **Grid View**

Airplane mode settings

Airplane mode allows you to turn off calling, messaging and data network features. It also turns off connectivity features such as Wi-Fi and Bluetooth. To use Wi-Fi and Bluetooth, turn them on in Settings or on the notification panel.

(2) In the Turn On Airplane Mode dialog box, confirm by tapping OK. The Airplane mode indicator appears in the status bar; cellular connections, Wi-Fi, and Bluetooth are automatically disabled.

(3) Restore normal calling and data transmission functionality by disabling Airplane mode by reversing any of the actions described in Step 1. Tap OK in the Airplane Mode dialog box.

Turn on Airplane mode

Airplane mode allows you to turn off calling, messaging and data network features. It also turns off connectivity features such as Wi-Fi and Bluetooth. To use Wi-Fi and Bluetooth, turn them on in Settings or on the notification panel.

| Cancel | OK |

(2)

Airplane mode

Airplane mode will be turned off.

| Cancel | OK |

(3)

Configuring Call Settings

You can set preferences for many phone operations in Call Settings. Although the default settings will suffice for most calling situations, you should still familiarize yourself with them.

To review or change the settings, launch Phone, tap the menu icon, choose Settings, and tap Call. Or you can open Settings and tap the Call icon (in the Applications section). Here are some of the most useful Call Settings:

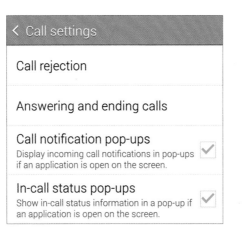

- *Call Rejection.* Enable/disable Auto Reject mode for blocked callers (or to temporarily reject *all* incoming calls), as well as add or remove numbers from the Auto Reject List. Rejected calls are sent straight to voicemail. You can also create or delete call rejection text messages. These can optionally be sent when manually rejecting an incoming call by dragging Reject Call with Message upward (at the bottom of Phone's main screen).

- *Answering and Ending Calls.* See the "More Ways to Accept and End Calls" sidebar, earlier in this chapter.

- *Call Notification Pop-ups.* When this setting is enabled, rather than commandeer your entire screen whenever there's an incoming call, a smaller, less intrusive pop-up window appears. You can tap a button to answer or reject the call, expand the window to its normal full-screen view (in order to view additional information or reject with a text message), or drag the pop-up to a different screen location.

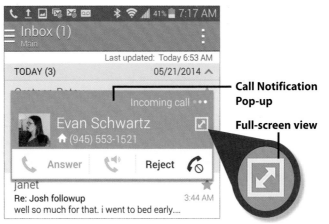

- *In-call Status Pop-ups.* When you dial a number or receive a call, a window above the Accept and Reject icons shows your most recent interactions with the person or company (as a reminder of when you last talked, for example).

In-Call Status Pop-up

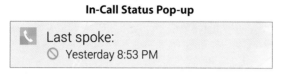

- *Call Alerts.* Specify whether the phone vibrates when the call recipient answers and when the call ends, whether tones denote each call connection and end, and whether alarms and new message notifications are active during calls. When Minute Minder is enabled, the phone beeps twice whenever another minute of connect time passes.

Call Alerts Settings

< Call alerts

CALL VIBRATIONS

Vibrate on connection to netwo..

Call-end vibration

CALL STATUS TONES

Call connect tone ✓

Minute minder

Call end tone ✓

ALERTS ON CALL

Notify during calls
Allow alarms and notifications to sound/
vibrate during calls. ✓

- *Call Accessories.* Configure the phone for use with a Bluetooth headset. You can enable the headset to automatically answer incoming calls and specify a delay period prior to answering. Outgoing Call Conditions determines whether calls can also be initiated with the headset when the phone is locked.

- *Additional Settings.* Configure settings for the deaf and those who wear hearing aids.

- *Ringtone and Sound Settings.* Specify the sounds that announce an incoming call and govern call sound quality. Tap Ringtones and Keypad Tones to select or create a ringtone for incoming calls, change the vibration pattern, enable or disable vibration when ringing, and enable or disable the playing of tones when tapping numbers on the keypad. Tap Personalize Call Sound to adapt the call audio to your needs (see the "Personalize Call Sound" sidebar at the end of this section). Enable Noise Reduction to suppress background/ambient noise during calls.

RINGTONE AND SOUND SETTINGS
Ringtones and keypad tones
Personalize call sound Adapt sound
Noise reduction Suppresses background noise from your side during calls.

- *Voice Privacy.* When enabled, this setting causes your calls to be encrypted using Enhanced Encryption (when available).

>>>Go Further

PERSONALIZE CALL SOUND

To improve audio quality during phone calls or while listening to music, you can enable the Adapt Sound feature. Based on a hearing test, the phone adjusts sound so it's optimal for you. If you haven't already set up Adapt Sound from within the Music app, you can do so now.

1. Launch Phone, tap the menu icon, choose Settings, and tap Call.

2. Scroll down and tap Personalize Call Sound.

3. Plug in your earphones and, following the instructions, take the audio test.

4. At the test's conclusion, tap icons to compare unaltered (Original) audio in the left, right, and both ears with that of the Adapt Sound (Personalized) audio.

5. Set options in the Adapt Sound Settings section of the screen. To enable Adapt Sound during calls and listening to music, tap their check boxes. Tap Frequently Used Side to specify the side of your face that you typically use when speaking on the phone.

ADAPT SOUND SETTINGS	
Call sound	☑
Music sound	☑
Frequently used side Left	

6. Tap Done.

During a call, open the menu in Phone, choose Personalize Call Sound to disable or enable the feature, and then select Adapt Sound (for your personalized setting) or one of the other audio options. When using earphones to listen to songs in Music, you can enable or disable Adapt Sound by opening the menu, choosing Settings, and tapping Adapt Sound. (Without earphones, Adapt Sound is automatically disabled.)

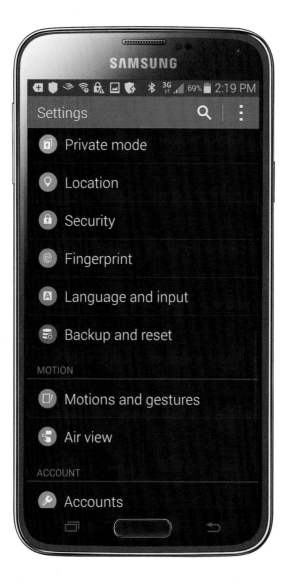

In this chapter, you become familiar with the Samsung Galaxy S5's keys and gestures. Topics include the following:

→ The keys: using Menu, Home, and Back
→ Gestures: enabling motion

Using the Keys and Gestures

The Galaxy S5 has a touch-sensitive screen (touchscreen) that detects location, pressure, and motion. The system determines how the phone and its apps react to various kinds of touches and gestures, including some that don't touch the surface. This chapter goes into more detail about how these touches work.

The Keys

What's a Key?

Something I mentioned in Chapter 2 bears repeating here: In this book, the word "key" means the same thing as "button." There aren't actually any keys or buttons on the Galaxy S5 (except for the Power button at the bottom of the front screen). Both "key" and "button" refer to the symbol for a key, which might look like an icon or it might look like an actual key on a keyboard.

The standard keyboard on the Galaxy S5 looks like a normal keyboard layout, except that it has some extra symbols in the bottom row. It operates much the same way a normal keyboard does, but you touch the symbol representing the key rather than pushing a key or a button.

Keyboard Letters and Symbols

1. Tapping any of the letter keys results in the equivalent lower-case key. For a capital letter, press the up arrow (the Shift key) and the next letter you tap will be an uppercase letter.

2. Tapping the SYM key results in a display of symbols. Note that the up arrow changes to 1/2.

3. Tapping the SYM key again results in a second display of symbols. Note the up arrow changes to 2/2. Use this key to toggle back and forth between the two sets of symbols.

4. Tapping the microphone key results in turning on the audio recording capability, which lets your spoken message be translated into text. See Chapter 9, "Using Voice Services," for more information on using voice input with your Galaxy S5. (You might need to spell email addresses and other text until the Galaxy S5 gets used to your voice.)

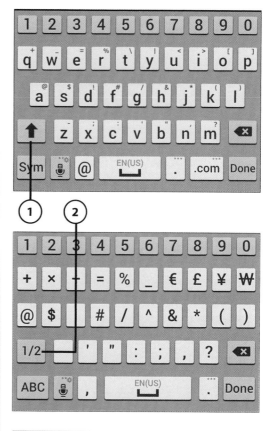

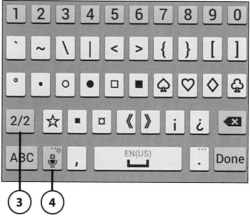

Keyboard Language

Note that the space bar has **EN(US)** above the space symbol. This means the default language set for this session is U.S. English. You can change the default language, as described in the "Changing the Default Language" section of Chapter 10.

Other Buttons and Keys

You may encounter other kinds of buttons or keys. Following are some examples:

- In the Calculator app, you tap numbers and symbols to perform various arithmetic operations.

- You tap buttons to respond to requests from an app.

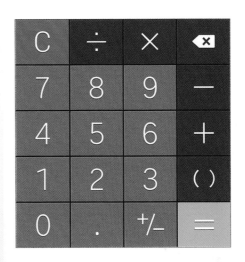

Tap a button to respond to the app's question

- Sometimes you use buttons to indicate that you want to skip a step or complete an action.

Remedy for Fat Finger Syndrome

Some of us are afflicted with "Fat Finger Syndrome." This occurs when you mean to tap one key or button and inadvertently tap another close by. Don't worry—just press the Delete or Backspace key and correct your mistake.

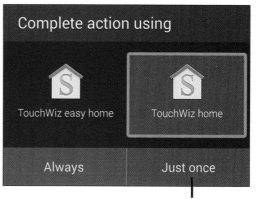

Tap a button to complete an action

The Delete key

Using Motions and Gestures

The Galaxy S5 responds to some motions of the phone without your touching it. And in addition to touching, flicking swiping, dragging, and spreading or pinching, there are other gestures that can affect the Galaxy S5. However, you need to enable these by touching the Settings icon and scrolling down.

Enabling Motions and Gestures

1. Tap the Settings icon, scroll down to Motion, and tap the Motions and Gestures icon.

2. Each Motions and Gestures setting operates as an on/off toggle. They work as follows:

   - *Air Browse.* When enabled, you can wave your hand over the sensor at the top of the phone to instruct it to scroll in various apps, such as Gallery, Music, Email, and Internet.

   - *Direct Call.* When viewing a person's contact record, log entry, or message conversation, you can move the phone to your ear to automatically call the person.

   - *Smart Alert.* When you pick up the phone, it vibrates to notify you of missed calls or messages.

- *Mute/Pause.* When enabled, you can specify methods that can be used to pause media playback and mute alarms or incoming calls. Unlike the two natural motions for silencing the phone, Smart Pause relies on the front camera to detect when you're looking at the screen. If it senses you've looked away, video playback is automatically paused. It restarts again when it detects that you're looking at the screen.

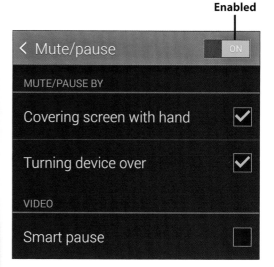

Enabled

- *Palm Swipe to Capture.* When enabled, you can create screen captures by placing the edge of your hand on the screen and dragging across it. Captured screens are saved in the Gallery. (You can also create screen captures by simultaneously pressing the Home key and Power button.)

Enabling Air View

When enabled, Air View instructs certain apps to respond when they sense that your finger is hovering slightly above the screen. For example, Calendar can pop up an event's details and Phone shows the person and number you have associated with a speed dial number. To enable or disable Air View, open Setting and tap the Air View icon (in the Motions section).

Air View (Speed Dial Assignments)

One-Handed Operation

If you sometimes need to operate the phone entirely with one hand, you can enable One-Handed Operation. When enabled, the screen is reduced in size and shifted so it's closest to the operating hand. To avoid the need to press the hardware buttons at the bottom of the phone and other essential controls, onscreen controls are added to the reduced display within reach of your thumb.

1. Tap the Settings icon on the Home screen.

2. Tap the One-Handed Operation icon (in the Device section).

3. Enable One-Handed Operation mode by moving the slider to the On position.

4. Follow the onscreen directions by sliding your thumb from the outer edge to the center and then back. When successful, the screen reduces in size. Where you start the swipe determines the new side of the screen.

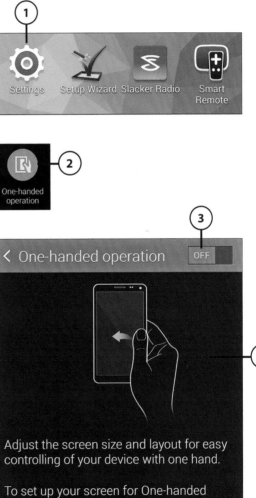

Adjust the screen size and layout for easy controlling of your device with one hand.

To set up your screen for One-handed operation, hold the device in one hand. Slide your thumb from the edge of the screen to the middle and back, in one quick motion.

⑤ To configure and use the reduced screen, you can do either of the following:

- Drag the upper-right corner to adjust the display size.

- Tap icons at the bottom of the screen rather than trying to press the keys they represent.

- Tap icons at the top of the screen to display your favorite contacts or favorite apps on the right edge of the window. With the contacts or apps icon selected (dark), you can tap the pencil icon to modify the listed contacts or apps. To hide the favorites, tap the same icon at the top of the screen again.

⑥ When you're done using One-Handed Operation, tap the icon at the top left or turn off the phone.

One-Handed Operation mode

Restore display

Favorite contacts

Favorite apps

Resize window

Recent Apps   Home   Back   Volume Up

Volume Down

Edit favorite apps or contacts

Search

Tabs

Menu

Create a contact

Owner's contact record

Section letter

Index letters

Contact record

In this chapter, you learn how to use the Contacts app to create and manage your business and personal contacts. Topics include the following:

→ Understanding the Contacts interface
→ Creating, viewing, and editing contact records
→ Joining multiple contact records for the same person
→ Defining and working with contact groups
→ Backing up your contacts to built-in memory or a memory card
→ Exporting contacts from Outlook (Windows) and Contacts/Address Book (Mac) and importing them into Google Contacts
→ Setting display options for the Contacts record list

Managing Contacts

Contacts is the built-in address book app on the Galaxy S5. It's populated by contact records created on the phone, in your Google Contacts account on the Web, and in other information sources that you sync to it, such as Facebook, LinkedIn, and Exchange Server accounts. The Contacts app links to Phone for dialing numbers, Email for selecting email recipients, and Messages for selecting text and multimedia message recipients.

Verizon and Other Carriers

The tabs across the top of the Contacts screen are slightly different for Verizon phones. Verizon users will see a *Recent* tab, whereas everyone else will see a *Logs* tab. Both tabs and their uses are discussed in this chapter, but the figures shown are a mixture of Verizon and non-Verizon ones.

The Contacts Interface

Contacts has four sections, each represented by a tab at the top of the screen. Here's what you can do in each section:

- *Keypad.* Tap the Keypad tab to switch to the Phone app to make a call. (Phone and Contacts are linked; you can quickly switch between them by tapping the appropriate tab. Chapter 4, "Using the Phone," covers the Phone app.)

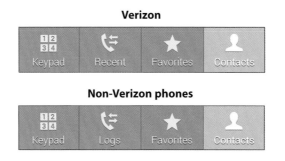

- *Logs (all carriers other than Verizon).* Tap the Logs tab to view your call records (dialed calls, missed calls, received calls, and rejected calls), enabling you to easily return calls and assign numbers to your Auto Reject List.

- *Recent (Verizon only).* Tap the Recent tab to view a list of people and companies that you have recently called or have received calls from.

Non-Verizon Phones

If Verizon isn't your carrier, you can view the people you frequently call by selecting the Favorites tab and scrolling to the Frequently Contacted section.

- *Favorites.* Tap the Favorites tab to view a list of only those contact records that you've marked as favorites. For more information about favorites, see "Mark Contacts as Favorites," later in this chapter.

Grid Versus List View

If you've added photos to your favorite contacts, tap the menu icon and choose Grid View to display favorites as photo thumbnails. (To restore the Favorites scrolling list, tap List View.) With Verizon phones, each contact appears with the related photo, if any.

- *Contacts.* The default tab is Contacts. It displays a scrolling list of your contact records. You can tap a person's name to view her contact record. This section of Contacts, or part of it, can optionally be displayed by Phone, Email, and Messages to enable you to select a call, email, or message recipient. The Contacts list is discussed throughout this chapter.

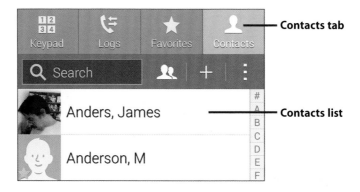

Creating a Contact Record

In addition to creating contacts in Google Contacts or another address book utility that you're syncing with your phone, you can create new contact records directly on the phone.

(**1**) Tap the Contacts icon on the Home screen or select it in Apps.

Other Contacts Launch Options

You can also launch Contacts by tapping the Contacts tab in the Phone app or the Contacts icon in Email or Messages when selecting message recipients.

2 Tap the Contacts tab if it isn't already selected.

3 Tap the + (plus) icon to create a new contact record.

4 *Verizon only:* Choose where the new contact will be created. Select Phone for a contact that will reside only on the phone. Select the account from where you usually receive email to share this record with the account's contact list. (Other carriers specify where the record is created in Step 6.)

Adding Accounts

Chapters 7, "Setting Up Accounts," and 11, "Using the Calendar," provide examples of adding accounts to the phone.

5 The screen for creating a contact appears, ready for you to enter the person or company's contact information.

6 The top entry shows the account in which the contact will be created and shared. Tap the entry to change the location.

Storage Location and Sharing

To create and store the record only on the phone, choose Phone (Verizon) or Device (carriers other than Verizon).

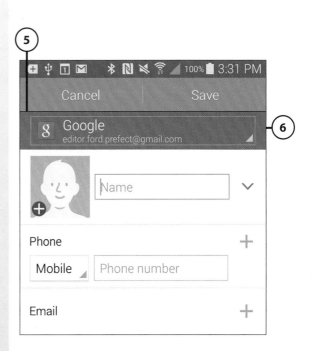

7 Enter the person's name. You can type the full name in the Name field or—to enter more detailed name information, such as a prefix, suffix, or middle name—tap the expand/collapse arrow beside the field. When you finish entering the name components, you can collapse the name by tapping the same arrow.

8 Enter a phone number for the person in the Phone field. If the label (Mobile, for example) is incorrect, tap the label and select the correct one from the drop-down list. (Select Custom or Other—at the bottom of the list—if you want to create your own label.)

Add more numbers by tapping the Phone field's plus (+) icon. To remove an unwanted or blank number, tap its minus (–) icon.

Text Messaging

To send text or multimedia messages to this person, you must enter at least one number that's designated as Mobile.

Expand/collapse

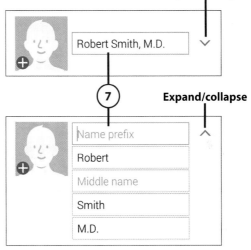

Expand/collapse

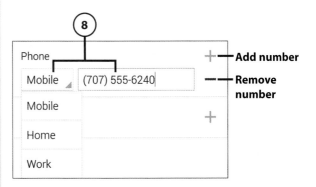

Add number

Remove number

9 Tap the + (plus) icon beside the Email field to record an email address for the person. Use the same process as you did for the Phone field (see Step 8).

10 Add fields that aren't currently shown by tapping Add Another Field at the bottom of the screen. As an example, Steps 11–12 explain how to add an Address field to the record.

11 Select Address in the Add Another Field dialog box and tap OK.

12 Use the same method that you used to enter Phone and Email information. Address is a composite field with separate entries for Street, City, State, ZIP Code, and Country. To add other elements, such as P.O. Box and Neighborhood, tap the expand/collapse icon. You can also select the Custom tab to enter other addresses, such as Beach House.

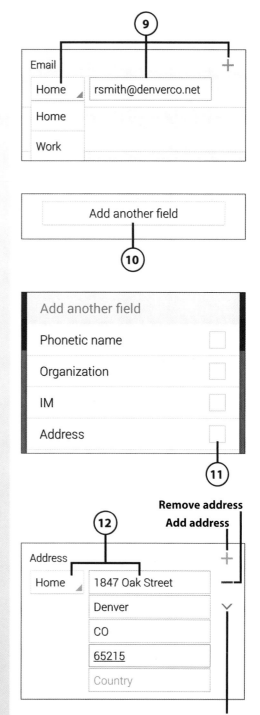

9

Email		+
Home	rsmith@denverco.net
Home	
Work	

Add another field

10

Add another field

Phonetic name	☐
Organization	☐
IM	☐
Address	☐

11

Remove address
Add address

12

Address		+
Home	1847 Oak Street	—
	Denver	⌄
	CO	
	65215	
	Country	

Expand/collapse

13 *Optional:* You can assign the person to one or more contact groups. With groups, you can text or email all members of the group by addressing a message to the group rather than to each member. To assign the person to groups, tap the Groups field, select the check box of each appropriate group, and tap Save. (To learn how to create and use groups, see "Working with Contact Groups," later in this chapter.)

14 *Optional:* To specify a distinctive ringtone that will announce calls from this person, tap Ringtone, select an option in the Ringtones dialog box, and tap OK.

15 *Optional (Verizon only):* To choose a distinctive alert for messages from this contact, tap Message tone, select an alert tone in the Message tone dialog box, and tap OK.

16 *Optional (Verizon only):* To assign an identifiable vibration pattern to the contact, tap Vibration Pattern, select a pattern in the Vibration Pattern dialog box, and tap OK. To create a custom vibration, tap Create and touch and release the screen with varying lengths of time to create the pattern on the Create Pattern screen.

Groups Co-workers	**13**
Ringtone Default	**14**
Message tone Default	**15**
Vibration pattern SOS	**16**

Cancel	Save
Create	
☐ Not assigned	
☐ ICE - emergency contacts	
☑ Co-workers	

13

Specifying a Ringtone

You can select ringtones from those provided with the phone (Ringtones) or use any audio file—such as a down-loaded ringtone or a complete song—that you've stored on the phone. To assign such a custom ringtone to the record, tap the Add button and locate the audio or music file. Ringtones are discussed in detail in "Choose Ringtones and Vibrations" in Chapter 10, "System Functions and Tools."

(17) When you finish entering the initial information for this contact, tap the Save button at the top of the screen or tap Cancel to discard the record.

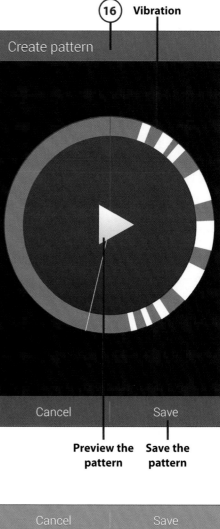

(16) Vibration

Preview the pattern   Save the pattern

(17)

Adding a Photo to a Contact Record

To help identify a contact, you can add a photo to the person's record. You can use any photo that's stored on the phone or use the phone's camera to shoot the picture.

(1) Associate a photo with the contact by tapping the photo placeholder in the upper-left corner while creating or editing the contact record. (If the record already has a photo, you can tap it to replace it with a new photo.)

(2) Select the appropriate option in the Contact Photo dialog box. Tap Image to use a photo stored on the phone. Tap Tagged Pictures to use a previously shared image. Tap Take Picture to use the phone's camera to shoot the picture now.

(3) If you tapped Image or Tagged Pictures in Step 2, Gallery launches. Tap the folder that contains the photo, tap the photo's thumbnail, and go to Step 5.

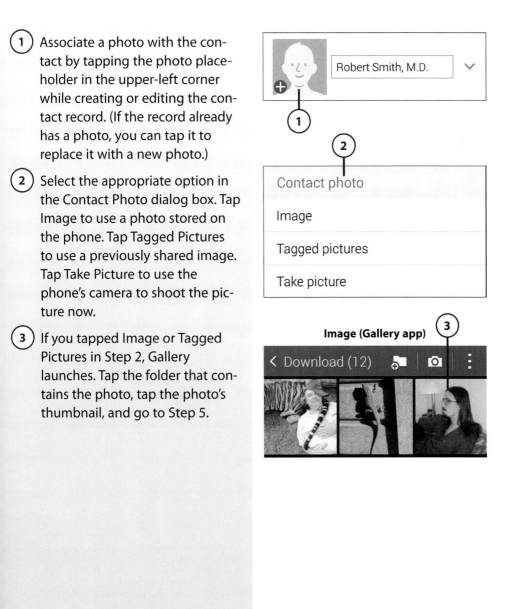

Robert Smith, M.D.

Contact photo

Image

Tagged pictures

Take picture

Image (Gallery app)

< Download (12)

4 If you tapped Take Picture in Step 2, Camera launches. Tap the Camera button to take the person's picture. If you don't care for the shot, tap Discard and try again; otherwise, tap Save.

5 On the cropping screen, move and resize the blue cropping rectangle to select the area of the photo that you want to use, and then tap Done. The cropped photo is added to the contact record.

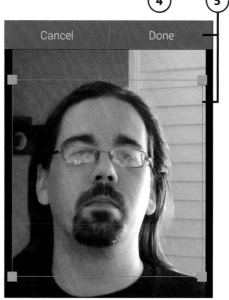

6 If you're done creating or editing the record, tap the Save button at the top of the screen.

Viewing Contacts

The bulk of what you do in Contacts involves finding and viewing individual contacts so you can call, email, or text them.

1 Launch Contacts by tapping its Home screen icon.

2 With the Contacts tab selected, contacts are displayed in an alphabetical scrolling list. By default, all contacts from all sources are listed. You can restrict contacts to a single source (LinkedIn, for example) and set other display options by following the instructions in "Setting Display Options" at the end of this chapter.

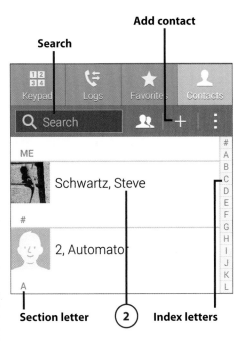

Section letter   **2**   **Index letters**

3 To find a particular contact, you can use any of the following techniques:

- Flick up or down to scroll the list.

- Tap an index letter on the right edge of the screen to go to that approximate spot in the alphabetical list.

- Press and drag in the index letter list. As you drag, a large version of each index letter appears. Remove your finger when the correct letter is shown. For example, to find a person whose last name is Jones, release your finger when J appears.

- Search for someone by tapping the Search box and entering any element of the person's record, such as first or last name, street name, phone number, email address, or notes. As you type, a list of likely matching contacts appears. When you see the correct record, tap the person's entry.

4 When you find the contact, tap it to view the person's record. Depending on the information recorded for the contact, you can dial any listed number by tapping the green phone icon, send a text message to the person by tapping the orange envelope icon, or address a new email to the person by tapping an email address' envelope icon.

Editing Contact Records

Contact records sometimes require editing. You might have to add or change an email address or phone number, or you may want to substitute a better picture. Editing a contact employs the same techniques that you use to create contact records. In this section, you discover several ways to edit records, as well as delete them.

Edit Contacts

When changes to a record are necessary to bring it up to date, here's what you need to do:

1. Select the record that you want to edit in Contacts. The complete record displays.

2. Tap the Edit icon.

3. Using the techniques described in "Creating a Contact Record," make the necessary changes to the person's information.

4. Tap Save to save your edits, or tap Cancel if you decide not to save the changes.

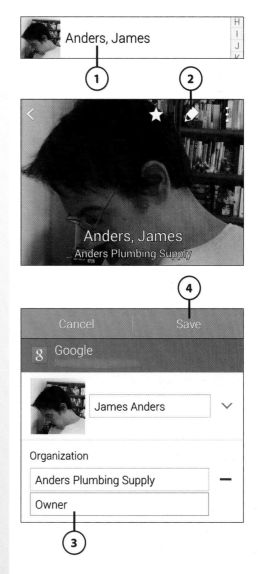

Set Defaults for a Contact

Several contact fields can have multiple entries. For example, a record can have several phone numbers, email addresses, IM usernames, and mailing addresses. For some of these fields, you can optionally specify a *default entry*—that is, one that you want to treat as primary.

(1) In any Contacts list, select the record for which you want to view, set, or change defaults. The complete record displays.

(2) Tap the menu icon and choose Mark as Default. All items for which you can set a default are displayed.

(3) Tap a radio button to set an entry as a default. If necessary, scroll to see any additional items.

(4) Tap Save to set the new defaults for the record.

(5) Whenever you view the record, default entries are denoted by a blue check mark.

Link and Unlink Contacts

Your contact records probably come from multiple sources. Some are created on the phone; others might originate in Google Contacts, LinkedIn, an Exchange Server account, or a social networking site. As a result, when you scroll through the entries in Contacts, you might find some duplicates. You can use the Link Contacts command (formerly known as Join Contact) to merge the duplicates for a person into a single contact record.

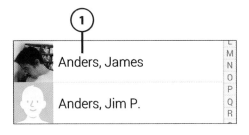

1 In the Contacts list, locate a pair of records for the same person by browsing or searching. This example uses a person with a record that was created on the phone and another created in Gmail. Tap the record that you want to serve as the primary record.

2 Tap the menu icon and choose Link Contacts. The Suggested Contacts list appears.

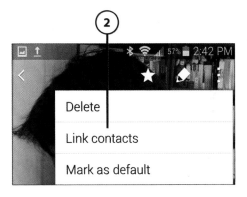

3 If the list includes the person's other record, select it and tap Done. Otherwise, scroll down to locate the record, select it, and tap Done.

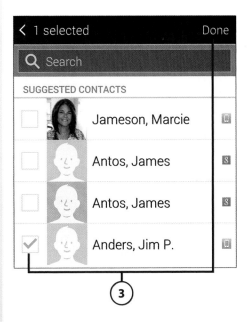

(4) The two records are linked to create a single record. If you view the record, you can see the sources of the linked records. If more records exist for this person, you can link those as well by using the Link Contacts command again.

Google

Device/Phone

(4)

Unlinking Contacts

If necessary, you can unlink records, re-creating the original, individual records. Open the linked record, tap the Link icon (which looks like a chain link) or choose Unlink Contacts from the menu, and tap the minus (–) sign beside one of the listed records.

Mark Contacts as Favorites

To make it easy to quickly find people with whom you're in regular contact, you can mark records as *favorites*. Doing so adds those people to the contacts in your Favorites list.

(1) In a Contacts list, tap a contact name.

(2) Tap the star icon at the top of the screen to add the contact to your Favorites. When marked as a favorite, the star is gold. If you subsequently need to remove the contact from Favorites, open the record and tap the star icon again.

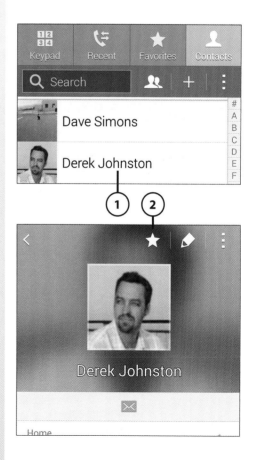

Simultaneously Removing Multiple Favorites

To remove *multiple* contacts from Favorites, select the Favorites tab, tap the menu icon, and choose Remove from Favorites. Tap the check box of each person that you want to remove, and then tap Done. (When removing favorites, you can also remove people from the Frequently Contacted list by tapping their check boxes.)

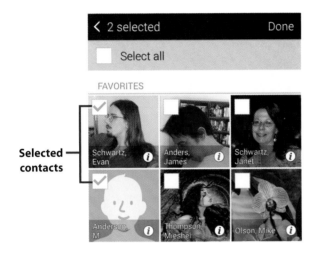

Grid Versus List View

If you've added photos to your favorite contacts, tap the menu icon and choose Grid View to display favorites as photo thumbnails. (To restore the Favorites scrolling list, open the menu and choose List View.)

Delete Contacts

People leave your personal and business life for many reasons. When you're certain that you no longer need certain contact records, you can delete them.

(1) To delete one or more records while viewing any Contacts list, press and hold any of these records. (Alternatively, you can open the menu and choose Delete.)

(2) Select other contacts that you also want to delete, if any. Selected contacts have a green check mark.

(3) Delete the selected contacts by tapping the Trash icon or Done, respectively (depending on the technique employed in Step 1). Tap OK in the Delete Contact confirmation dialog box.

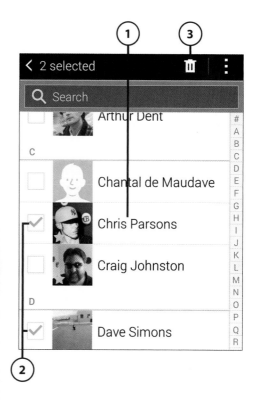

Deleting an Open Record

You can also delete a record while you're viewing it. Tap the menu icon, choose Delete, and tap OK in the Delete Contact confirmation dialog box.

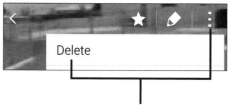

Deleting an open record

Working with Contact Groups

A *group* is a collection of contacts that have something in common, such as membership in a club. Because each group is a subset of Contacts, you can use groups to quickly find every important person of a particular type. You can also use a group as the recipient for an email or text message, automatically sending it to all members.

Create a Group

(**1**) In Contacts, tap the Groups icon.

(**2**) Tap the plus (+) icon to create a new group.

(**3**) *Optional:* Specify the account of which this group will be a subset by tapping Create Group In.

(**4**) Enter a name for the group.

(**5**) *Optional:* Specify a ringtone that will announce calls from group members.

(**6**) *Optional:* Specify an alert for text messages from group members.

(**7**) *Optional:* Specify a vibration pattern that will announce calls or text messages from group members.

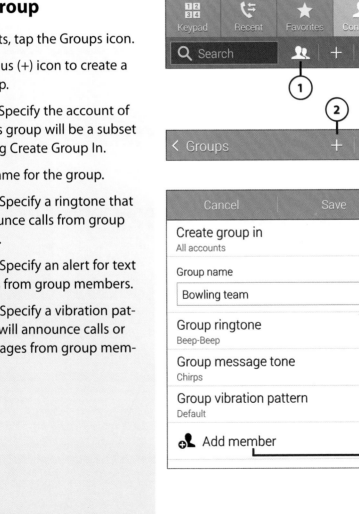

8 *Optional:* Tap Add Member to set the initial group membership. Select members by tapping their names and then tap Done. (Note that you can add members at any time.)

9 Tap the Save button to save the group name, membership, and settings. The group name is added to the Integrated Groups list. Whenever you want to view the group's membership, tap the Groups icon (refer to the figure for Step 1) and tap the group's name in the Integrated Groups list.

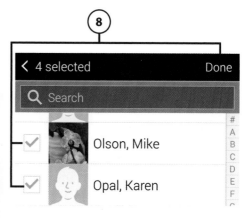

Changing a Group's Definition or Membership

You can quickly change a group's settings or membership. Tap the Groups icon, tap the group's name, and then open the menu and choose Edit Group. When you finish making changes, tap Save.

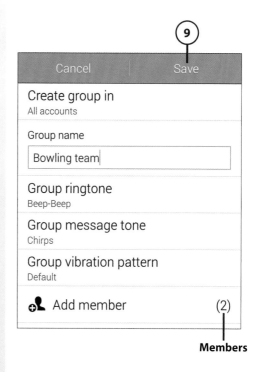

A Hidden Groups Feature

Below the Integrated Groups list are two categories labeled Accounts and Organizations. Tap Accounts to view contacts grouped by account, such as your LinkedIn associates. Tap Organizations to view all people affiliated with the same organization, such as all Google employees. If you aren't great at remembering names, opening an organization group might be just the help you need to find the name, phone number, or email address of the person you're trying to contact.

Change a Group's Membership

(1) With the Contacts tab selected, tap a person's name to open her record.

(2) Tap the Edit icon.

(3) Tap the Groups entry.

(4) Add or remove check marks to assign or remove the person from the listed groups. Tap Save to save the changes. (Note that a person can be a member of multiple groups.)

Quickly Removing Members from a Group

In addition to adding new members to a group, you can easily remove one or more members. Open the group to display its membership. Then tap the menu icon, choose Remove from Group, select the members that you want to remove, and tap Done.

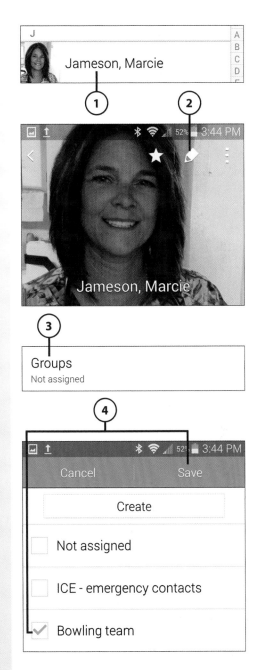

Email or Text a Group

1. In Email or Messages, tap the Compose icon.

2. Tap the Contacts icon to select email or message recipients.

3. In Contacts, tap the Groups tab and select the group that you want to email or message.

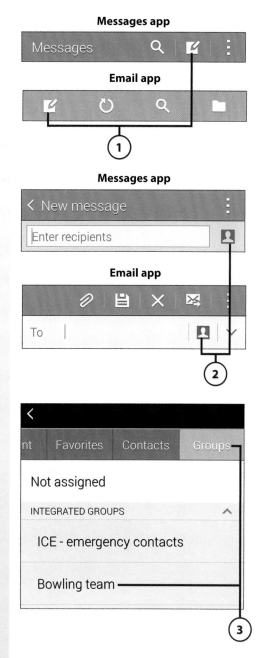

Messages app

Messages

Email app

Messages app

New message

Enter recipients

Email app

To

Favorites   Contacts   Groups

Not assigned

INTEGRATED GROUPS

ICE - emergency contacts

Bowling team

4 Select the individual group members that you want to email or message, or tap Select All to include the entire group as recipients.

Multiple Choice

If a selected individual has multiple email addresses or mobile phone numbers, a dialog box appears in which you must select the correct address or number.

5 Tap Done to transfer the selected members' email addresses or mobile numbers to Email or Messages, respectively. Complete your email or compose your message as you normally do.

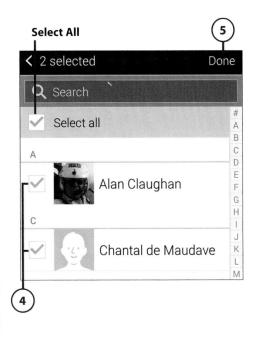

Select All

Start an Email or Text Message from Contacts

You can also initiate a group email or text message from within Contacts. Choose the Send Message or Email command and then select a group and specify members who will be recipients.

Send a text message or email

Delete a Group

1. Tap the Groups icon, and then open the menu and choose Delete Group.

2. Select the groups you want to delete by tapping check boxes, and then tap Done.

3. Indicate whether you want to delete only the selected group(s)—leaving the associated contact records intact—or the group(s) *and* member contact records. If you choose Groups and Members, all information for the selected contacts will be deleted from your contact list.

4. Confirm the deletion(s) by tapping OK or tap Cancel if you've changed your mind.

Deleting a User-Created Group

To quickly delete a group that you created, press and hold its entry in the groups list and tap the Trash icon.

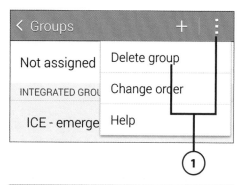

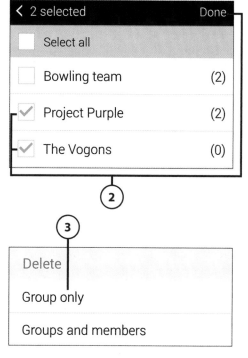

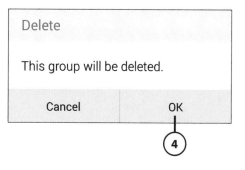

Backing Up/Restoring and Exporting/Importing Contact Records

As security against phone-related disasters or in preparation for switching to a new phone, you can back up your Contacts data to a memory card or built-in memory, or you can merge the data with your Google or Samsung account. Normally, your Contact information is backed up automatically on Google servers.

You can also use export/import procedures to manually move copies of contact records from your computer-based email and address book utilities into Contacts.

Carriers Differ

Each carrier decides the Contacts backup and restore procedures that it supports, as well as the steps required. However, regardless of which carrier you have, you should find several procedures in this section—occasionally with small variations—that are applicable to *your* phone.

Importing Contact Data from Other Sources into Google Contacts

Although Google Contacts (Gmail's address book) is the *de facto* source for Android contact data, it's not the place in which many of us have chosen to store our contacts. You may already have years of contacts stored in email clients and address book utilities on your computer. This section explains how to export your existing computer contacts and then import them into Google Contacts.

Exporting Your Computer's Data

Here's how to export your data from your existing contact-management application on your Mac or PC:

- *Address Book or Contacts (Mac).* Select the contacts to export and then choose File, Export, Export vCard (or Export Group vCard). Alternatively, drag the contacts out of the Address Book or Contacts window to your Desktop or a convenient Finder window.

- *Outlook 2010 or 2013 (Windows).* Click the File tab, click Options, and then click Advanced. Click the Export button to launch the Import and Export Wizard, click Export to a File, and click Next. Select the Comma Separated Values (Windows) option and click Next. Select the Contacts folder and click next. Click Browse, select the folder in which to place the exported file, and click Next. Finally, click Finish to export the data.

Import the Exported Data into Google Contacts

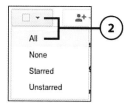

(1) In your computer's browser, go to mail.google.com or gmail.com and log in to your account. Open the Gmail menu and choose Contacts.

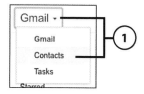

Just in Case...

As a safety measure, you might want to back up the Google Contacts data by opening the More menu and choosing Export. If the import described in this task doesn't go as planned, you can then restore your original Google Contacts data by choosing More, Import or by choosing More, Restore Contacts. The former command restores from your backup file, whereas the latter restores from one of several Google-provided backups.

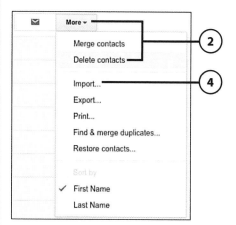

(2) To replace all current data in Google Contacts with the new data, you must delete all the records. From the first Contacts menu, choose All to select all visible records. Then from the More menu, choose Delete Contacts.

Caution: Selective Deletions

If Google Contacts contains records that do *not* exist in the imported data, you may want to delete all records *except* those.

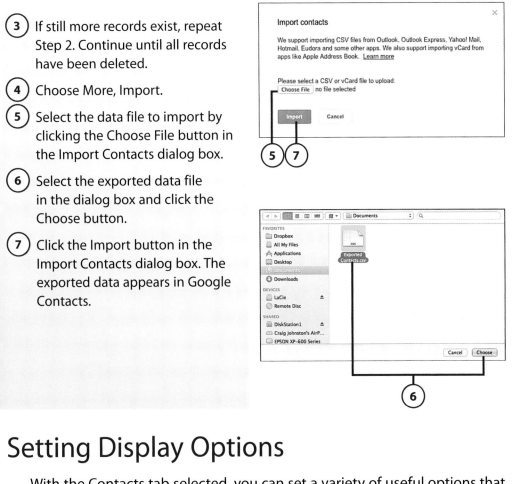

(3) If still more records exist, repeat Step 2. Continue until all records have been deleted.

(4) Choose More, Import.

(5) Select the data file to import by clicking the Choose File button in the Import Contacts dialog box.

(6) Select the exported data file in the dialog box and click the Choose button.

(7) Click the Import button in the Import Contacts dialog box. The exported data appears in Google Contacts.

Setting Display Options

With the Contacts tab selected, you can set a variety of useful options that determine which records are displayed and the order in which they appear.

1 Tap the menu icon and choose Settings.

2 Tap Contacts.

3 Tap the Only Contacts with Phones check box to hide contact records that don't include a phone number. (To restore the full contacts list, tap it again to remove the check mark.)

(4) You can sort contacts alphabetically by first name or last name. To change the current sort order, tap Sort By and then select an option in the Sort By dialog box.

Sort by	
First name	◉ —— **(4)**
Last name	○
Cancel	

(5) Regardless of the Sort By order specified in Step 4, you can display each contact as first name first (Bob Smith) or last name first (Smith, Bob). Tap Display Contacts By, and then select an option in the Display Contacts By dialog box.

Display contacts by	
First name first	◉ —— **(5)**
Last name first	○
Cancel	

(6) When you finish making changes, tap the Back icon or press the Back key.

Specifying Contacts to Display

There's also an option to view only those contacts associated with a particular account. For instance, you can view only your Facebook friends or LinkedIn colleagues. On the Settings screen, tap Contacts to Display, and select the account that you want to view. To create a custom view that combines several accounts, tap the Settings icon to the right of the Customized List option.

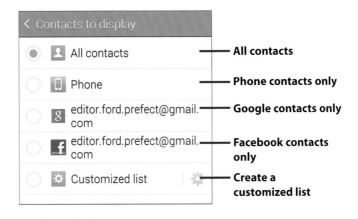

Menu for other options

Send button

Sender's account

Recipient email address

Title of email

Message body

In this chapter, you become familiar with the basics of setting up and operating your new phone. Topics include the following:

→ Setting up a Gmail account
→ Registering your Gmail account
→ Creating another email account
→ Setting up a Samsung account
→ Creating a Dropbox account

Setting Up Accounts

For some applications, such as your email account or apps for music, you need to set up an account. This chapter tells you how to set up your email, Samsung, and Dropbox accounts, which work with three of the more commonly used apps.

Gmail and Your Phone

Your phone runs on Android, the Google operating system. To use and connect to any Google service (such as Google Play, a source for Android apps that run on your phone), you must have a Google (Gmail) account. Gmail is Google's free email service. If you don't have an account, you should create one, as described in the next section. The final step is letting your phone know your Gmail account username and password, enabling it to access Google services.

Do It the Easy Way

Although you can create a Gmail account using your phone, a lot of typing is required. It's easier to use your computer's web browser (as described next). On the other hand, if you don't have access to a computer or would prefer to create the account using your phone, open Settings and tap Accounts, Add Account, Google, New. You can have more than one Google account, if you like.

Create a Gmail Account

1. On your PC or Mac, launch your web browser: Internet Explorer, Safari, Firefox, or Chrome, for example. Type www.gmail.com in the address box and press Enter/Return.

2. Click the Create an Account button in the page's upper-right corner.

3. Enter the requested registration information on the Create a New Google Account page.

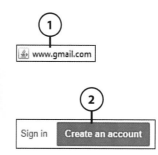

>>>Go Further

ACCOUNT-CREATION TIPS

The most common, desirable Gmail usernames are taken. To get one based on your name or your company's name, try adding numbers at the end (etymes529), separate words with periods (elna.tymes), or combine two or more unusual words (hamstringwarrior). Your username can be any combination of letters, numbers, and periods.

Your password must contain at least eight characters and can be any combination of uppercase letters, lowercase letters, numbers, or symbols. The Password Strength rating indicates how secure your proposed password is.

If possible, resist the temptation to use your Internet service provider (ISP) account password for Gmail, too. If you use one password everywhere on the Internet and someone learns it, all your accounts could be compromised. The most secure passwords combine uppercase letters, lowercase letters, and numbers (such as hA73rTv91).

Register Your Gmail Account

If you just created a Gmail account using your computer's browser, you need to add the account to your phone.

Once Will Suffice

To see if the account is already registered, open Settings and tap Accounts. If Google is listed in the My Accounts section, the account is registered, and you can skip the following task.

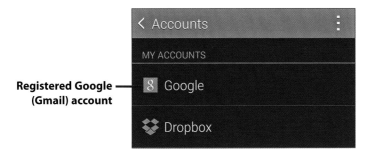

Registered Google — (Gmail) account

---

1. Open Settings, and then tap Accounts.

2. Tap Add Account at the bottom of the Accounts list.

3. Tap Google.

4. On the Add a Google Account screen, tap Existing. (If you don't have a Google/Gmail account, tap New and follow the onscreen prompts, or perform the steps in the "Create a Gmail Account" task.)

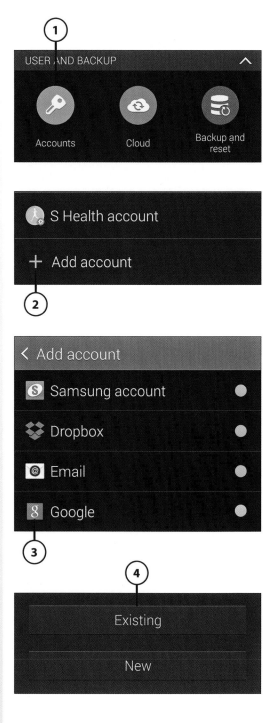

5. Enter your Gmail username and password. Tap the right-arrow icon to continue.

6. Tap OK to agree to the terms of service. An attempt is made to sign into the account.

7. Decide whether you want to receive news and offers from Google Play. Tap the right-arrow icon to continue.

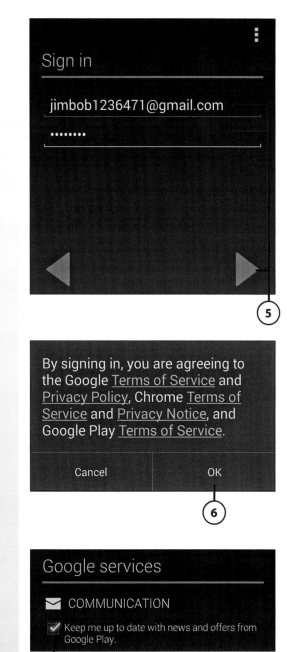

8 Enter payment information for purchases that you may later make in Goggle Play, or tap Not Now to skip this step. The phone attempts to sign into your new account.

9 On the Account Sign-In Successful screen, the check boxes determine the types of important phone data that will be regularly synced with your Gmail account. Ensure that each box is checked or unchecked according to your preference, and then tap the right-arrow icon. An account sync is automatically attempted.

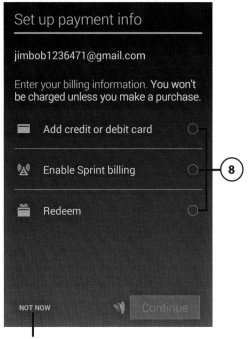

Not Now

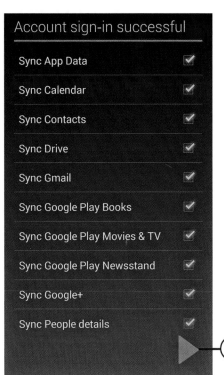

Creating Another Email Account

If you want to create an email account other than via Gmail, it's easy to do.

(1) Click the Email icon.

(2) Choose the type of email account you want to set up from the icons available. For instance, if you want to set up a Verizon.net account, click that icon.

(3) Enter an existing email address and password for this account and click the Next button. If you need to create the account, exit the screen and go to the account setup web page for your provider.

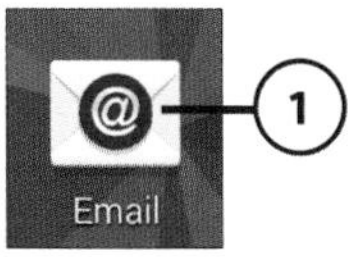

@ Email — 1

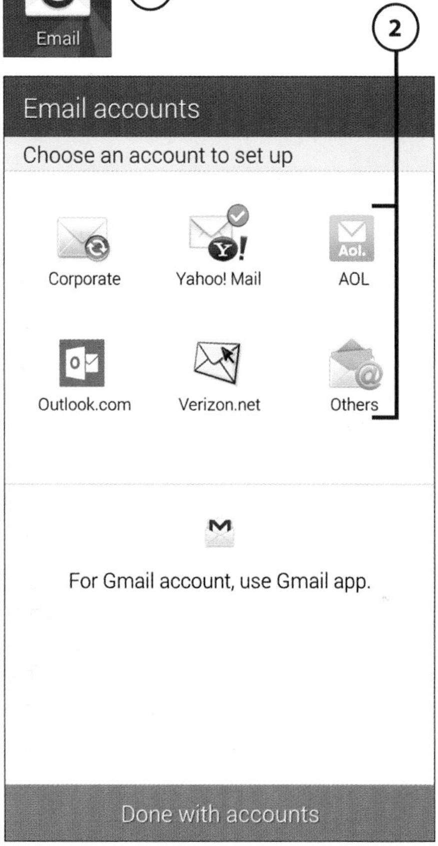

2

Email accounts

Choose an account to set up

Corporate   Yahoo! Mail   AOL

Outlook.com   Verizon.net   Others

M

For Gmail account, use Gmail app.

Done with accounts

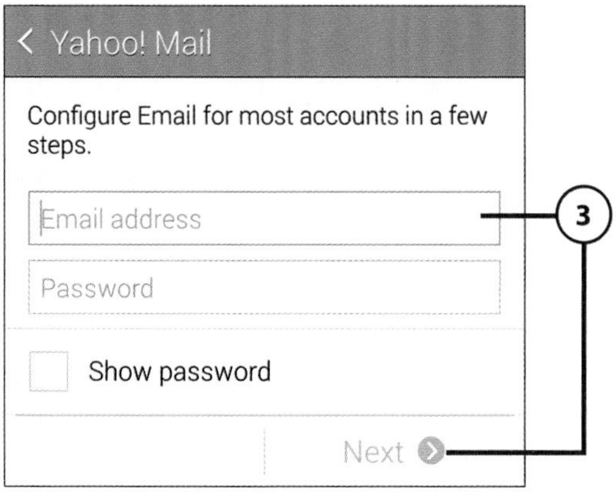

< Yahoo! Mail

Configure Email for most accounts in a few steps.

Email address — 3

Password

☐ Show password

Next ❯

(4) Your Galaxy S5 might ask for the type of account, such as whether it's a POP3 or IMAP account. Tap the option that applies to your account.

What's My Account?

If you don't know which type of account to choose, contact your service provider, such as Verizon or AT&T.

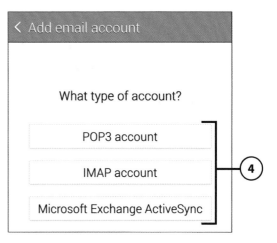

(5) When the Galaxy S5 detects the setup information for the account on this provider, it displays incoming and outgoing verification screens (not pictured). What comes next depends on what kind of email account you've set up. Provide any necessary details and tap Next.

(6) The S5 displays your completed email information (not pictured). You can now send and receive email via this account.

>>>Go Further
MULTIPLE EMAIL ACCOUNTS

If you have another email account, such as Gmail, you need to specify which account is your primary email account. The primary email account is the one that your phone will use for sending email by default. You can still use other email accounts, but you'll need to specify which of the other accounts you want to use each time. Set up additional accounts under the Accounts section when you tap the Settings icon, and specify whether the new one is the primary account on the screen that appears after you tap Next.

Creating a Samsung Account

Certain Samsung applications that are supported on the Galaxy S5 require you to sign up for a free Samsung account. Having a Samsung account also enables you to easily back up some types of data, such as your phone logs and messages. If you didn't create the account or log into an existing one when you ran the setup wizard described in Chapter 3, you can create the account now—or the first time you use an application that requires an account.

(1) Open Settings, and then tap Accounts.

(2) Tap Add Account at the bottom of the Accounts list.

(3) Tap Samsung Account. (If the account's status dot is green, you've already added a Samsung account to this phone and can skip the remaining steps.)

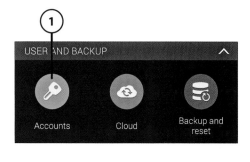

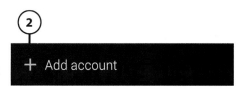

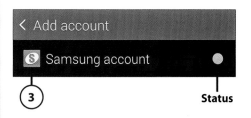

4 Tap Create Account.

5 Create the account by entering an email address and password to use for the account, as well as the other requested information. Tap the Sign Up button.

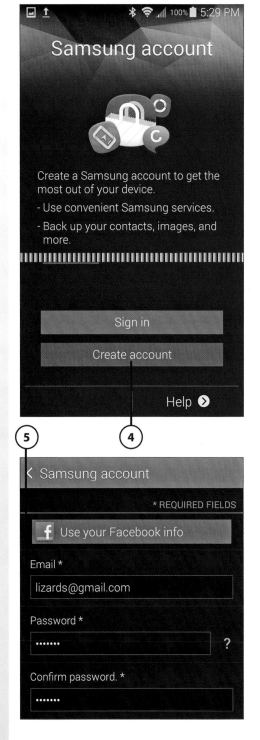

6 Review the Terms and Conditions, Special Terms, Privacy Policy, and Data Combination information by tapping each entry. Tap the check boxes, and then tap the Agree button.

7 Open the account verification email message on your phone or computer and follow the account activation instructions. When you finish, the Samsung account is marked with a green dot on the Add Account screen, indicating that it's recorded on your phone.

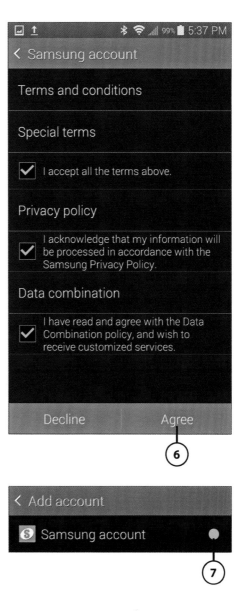

Creating a Dropbox Account

With Dropbox installed on your phone, tablet, and computers, you can use cloud storage to share your videos, photos, and other files among your devices and with other users. Normally, a free Dropbox account provides 2GB of online storage. If your carrier is one of those participating in the Galaxy S5 promotion, you're eligible for an upgrade to 50GB—free for the first two years.

Getting the App and Desktop Versions

If the Dropbox app isn't preinstalled on your Galaxy S5, you can download it from Google Play. You can get versions for PCs, Macs, tablets, and other devices from the Dropbox website at www.dropbox.com. Instructions and tutorials for using Dropbox are there, too.

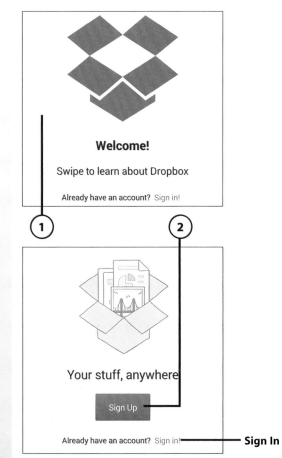

(1) To create a free Dropbox account, do either of the following:

- From any Home screen, tap Apps and then Dropbox.

- Perform Steps 1 and 2 of "Creating a Samsung Account," and then tap Dropbox.

The Dropbox Welcome screen appears.

(2) Swipe repeatedly until you reach the last page. Tap Sign Up. (If you already have an account, tap Sign In and provide your log-in information.)

Welcome!

Swipe to learn about Dropbox

Already have an account? Sign in!

Your stuff, anywhere

Sign Up

Already have an account? Sign in! — **Sign In**

3 Enter your first and last name, an email address with which to associate the account, and a password for the Dropbox account. Tap Create Account.

4 Review the Terms of Service, and tap I Agree.

✦ Sign up for Dropbox

First name

Last name

Email

Password

Create account

3

Terms of Service

Before you can complete your registration, you must accept the Dropbox Terms of Service

I Agree   View Terms

4

5 To instruct Dropbox to automatically back up photos and videos that you take with the phone, tap Turn On Camera Upload; otherwise, tap Skip This. (You can enable this feature within the Dropbox app whenever you like.)

6 The Dropbox account is marked with a green dot on the Add Account screen, indicating that it's recorded on your phone.

Camera Upload

Keep your memories safe

Dropbox can automatically back up photos & videos right after you take them.

Include videos   ON

Turn on Camera Upload

Skip this ›

Include/exclude videos

< Add account

Samsung account   ●

Dropbox   ●

In this chapter, you become familiar with the basics of working with networks on your new phone. Topics include the following:

→ Using the Galaxy S5's automatic network detection
→ Working with Wi-Fi
→ Setting up a connection method
→ Printing from your phone

8

Connecting to a Network

This chapter explains how to connect to a network—in particular, a Wi-Fi network—so that you can then connect to the Internet. Through your network connection, you can send and receive email; store and retrieve information; download and play music, TV shows, and movies; and take advantage of the apps stored on your Galaxy S5, such as the GPS.

Automatic Network Detection

When you first turn on your Galaxy S5, by default it searches for an available Wi-Fi connection and automatically connects you. Thus, if you already have a Gmail account, you're connected to the network the first time you press the Gmail icon. However, you need to supply your login and password.

If you have set up a Contacts list on another computer or device that uses Google for email, you'll automatically be connected to that, too. This means that you can make a phone call directly to one of the people on your Contacts list without going through any setup procedure. However, this isn't necessarily true if you're using another program (such as Outlook) on the other computer or device.

Further, because most of your information is stored "in the cloud" and not on your Galaxy S5, you'll have instant access to all that information. What you first see when you see your Contact list is accounting information about your phone account, followed by all your contacts.

The Good and the Bad About the Cloud

What is "the cloud"? Very simply, it's another place where your data is stored and can be quickly retrieved. Although some data is stored on your Galaxy S5, your phone would have to be the size of a large brick to accommodate even a modicum of your personal data. Samsung provides a transparent (to you) method of retrieving whatever you request. The good news is that, thanks to Wi-Fi connections, the Galaxy S5 can retrieve whatever is necessary very quickly. The bad news is that, if you're in an area with little cell phone coverage (such as parts of New Mexico, Montana, or Wyoming) or in airplane mode you might not be able to retrieve any data that isn't currently stored on your phone. However, some airplane flights offer Wi-Fi connections in-flight (for a fee), which means you can use your contacts and send and retrieve email as long as Wi-Fi is in service. (Normally such service is shut down during takeoff and landing.)

Enabling and Disabling Wi-Fi

Any activity that transmits data to and from your phone over the cellular network counts toward your plan's data limit. The same data transmitted over Wi-Fi, on the other hand, doesn't count. By tapping icons in the Notification panel, you can manually control the method by which data transmissions occur, ensuring that the least expensive and fastest method is used. In this section, you learn how to enable and disable Wi-Fi, as well as how to connect your phone to a wireless (Wi-Fi) network.

Connection Methods

At any given time, only a Wi-Fi or 2G/3G/4G cellular connection can be the active data connection method.

When Wi-Fi is enabled and you're connected to a network, the 2G/3G/4G connection is automatically disabled. When Wi-Fi is disabled or unavailable and you perform a data-related activity, the 2G, 3G, or 4G cellular connection is automatically used, depending on what's available at your current location. (Note that there's an exception to the Wi-Fi *or* cellular connection rule. If your carrier is one of the few that supports the Download Booster feature, Wi-Fi *and* a cellular connection can be simultaneously active, enabling you to improve download speeds for files larger than 30 MB. Check with your phone service provider to find out if it supports the Download Booster feature.)

You can also use Bluetooth to exchange data directly between the phone and any Bluetooth-capable computer or laptop.

Manually Set a Connection Method

(1) Open the Notification panel by touching the status bar at the top of the screen and dragging downward.

(2) The Wi-Fi icon toggles between a Wi-Fi and cellular (2G/3G/4G) data connection. Wi-Fi is enabled when the icon is green; a cellular connection is active when the Wi-Fi icon is dim. Tap the Wi-Fi icon to toggle its state.

(3) Close the Notification panel by touching the bottom of the panel and dragging upward.

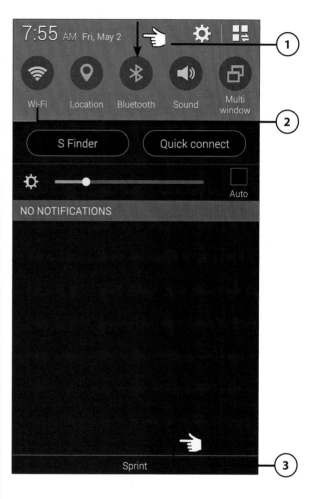

Which Wi-Fi Network?

In Settings, Wi-Fi shows the Wi-Fi network to which you're connected, as well as other available networks. Open Settings and tap Wi-Fi, or press and hold the Wi-Fi icon in the Quick Setting buttons. You can tap any network name to view its speed and signal strength.

Monitoring Data Usage

If your data plan isn't unlimited, you can use the Data Usage setting to monitor your usage and warn when you're close to the cellular data plan limit.

Connect to a New Wi-Fi Network

Because it's free and often a faster connection than using a 2G, 3G, or 4G cellular connection, it's advantageous to use a Wi-Fi connection whenever it's available. After you successfully connect to a given network (such as your home network or one at a local coffee shop), your phone can reconnect without requesting the password again.

(1) To go directly to the Wi-Fi screen, open the Notification panel, and then press and hold the Wi-Fi icon in the Quick Setting buttons. (Alternatively, you can open Settings and tap the Wi-Fi icon.)

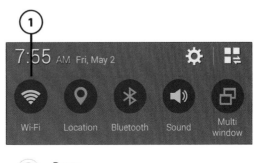

Press and hold

(**2**) Ensure that Wi-Fi is enabled by dragging its slider to the On position.

(**3**) A list of nearby networks appears. If a network to which you've previously connected is found, the phone automatically connects to it. If no network is automatically chosen or you want to connect to a different network, tap the name of the network to which you want to connect and continue with Step 4.

(**4**) Do one of the following:

- If the network is unsecured (there's no lock icon), tap the Connect button. No password is required to connect.

- If the network is secured (password protected—has lock icon), enter the requested password, and then tap the Connect button.

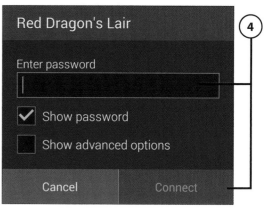

Secured network

Proceed with Caution

Always be cautious when using a Wi-Fi network you don't know—especially one that is not password protected. On unprotected networks, anyone can see your information; even on protected networks anyone with a password can potentially see your information. Be especially cautious with important information such as bank transactions.

(**5**) If successful, the Settings screen shows that you're connected to the network.

Show Password

When entering a lengthy or complex password, you might find it helpful to tap the Show Password check box. Otherwise, each character in the password is only momentarily visible as you type it.

>>>Go Further

WI-FI NETWORK TIPS

If you have occasion to connect to more than one Wi-Fi network, here are a couple of tips you might find helpful:

- To forget a network to which you've previously connected, press and hold the network name in the Wi-Fi Networks list, and then tap Forget Network.

Forget this network — NETGEARSS_Guest1 / Forget network / Modify network config

- To view information about the network to which you're connected, tap its name in the Wi-Fi Networks list. If there are multiple unsecured networks within range, you can connect to each one and compare their signal strength and speed.

Network properties

Siliconwasteland-5Ghz

Status
Connected

Signal strength
Very strong

Link speed
270Mbps

Security
WPA2 PSK

IP address
192.168.1.8

Cancel   Forget

Using Bluetooth

Bluetooth is a short-range communications technology that lets you connect wirelessly to a number of Bluetooth-enabled devices—most commonly headsets and in-car hands-free systems within a range of about 30 feet. With Bluetooth, you can also set up your phone to receive files sent by another Bluetooth device.

(1) Tap the Apps icon and then tap the Settings icon.

(2) Tap Bluetooth.

(3) Slide the switch to On.

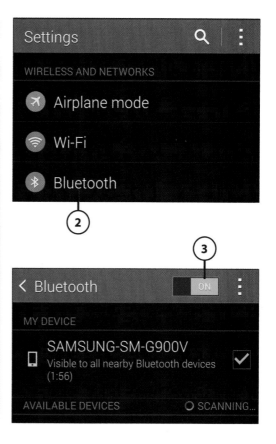

4 Give your Galaxy S5 a user-friendly name, such as My Bluetooth or Molly, by tapping the menu icon in the upper right and then selecting Rename Device.

5 Read the instructions about renaming, and tap OK.

6 Tap Device Name.

7 Enter the new name and tap OK.

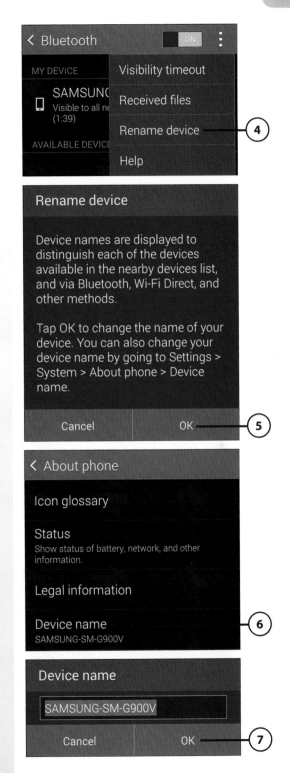

(8) Your phone needs to be visible to other Bluetooth devices. On the Settings menu, tap Bluetooth, as shown in the figure for Step 2. Tap the menu icon and select Visibility Timeout.

(9) Specify a length of time where your phone will remain visible to other Bluetooth devices after you turn on visibility.

(10) To connect with another Bluetooth device, on the Bluetooth menu make sure the On/Off button is set to On (as shown in the figure for Step 3), and then tap Scan to see other Bluetooth-enabled devices in the vicinity. Tap one of the devices and follow the prompts to complete the connection.

(11) When another device has sent you a file, you can access it from your phone. On the Bluetooth menu, tap Received Files.

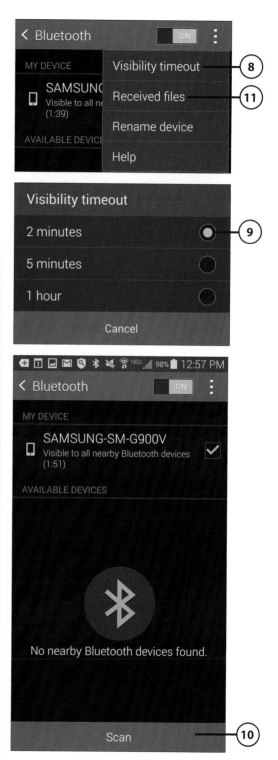

(12) The received file is automatically stored in the Files section of your phone. (Tap the My Files icon on the Apps screen to see what's there.)

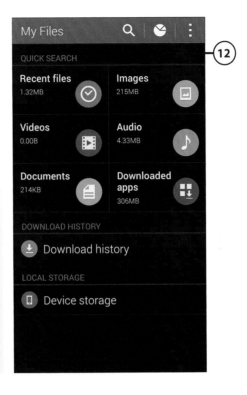

(12)

Wireless Printing

If you own or have access to a wireless printer, you can print from any app that provides a Print command, such as Gallery. Prior to printing, you must install print service software for your printer. You also need to know the IP (Internet protocol) address of the printer on the wireless network. See the printer manual for this information. (If you know your router's IP address, you can turn on the printer, enter the router's IP address in your browser, and discern the printer's IP address.)

Install the Print Services Software (First Time Only)

(1) On the Home screen, tap Apps, followed by Settings.

(2) In the Connect and Share section, tap Printing.

(3) If a print service plug-in isn't listed for your printer, tap the plus (+) button. Play Store launches.

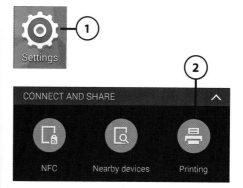

4 In the list that appears, locate a print service app from your printer's manufacturer. Tap to select the software.

5 Review its description, ensure that your printer model is supported, and tap Install.

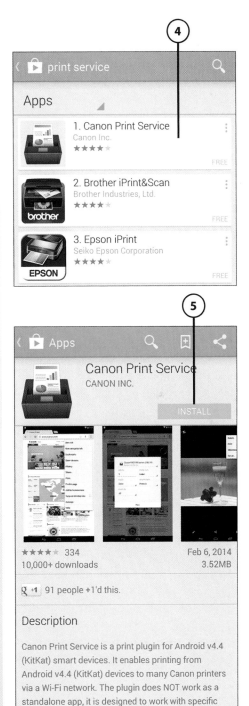

6 When installation finishes, press the Back key repeatedly until the Printing screen reappears. The new print service software is added to the list. Tap its name to enable and configure it. The system automatically searches for the printer. Be sure your printer is on.

7 When you print from an app, select your wireless printer from the Available list. When you print from your phone, the formatting might not be as accurate as when you print from a PC or a Mac.

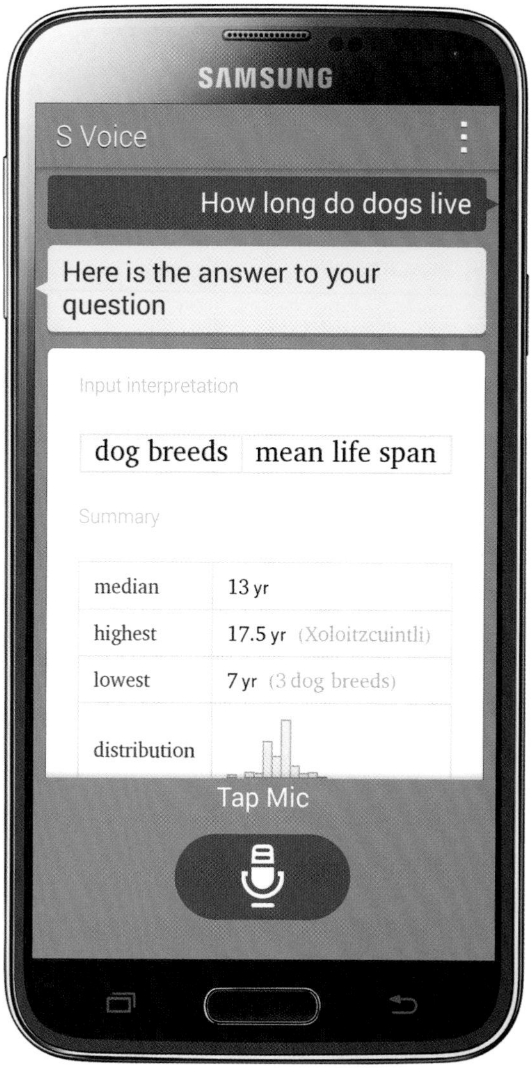

SAMSUNG
S Voice
How long do dogs live
Here is the answer to your question
Input interpretation
dog breeds | mean life span
Summary
median 13 yr
highest 17.5 yr (Xoloitzcuintli)
lowest 7 yr (3 dog breeds)
distribution
Tap Mic

In this chapter, you learn about controlling your Galaxy S5 using voice commands. Topics include the following:

→ Using and configuring S Voice
→ Using and configuring Google/Voice Search

Using Voice Services

The Galaxy S5 ships with a pair of competing voice-command apps: S Voice (a Samsung app) and Google/Voice Search. Both operate in a similar fashion, letting you speak English-like commands and queries to control the phone and its apps, perform Web searches, and find answers to your questions.

Using S Voice

S Voice is a voice app that lets you ask questions in natural language ("Where can I find pizza?") and command the phone ("Open Calculator"). The result may be a direct answer, a Web search, launching an app, or performing a specific command within an app.

(1) Launch S Voice by tapping Apps, S Voice or by double-tapping the Home key.

Using the Home Key

If double-tapping the Home key doesn't launch S Voice, tap Apps, S Voice; tap the menu icon and choose Settings; then enable Open Via the Home Key. On subsequent uses, double-tapping the Home key will work properly. To learn more about S Voice settings, see the "Configure S Voice" task later in this chapter.

(2) The S Voice screen appears. Say your first question or command. For example, you might ask, "What's the weather like today?" to see the weather forecast for your city. S Voice displays the information it finds.

(3) To ask S Voice the next question or give it a new command, tap the microphone button or say the wake-up phrase. ("Hi, Galaxy" is the default phrase.)

Help with S Voice Commands

If you want assistance with question and command phrasing, say "Help," or tap the menu icon and choose Example Commands.

Commanding the Phone

When using S Voice to control the phone or specific apps, there are some important commands you need to know and S Voice limitations of which you should be aware. In addition to the ones presented in this section, you'll discover other general and app-specific commands and limitations as you experiment.

First, if you leave the S Voice screen, you typically lose the ability to issue further commands—until you return to S Voice. This happens, for example, when you issue an Open app command. If you need to perform specific functions within the app, you have to do so manually or figure out if there's a way to issue a more complex command from S Voice. Instead of saying "Open Music," you might say "Play Black Oak Arkansas" (a group) or "Play Stagefright" (an album), for instance.

Play stage fright — **Command**

Playing Stagefright

Stagefright
The Band — **Response**

Second, in some circumstances, S Voice prompts you for missing details in order to complete a command or clarify what you want. For example, if you say "Create new event Shop for trombone," S Voice asks for a time (because you've requested a new event rather than a task) and then asks whether you want to save it to Calendar.

Third, when buttons are displayed (such as Cancel and Save), you can tap or speak the button name to indicate how the current item should be handled. Alternatives, such as saying "Yes" or "No," are often acceptable, too.

> Here's your appointment. Should I save it?
>
> **29** May
> Thursday
>
> Shop for trombone
> 10:00AM - 11:00AM
>
> Cancel   Save
>
> OK, I'll leave it off your calendar

Fourth, you can back out of or halt many commands by saying "Cancel."

To get you started, review some of S Voice's supported commands by opening the menu and choosing Example Commands. Here are some others you can use:

- *Launching apps.* To open an app, you can say "run," "open," "launch," or "start," followed by the app's name. After you finish using the app, you can frequently return to S Voice by pressing the Back key repeatedly until you exit the app.

- *Controlling settings.* Sadly, there are only a few system settings that you can command. You can enable or disable Wi-Fi or Bluetooth by saying "Turn on (or off) Bluetooth," "Enable (or disable) Wi-Fi." Because Settings is an app, you can open it by saying "Open Settings." You can also change the current volume by saying "Volume up (or down)" or "Raise (lower) volume."

I Can't Find a Network Connection

If Mobile Data (in Data Usage Settings) isn't enabled when you turn off Wi-Fi, you won't be able to turn it back on with a voice command. In fact, you won't be able to use S Voice at all because it requires an active Wi-Fi or cellular connection. To resume using S Voice, manually enable Wi-Fi by tapping its Quick Setting button or open Settings, tap Data Usage, and enable Mobile Data.

- *Safer navigation.* Open the Notification panel and enable Car mode by tapping its Quick Setting button. A version of S Voice with huge text and icons launches.

- *Calculations.* Rather than launch Calculator, speak the calculation that you want to perform. Examples include "472.43 divided by 17.6," "Multiply 6 by 17.5," "Square root of 87.5," "Minus 6.5 times 8," "What is three-fourths of 17.65?" and "Calculate 15% of $84.35."

Calculation Difficulties

It can be difficult discovering acceptable phrasing for calculation commands, and many such commands can't be answered—even when S Voice shows that it understands the numbers and operators. For example, you can multiply by a number less than one (such as 18 * 0.12) either by stating "eighteen times zero point one two," or by stating the decimal number as a fraction: "18 times 12 divided by 100."

- *Units of measure and currency conversions.* Examples include "How many pints in a liter?" "How many millimeters in a yard?" "How many British pounds can I get for $14?" and "Convert dollars to yen."

- *Just-for-fun commands and queries.* Try asking/saying the following: "How much wood could a woodchuck chuck if a woodchuck could chuck wood?" "Sing," "Where is Carmen Sandiego?" "What's the ultimate answer to life, the universe, and everything?" and "Tell me a joke."

What About Web Searches?

Like Voice Search (discussed later in this chapter), S Voice can perform Web searches. In fact, when it doesn't hear you clearly or can't determine what you want, it *offers* to search the Web. Interestingly, when you *do* request a search, the request is often handed off to Google Search.

Commanding Apps: Calendar

In addition to merely launching apps, you can use S Voice to issue commands to some of them. As an extended example, here are some ways that you can control Calendar.

You can give voice commands to schedule new appointments (events) or tasks. Examples of creating new tasks include: "Create new task give Jethro a bath next Sunday," "New task install vertical blinds" (when no date is provided, S Voice assumes the task's due date is today), and "Create task wash car on Saturday reminder on Friday" (adding "reminder on…" instructs Calendar to present a reminder notification on the specified day). Another way to add a reminder is to include a time in the command, such as "New task take out garbage tonight at 10:00 p.m." Although tasks don't have scheduled times (only events do), the mention of 10:00 p.m. is interpreted to mean that you want to be reminded at that time.

Scheduling appointments works in much the same way, but events contain additional components. You might say, for example, "Schedule operation at hospital for 7:00 a.m. Wednesday for 4 hours." Because it includes all essential details for a new appointment, S Voice offers to save it as-is. If it's lacking an important element (such as the time), S Voice prompts for it. When asked, you can specify *both* the time *and* date, such as "Saturday at 11:30 a.m."

To view a list of your upcoming tasks or events, you can say "Show my tasks" or "Show my appointments." Each command results in a list, but appointments are read aloud.

Deleting and Editing Tasks and Events

To delete upcoming or recent tasks and events without launching Calendar, you can say "Delete task (or appointment)." S Voice presents a list of tasks or events, asks you to specify the one to delete, and then asks you to confirm the deletion.

You can also be more specific, such as "Delete wash car." If there are multiple instances of a wash car task, S Voice lists them and asks which one to delete. You can select an item by position by saying "the second one," for example.

If you notice an error in a saved appointment or event, say "Edit appointment (or task)." S Voice asks you to select the appointment or task to edit and then prompts for the change(s).

Configure S Voice

Like other apps, you can customize the way that S Voice works.

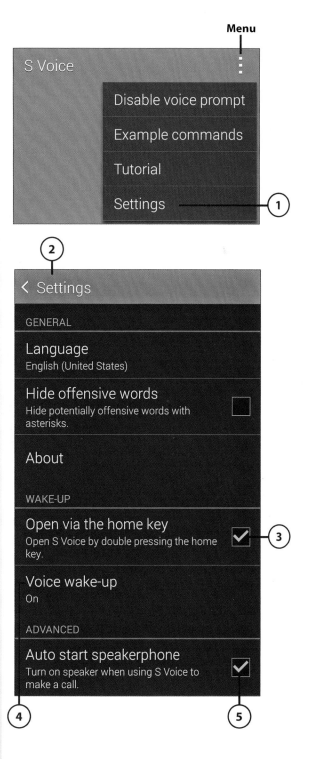

Menu

1. In S Voice, tap the menu icon and choose Settings.

2. The Settings screen appears. Following are some of the most important S Voice settings.

3. *Open Via the Home Key*. When enabled, you can launch S Voice by double-pressing the Home key from almost anywhere on the phone.

4. *Voice Wake-up*. When Voice Wake-up is enabled and S Voice is onscreen, you can speak a phrase (such as "Hi, Galaxy") to get the app's attention; otherwise, you must tap the microphone icon. Tap this item to enable, disable, or change the wake-up command.

5. *Auto Start Speakerphone*. When this option is checked and you instruct the Phone app to place a call, Speakerphone mode is automatically enabled.

(6) *Show Body of Message.* When a text message arrives, S Voice can display the message body (checked) or only the sender's name (unchecked). If the latter option is chosen, you can ask S Voice to read the hidden message text aloud.

(7) *Check Missed Events, Personal Briefing.* When enabled, missed events and/or your schedule are displayed when you first launch S Voice.

(8) *Home Address.* Tap this setting to record your home address, enabling S Voice to use it to generate responses to you.

(9) *Log In to Facebook, Sign In to Twitter.* If you want to use S Voice to post to a Facebook or Twitter account, you must log into your account(s)—enabling S Voice to do so in later sessions. When enabled, you can say commands such as "Facebook update Has anyone seen the new Godzilla movie?" If the appropriate app isn't already installed, you'll be taken to the appropriate Google Play page to download and install it.

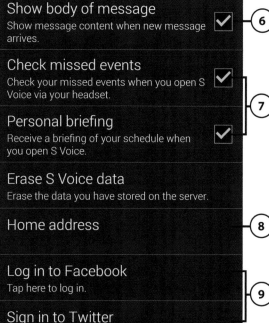

Show body of message
Show message content when new message arrives. — 6

Check missed events
Check your missed events when you open S Voice via your headset. — 7

Personal briefing
Receive a briefing of your schedule when you open S Voice.

Erase S Voice data
Erase the data you have stored on the server.

Home address — 8

Log in to Facebook
Tap here to log in. — 9

Sign in to Twitter
Tap here to sign in.

(7)

Schedule

Dr appointment
9:00 AM - 10:00 AM

It's Not All Good

It's Only a Start

There are several immediately apparent problems with S Voice. (Many of these criticisms apply equally to Google/Voice Search.) First, commands and queries can only be issued from the voice app's screen. You can control music playback, set or check your schedule, create text messages and memos, and perform calculations, but you can't issue any commands from *within* an app—even if S Voice opens the app for you.

Second, because S Voice is designed to recognize English-like commands, there's no simple way to determine what commands will work without experimentation. You never can tell whether certain commands are impossible or you're simply phrasing them in a way that S Voice doesn't understand. For instance, if I request the song "Happy Together," S Voice ignores the song with that name that's stored on my Galaxy S5 and instead attempts to play a song that it thinks is a *happy* one. (In point of fact, it failed badly, playing the saddest song I had.)

Third, S Voice is inconsistent. When I'm asked which of two appointments to delete and I say "the second one," it dutifully deletes the correct appointment. But when I ask it to play a song that's available on three albums, regardless of whether I tap one or say "the third one," it ignores me and plays the first.

Like many compelling Galaxy S5 features, I'm torn between marveling at the fact that S Voice works at all and being annoyed that it doesn't work well enough. For now, I consider it something fun to play with that will undoubtedly get better with each update—much like the improvements I've seen in the accuracy of converting voice input into text.

Using Google/Voice Search

Google, Voice Search, and Google Now are interrelated apps. As a result, you can perform several different launch actions to end up in the same place; that is, ready to issue voice commands and requests.

(1) Launch Google/Voice Search by doing one of the following:

- Tap Apps, Google or Apps, Voice Search.

- With the Google Search widget displayed on the current Home screen, tap the widget or say "OK, Google."

(2) The opening screen that appears depends on whether Google Now is enabled (see "Configuring Google/Voice Search," later in the chapter) and the launch method used in Step 1.

(3) If the screen doesn't automatically request your voice input, tap the microphone icon or say the wake-up phrase ("OK, Google").

4 Speak a voice command or search request.

5 Depending on the nature of your voice input, an app, web page, or Settings screen opens (taking you to a different screen) or the result is displayed on the Google screen. If you want to issue more commands or requests, do the following:

- If you're still on the Google screen, tap the microphone icon or say "OK, Google," and then issue your new command or request.

- If a different app or a Settings screen is onscreen, press the Back key until you reach the Google screen, or press the Home key and start over again at Step 1.

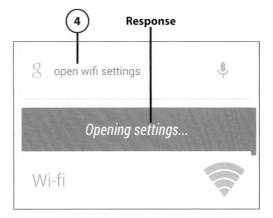

4   **Response**

open wifi settings

Opening settings...

Wi-fi

>>>Go Further

GOOGLE/VOICE SEARCH VERSUS S VOICE

As you experiment with Google/Voice Search, you'll see that it's *very* much like
S Voice. You can issue similar commands in similar language and get similar results. Both
require that you have an active Internet connection in order to function. Here are some of the
ways in which the Google and Samsung utilities differ:

- In addition to being able to launch apps by saying "run, open, launch, or start *app name*,"
  Google can open many Settings screens. Say "Open *settings name*," such as "Open Display
  Settings." S Voice, on the other hand, is limited to opening the Settings app.

- Google excels at opening websites when compared to S Voice's ability to do so only with
  very common sites. Say "Go to" or "Open," followed by the website name, such as "Open
  kitco dot com." (This advanced capability shouldn't come as a surprise. After all, this *is*
  Google's business.)

- You can dictate and send email using Google ("Email Evan Wonderful dinner tonight. Good
  job!"). S Voice doesn't support email.

- S Voice does a better job of handling in-app commands—primarily in Music. You can issue
  additional commands while a song is playing—as long as you do so from the S Voice
  screen. If you return to Google while a song is playing (in Google Play Music rather than
  Music) and issue a music-related command, Google responds with "Controlling media is
  not supported on this device." Google appears to be unable to issue additional commands
  of any sort after a target app launches.

- Google doesn't have some calculation restrictions from which S Voice suffers. In addition,
  an appropriate calculator frequently appears onscreen, enabling you to try similar calculations and variations. (Note that it's *essential* that you speak slowly and clearly.)

- Although Google can schedule appointments (events), it doesn't understand tasks.
  When you state the essential elements of an appointment (such as "Meet with Jeremy on
  Sunday"), Calendar launches and displays a new event containing the information that you
  spoke. You must manually complete the item by providing the remaining details and then
  tapping Save. Thus, although it's far from perfect, S Voice is the better choice for creating,
  editing, and deleting events—and the *only* choice for creating tasks.

Configuring Google/Voice Search

After familiarizing yourself with the Google/Voice Search capabilities, you should review its settings.

(1) On the Google, Voice Search, or Google Now screen, open the menu in the lower-right corner and choose Settings. (If you can't see the menu, you can also open it by long-pressing the Recent Apps key.)

(2) The Settings screen appears. Following are some of the most important Google/Voice Search settings.

(3) *Google Now.* You can enable or disable Google Now by changing the position of the switch. (This setting has no bearing on the manner in which voice commands and search requests are performed.)

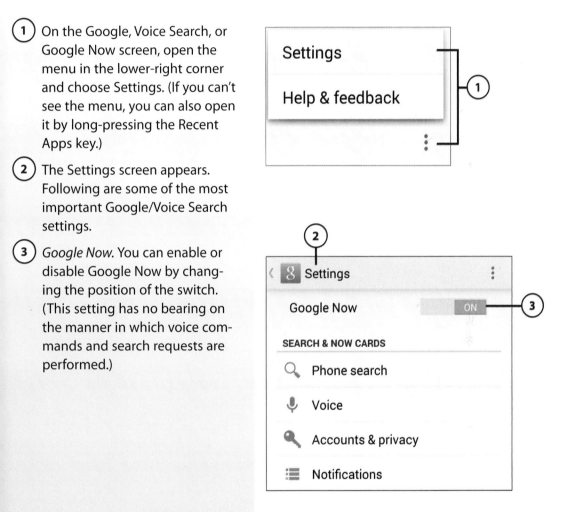

4 *Phone Search.* Checked items specify the types of information on your phone that will be examined when performing voice searches and commands. Generally, you'll want to leave all of these content areas checked.

5 *Voice.* These settings enable you to change the input language, specify whether Google responds audibly (Speech Output enabled) or only in text, whether it activates in response to the wake-up phrase ("OK, Google"), and whether it recognizes input from a Bluetooth headset.

6 *Accounts & Privacy.* The only setting that has a significant effect on voice commands and searches is Contact Recognition. When checked, Google uses your Contacts records to determine who you're trying to reach when calling people or creating text messages and email, for example.

7 When you're done viewing and changing settings, press the Back key or tap the Back icon.

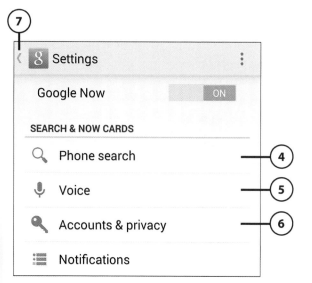

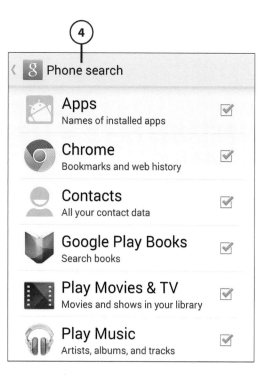

This chapter is all about some of the utility functions you will find on your Galaxy S5. Topics include the following:

→ Adjusting date and time
→ Enabling the kinds of notification sounds you want
→ Changing the default language
→ Using the calculator, the calendar, and the Gallery
→ Getting help
→ Downloading new apps, games, movies and TV shows, music, books, and other information with Play Store
→ Changing your settings
→ Printing from your phone
→ Storing your files on the Cloud

System Functions and Tools

Most of us have "that drawer" in the kitchen where we keep scissors, bottle openers, corkscrews, tea strainers, and other tools that just don't logically fit in with things in other drawers. This chapter is like that. Some of the utilities are located by tapping on the Settings icon, whereas others are located by tapping on separate icons.

Setting the Date and Time

Your Galaxy S5 is configured to maintain the correct date and time from the moment you take it out of the box. Normally it appears in the upper-right corner of the startup screen.

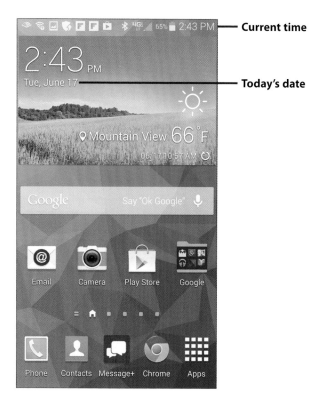

Current time

Today's date

Use the following steps if you need to adjust the date and time on your Galaxy S5:

(1) Tap the Settings icon.

(2) Tap Date and Time in the Settings window.

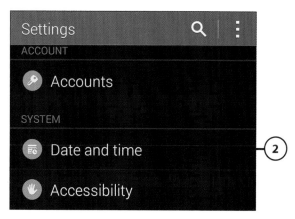

(**3**) The default (checked) option is to use the date and time provided by the network. Tap the green check mark to change either the date or time.

Change the Time or Date Format

You can also enable 24-hour format and change the date format after you have turned off the automatic date and time.

(**4**) Use the arrows to increase or decrease the date or time values, and then tap Set.

Daylight Savings Time

When your location switches to Daylight Savings Time (DST), the time shown on your Galaxy S5 automatically adjusts based on your location. (If you live in Arizona where you don't need to switch to DST, the time does not adjust; it remains Mountain Standard Time.)

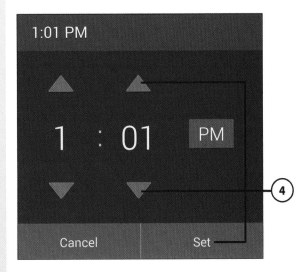

Specify a different date format here

Tap here to enable 24-hour format

Changing the Volume

You can change the volume of your ringtone, music, video, games and other media, and notifications in one place.

(1) Tap the Settings icon.

(2) Tap the Sound option.

(3) You can adjust sound levels for other applications here, including picking ringtones for a variety of calls. Tap volume to adjust volume.

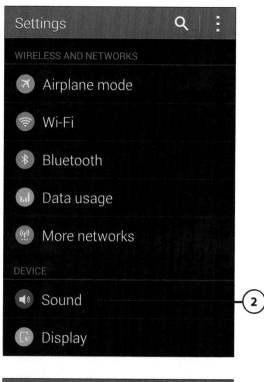

Settings

(**4**) Move the sliders for the various sounds and notifications to adjust the volume for each and then tap OK.

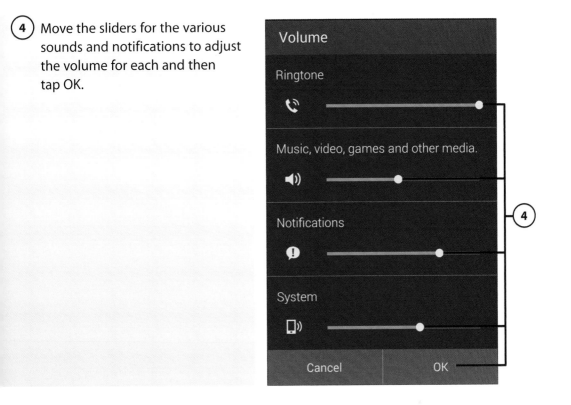

Enabling Mute, Vibrate, and Ringtones

Where you are and what you're doing can influence how you want your Galaxy S5 to notify you of incoming calls and messages. For instance, there are times—such as at a wedding or funeral or in a meeting—when you don't want your phone to ring. Your Galaxy S5 has a variety of tools to change how you're notified when things happen. Most of these (mute, vibrate, ringtone) are on screens you can find by tapping the Settings icon.

Mute Your Phone

(**1**) Tap the Settings icon.

(2) Tap the Sound menu item.

(3) Tap Sound Mode.

(4) Tap Mute so that the option button on the right turns green.

In Case of Emergency

Muting doesn't interfere with the emergency response mechanisms on the Galaxy S5. Regardless of what sound modifications you may have made on your phone, emergency tones and notifications will still sound.

Unmute the Phone

To unmute the phone, repeat these steps and tap the button next to Sound.

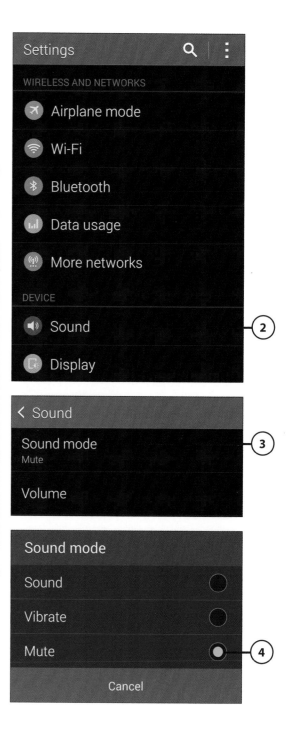

Control Vibration

Many of the feedback mechanisms on the Galaxy S5 use vibration to tell you what's going on. You can control the intensity of these vibrations.

(1) Tap the Settings icon.

(2) Tap Sound.

(3) Tap Vibration Intensity.

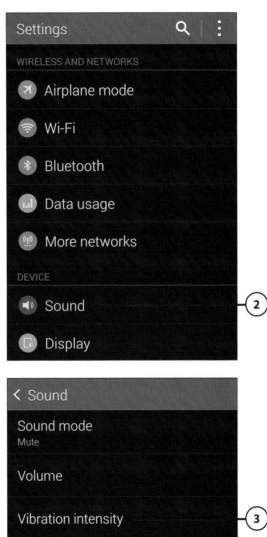

(4) Use the sliders to adjust the vibration intensity of various feedback options and tap OK.

What Is Haptic Feedback?

Haptic feedback is the mechanism by which your Galaxy S5 translates touch into various kinds of commands, from swiping to tapping to pressing and holding.

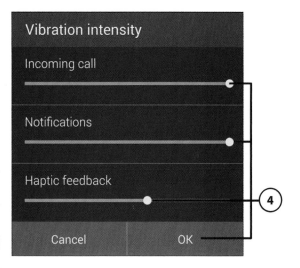

Choose Ringtones and Vibrations

By default, the sound of water dropping is the ringtone for your Galaxy S5, but it comes with a number of ringtones preinstalled. You can also import ringtones from the web, and then you can choose different ringtones for different types of messages and actions.

(1) Tap the Settings icon.

(2) Tap Sound, and then tap Ringtones.

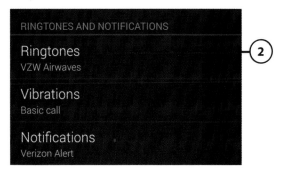

(3) Scroll through the various ring-tones and tap the one you want to use. Then tap OK.

Make It Louder or Softer

Remember that after you have speci-fied the ringtone, you can control the volume. See "Adjusting the Volume" in Chapter 1.

(4) If you want to specify what kind of sound you hear for different types of messages, repeat Steps 1 and 2 and scroll down to the Samsung Applications section. Tap one of the options. This example uses Call.

(5) Tap Call Alerts to specify call-related notifications, such as when you connect to a network, when your call ends, or when you receive an alarm or notification while on a call.

Ringtones

Peaceful Strum

Pure Tone

Quantum Bell

Rolling Tone

A Rustling in the Trees

Scampering Tone

Smooth Evening

Soft Breeze Waltz

VZW Airwaves

Writing Adventure — **3**

Cancel   Add   OK

SAMSUNG APPLICATIONS

Call — **4**

Messages

Email

Calendar

< Call

Call alerts
Set call alerts. — **5**

(6) Choose an alert style and then press the back arrow to return to previous screens.

‹ Call alerts

CALL VIBRATIONS

Vibrate on connection to netwo..

Call-end vibration

CALL STATUS TONES

Call connect tone ✓

Minute minder

Call end tone

ALERTS ON CALL

Notify during calls
Allow alarms and notifications to sound/
vibrate during calls. ✓

(6)

Choose a Ringtone

(1) To specify a ringtone, tap Ringtones and Keypad Tones on the Call screen.

(2) Tap Ringtones to specify which ringtone you want to hear when a call or message arrives.

‹ Call

Call alerts
Set call alerts.

RINGTONE AND SOUND SETTINGS

Ringtones and keypad tones (1)

‹ Ringtones and keypad tones

Ringtones (2)
VZW Airwaves

Vibrations
Basic call

Vibrate when ringing ✓

Dialing keypad tone
Play tone when the dialing keypad is tapped.

3 Choose from the ringtones provided and tap OK. If you'd prefer to add a new ringtone, tap Add and proceed to Step 4.

4 Tap either Cloud or Sound Picker as the source for your own ringtone, and tap either Always or Just Once to indicate how often the Galaxy S5 should return to this source for ringtones.

(5) If you pick Sound Picker, a menu of sounds appears. Explore what's available and tap one to hear a sample. You can tap others to hear their sounds. When you have decided on one, be sure that its button is green, and then tap Done. Tapping Cloud works the same way, except that you're looking at items you have already stored in your Cloud area, such as albums or individual sounds or songs.

Using Music as a Ringtone

You can use imported music as a ringtone. In the Samsung Applications section of the Sound settings, tap Advanced. Tap either SoundAlive or MusicFX to import music you choose from those sources to use as ringtones. Tap OK when you're done making changes.

Choose a Vibration

(1) Tap Vibrations on the Sound screen if you want to hear or feel a vibration when a call or message arrives.

(2) Choose Vibrations and tap OK, or tap Create to make your own vibration pattern.

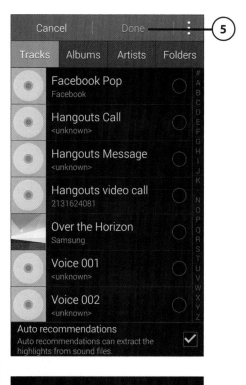

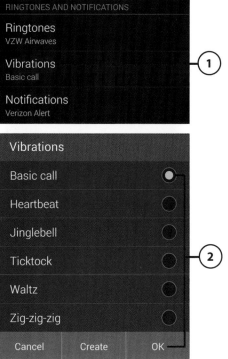

3 The circle represents the time you have for a vibration pattern. Start creating your pattern by tapping Tap to Create.

4 Tap the vibration pattern you want to use and tap Stop when you're done.

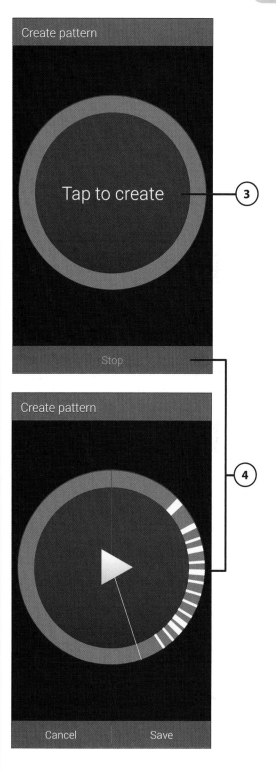

5 Tap Save to keep the vibration pattern now illustrated in the circle, or Cancel to discard it.

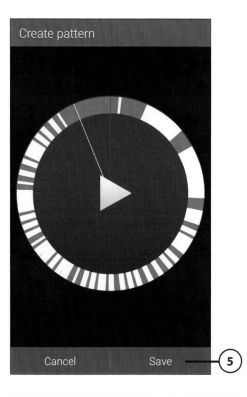

Create pattern

Cancel | Save — **5**

OTHER NOTIFICATION SOUNDS

You can also specify notification sounds (including ringtones) when a message arrives. Tap the Settings icon, then Messages, then choose the option you want.

Specify a notification sound when email from priority senders (for example, your spouse or one of your children) arrives. The sound you have previously chosen for email notification will be used when priority email arrives.

You can also specify a sound or ringtone when it's time for an item on your Calendar. For instance, if you have a 2:00 p.m. meeting, you can set up the item on your Calendar, tap the Settings icon, then the Sound icon, then tap Calendar.

SAMSUNG APPLICATIONS

Call

Messages

Email

Tap here to specify a sound —— Calendar
for Calendar notifications

Enabling Airplane Mode

Many airlines require that your cell phone be turned off or set to Airplane mode when your plane is in flight because sending and receiving signals might interfere with the airplane's operation. With the Galaxy S5, when you turn on Airplane mode, Bluetooth and Wi-Fi capabilities are disabled, although you can still receive FM radio and GPS signals. Although regulations are changing to allow more leeway for device use on planes, it's safer to turn on Airplane mode when you're in flight.

(1) Tap the Settings icon.

(2) Tap Airplane Mode.

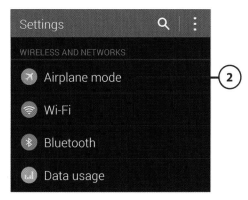

3 Tap the Airplane mode bar to turn it on.

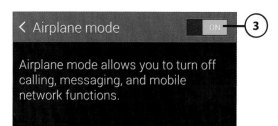

Airplane mode allows you to turn off calling, messaging, and mobile network functions.

A Friendly Reminder

When you land, remember to turn off Airplane mode or your phone might not operate normally. Just repeat the steps in this task, but turn the Airplane mode bar to the Off setting in Step 3.

Changing the Default Language

If English isn't your native language, you can change the phone's default language to another supported language.

1 On the Home screen, tap Apps, followed by Settings.

2 In the Personal section, tap the Language and Input icon.

3 Tap Language.

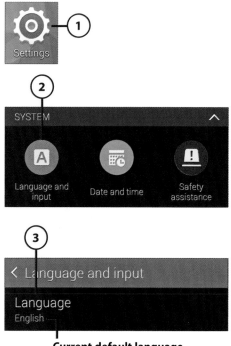

Current default language

(**4**) Tap the desired language. Icon names, display text, prompts, dialog boxes, and other text change to reflect the selected language.

< Language

English

Español — (**4**)

Tiếng Việt

한국어

中文

Change the Input Language

Options for the default language are limited. Although it won't affect system text, such as prompts and dialogs boxes, you can still change the input language (text that you type or speak) to your native tongue. See the "Changing the Default Language" section in Chapter 10 for more information.

Using the Calculator

Your Galaxy S5 includes a simple calculator for everyday use. The icons correspond to the same buttons you find on other simple calculators.

Data that you enter, including numbers, formulas, and operational symbols, appear in the top of the screen, along with the answer to your calculation.

Using the Calendar

Cell phone users often find that, next to the mobile phone applications, the most useful app is the Calendar. Because you carry your S5 with you, you are also carrying a way of keeping track of your daily appointments and meetings.

(1) Tap the Apps icon and then tap the Calendar icon.

(2) You see the calendar for today. Today's date is indicated by a blue dot.

(3) Move to the next month by tapping the > icon, or move to the previous month by tapping the icon.

(4) Tap the menu icon to change the display of the calendar to year, month and agenda, week, day, or just agenda.

(5) Tap the plus (+) icon to add an event to your current calendar. The add event screen opens.

	Sun	Mon	Tue	Wed	Thu	Fri	Sat
	29	30	1	2	3	4	5
		Alz. Co nference	SJC – S outhwe st to Bo ston			Indepen.. Update.. Past A G chair'..	STMR
	6	7	8	9	10	11	12
	BOS So uthwes t to San Jose			Marta ASC -Al zheime r's		HAC	
	13	14	15	16	17	18	19
				SAC m.. Linkage s Advis ory Com		Geront ology w orksho p, Stanf..	
	20	21	22	23	24	25	26
				Marta Alz. Scr eenings	Thursd ay nigh t live		
	27	28	29	30	31	1	2
						Agenda items t o SAC s taff	STMR
	3	4	5	6	7	8	9
				Marta	Thursd ay nigh t live		

Month   Today   +

< July, 2014 >

(6) Enter the title of the event and its location. If you want to identify the location using a map, tap the location icon to the right of the Location bar and move the icon to the correct place. Note that the address changes as you move and pause the icon, allowing you to find the correct address.

Color-Code Your Events

The blue square next to the title is so you can color-code events. The default for a new event is blue as shown, but if you tap the blue box you see other colors you can use for events.

(4)

☰ Calendar

Sat, Jul 12, 2014
3:50 PM

Year

Month

Month and agenda

Week

Day

Agenda

(6)

Add event ◢   Cancel   Save

▌ ████ @ ████ com

| Title | ████ | — Color code for the event |

| Location | ◉ | — Location icon |

Start   Wed, 07/16/2014 8:00 AM

End   Wed, 07/16/2014 9:00 AM

(7) Tap the start time and a calendar appears so you can select the correct date. Use the arrows to select the correct time and tap Set. Use the same procedure to set the end time of the event.

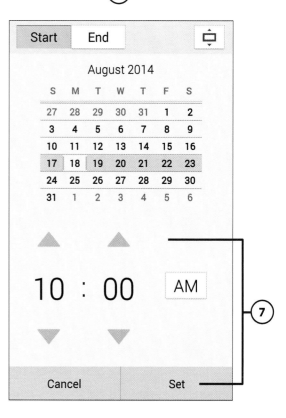

8 Tap Save when you are done entering the details of your appointment or Cancel to back out of it.

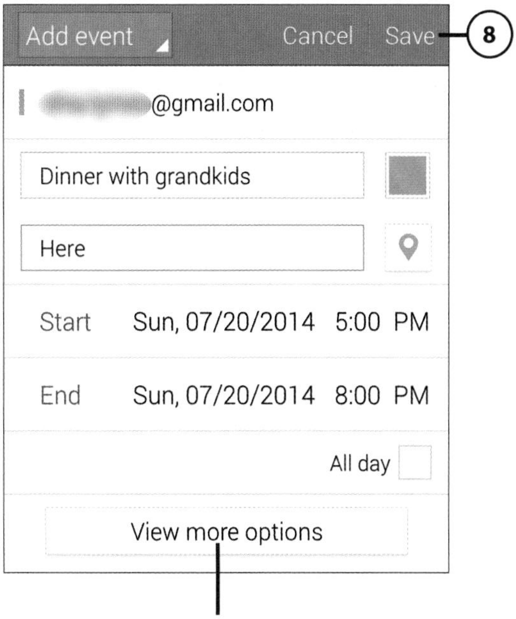

Add event ◢		Cancel Save

8

▮ ▦@gmail.com

| Dinner with grandkids | ◻ |

| Here | ◉ |

| Start | Sun, 07/20/2014 5:00 PM |

| End | Sun, 07/20/2014 8:00 PM |

All day ☐

View more options

Set other options for your event

>>>Go Further
OTHER EVENT OPTIONS

Below the basic Calendar page is a View more options button. Tap this to see additional options:

- Reminder options
- How the item on your calendar appears to others who have access to your calendar
- Repetition of the event
- Emoticons
- The time zone you want to use for this entry

Getting Help

When you have trouble with your Galaxy S5, you can tap the Help icon to get several types of assistance.

Help icon

- *How-to videos* walk you through basic navigation on your Galaxy S5 and demonstrate how to make and receive calls, how to send and receive text messages with Verizon Messages, how to set up email, and how to set up Wi-Fi and Bluetooth networking.

- *Useful tips* contain a lot of helpful information, organized by category, for getting the most out of your Galaxy S5. For this example, I tapped Emergency Alerts to get a description of the Emergency Alerts app.

> **‹ Useful tips**
>
> Emergency Alerts ⌃
>
> Emergency Alerts allows you to receive geographically-targeted messages. Alert messages are provided by the US Department of Homeland Security and will alert customers of imminent threats to their safety within their area. There is no charge for receiving an Emergency Alert message. To start, go to **Apps > Emergency Alerts**.
>
> There are three types of Emergency Alerts:
>
> - Alerts issued by the President
> - Alerts involving imminent threats to safety of life (Extreme and Severe)
> - AMBER Alerts (missing child alert)
>
> You may choose not to receive Imminent Threats (Extreme and Severe) and AMBER Alerts. Alerts issued by the President cannot be disabled.
>
> To disable Imminent Threats and AMBER Alerts:

Types of Emergency Alerts

- *User Manual* is an electronic version of Samsung's User Guide for the Galaxy S5. It provides detail about all the elements and features of your Galaxy S5.

> **‹ User manual**
>
> Manual > Connections > Bluetooth
>
> Bluetooth is a short-range communications technology that allows you to connect wirelessly to a number of Bluetooth devices, such as headsets and hands-free car Bluetooth systems, and Bluetooth-enabled computers, printers, and wireless devices. The Bluetooth communication range is approximately 30 feet.
>
> **Turning Bluetooth On and Off**
>
> 1. From home, tap ▦ **Apps >** ○ Settings.
> 2. Tap ✸ **Bluetooth**, and then tap the ON/OFF switch to turn Bluetooth on or off.
>
> **Bluetooth Settings**
> Configure your device's Bluetooth service.
>
> **Changing Your Phone's Name**
> This is the name others will use when pairing with your phone via Bluetooth.

The User Manual is handy for detailed explanations of how something works

- *Icon glossary* shows a list of commonly used icons that are likely to appear in the notification bar or on app-specific screens.

- *My Verizon Mobile* lets you explore information about your calling plan and your usage of online minutes.

Checking on Data Usage

Data usage refers to the monthly number of minutes in your carrier's plan. Anything over that gets billed at a higher amount. With the Data Usage setting, you can monitor how much data you have consumed for a given time period.

(1) Tap the Settings icon.

(2) Tap Data Usage in the Wireless and Networks section.

(3) Use the options at the top of the page to show mobile data usage (default), limit data usage (perhaps to conserve minutes on your plan), and set an alert to notify you when you are approaching a limit on data usage that you have specified.

White lines correspond to days in cycle

Orange line indicates maximum regular monthly mobile use you set for your carrier's plan

4 If you have specified a data limit, it appears as an orange line on the graph. For instance, the graph shows that you've been limited to 2.0 GB of data for the period Jul 5 – Aug 4, and for the week of Jul 29 – Aug 4 you have used only about 0.01GB. The largest users have been Google Play Store and Google Services. Most apps won't have a high amount of usage unless you have been using one or two for a great deal of data transmission, such as file transfers to and from the cloud or another service.

5 The period of time covered by the graph is shown just above the graph, and the white line on the graph shows where you currently fall within that time period. You can move the white lines to the right or left to identify data usage in a smaller period, such as a week.

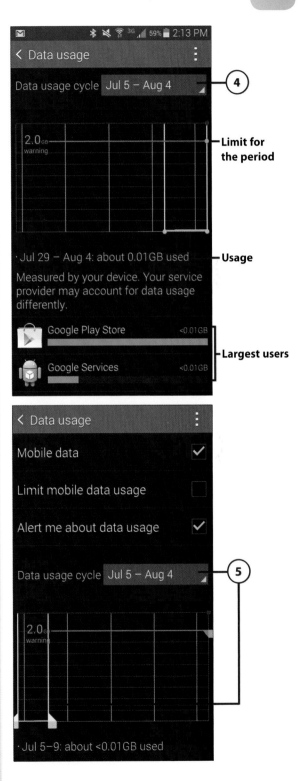

Changing Display Characteristics

Sometimes it's difficult to read the small type on the Galaxy S5. You can change the way information is displayed on your phone to make things easier to read.

(1) Tap the Settings icon.

(2) Tap Display in the Device section.

(3) You see a list of the various display options that you can adjust. Most of these are self-explanatory; you can adjust them till you find settings that work for you. Tap Brightness.

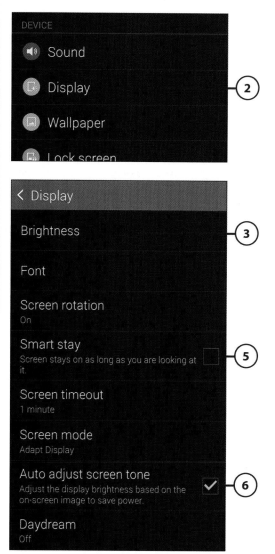

4 Use the slider to adjust the auto-matic brightness of the screen and then tap OK.

5 Tap Smart Stay to turn the feature on. The Smart Stay function uses the camera lens on the front of the Galaxy S5 to detect your face and will not turn off the screen until you turn away from the phone.

6 The Auto Adjust Screen Tone feature is enabled by default, and you probably should not change it. This lets your Galaxy S5 automatically adjust the intensity of what's shown on the screen, depending on the ambient light where you are. For instance, contrast is automatically greater when you're outdoors in the sun-light than when you're in a dark room.

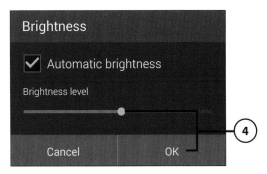

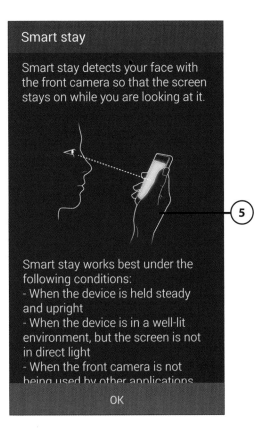

Backing Up Using the Cloud

The cloud is a nickname for online storage space that you rent, like a physical storage space. Rather than keeping your pictures, videos, documents, and other information (such as your will) on your computer, you can keep it in the cloud. You can also use it to back up other information, such as documents or spreadsheets in process.

Back Up in Batches

(1) Tap the Apps icon and then tap the Cloud icon. The menu of Cloud options appears.

(2) Choose what you want to back up. For instance, all the photos in this book were backed up to the cloud. Notice that they are listed as Enabled for Backup.

(3) Follow the instructions for the type of files, pictures, or documents you want to back up, tap the checkbox, and tap the Back Up Now button (not shown).

Knowing the Lingo

Terminology is important when dealing with the cloud. You "back up" to the cloud by sending files to it from any of several apps. You "download" files from the cloud by fetching files from it; these files are automatically stored in My Files.

≡   VERIZON CLOUD   ⋮

✓   Last backup: August 15, 10:34 PM

ENABLED FOR BACKUP

👤   8 Contact(s)

📷   515 Photo(s) — **(2)**

NOT ENABLED FOR BACKUP

▤   Start backing up your Videos now   ›

♫   Start backing up your Music now   ›

📄   Start backing up your Documents now   ›

💬   Start backing up your Messages now   ›

✆   Start backing up your Call Logs now   ›

Other types of files you could back up

Back Up Specific Apps

(**1**) Some of the apps on your Galaxy S5 have specific menu options to back up files onto the Cloud. For instance, when you tap the menu icon on the Gallery screen, you can choose Cloud as an option. This lets you specify which pictures or videos you want to store on the cloud. Tap the three dots in the upper-right corner.

(**2**) Choose the pictures you want to back up by scrolling through the categories and tapping on the photos you want to save. (Your carrier will bill you for their storage.)

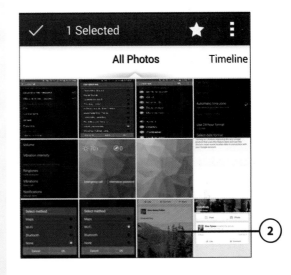

(**3**) Tap the menu icon and select Download.

Where Is the Cloud?

In the last few years, "the cloud" has become a nickname for offsite storage of files. For instance, if you want to store a copy of your will or other important electronic documents in a safe place that's not your home or office, you can create a space in the cloud, protect it with a password, and store your information there. You don't really care where that storage's physical location is—it could be in the California desert, for all you care—so long as it's safe and accessible when you need it.

The cloud is actually a collection of file servers, maintained by private companies, who contract with developers like Samsung to provide secure offsite storage for their customers. You don't usually have to type anything, just tap an icon on the Galaxy S5 and specify which document, picture, or video you want to save.

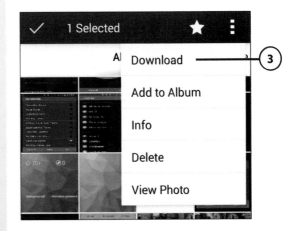

Month and Agenda view

Add an event or task

Today

Selected date

Agenda for selected date

Reminder

Task

In this chapter, you learn how to use Calendar to create, view, and edit events and tasks. Topics include the following:

→ Adding Calendar accounts to display events and tasks from your Gmail, Microsoft Exchange ActiveSync, and other account calendars
→ Creating events and tasks, viewing the calendar, and managing events and tasks
→ Responding to reminders for upcoming events and tasks
→ Setting Calendar preferences

Using the Calendar

Similar in design to a full-featured calendar application (such as the one in Microsoft Outlook), the Calendar app enables you to record upcoming events, meetings, and tasks and then receive reminders for them. If you already maintain calendars in Google, Facebook, Outlook.com (Microsoft Exchange ActiveSync), or a corporate Exchange Server account, you can synchronize your Calendar app data with that of your other calendars.

Adding Calendar Accounts

If you've used a Google/Gmail account on your phone to access any Google service, Calendar has two calendars that it can immediately associate with new events and tasks: your Google/Gmail Calendar and My Calendar, a phone-specific calendar created by the Calendar app. In addition to these sources, Calendar can use data from and sync with Samsung, Facebook, and Microsoft Exchange Server calendars.

1. To add a Facebook, Microsoft Exchange ActiveSync, Samsung, or Gmail calendar account (only these account types support calendar syncing with your phone), go to the Home screen and tap Apps, followed by Settings.

2. Tap the Accounts icon.

3. Tap Add Account at the bottom of the My Accounts list.

Multiple Accounts of the Same Type

Account types that are marked with a green dot have already been added. You can have multiple Exchange, Email, and Google accounts, but only one instance each of Samsung and Facebook accounts.

4. Select one of these account types: Facebook, Microsoft Exchange ActiveSync, Google, or Samsung Account. This example uses Microsoft Exchange ActiveSync.

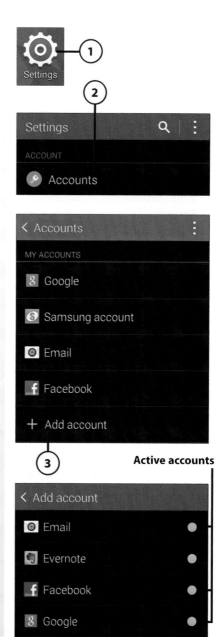

Active accounts

⑤ Follow the instructions to add the account. At a minimum, you need to supply your username and password (or use the provided option to create an account).

⑥ Ensure that Sync Calendar is enabled if that option is available on the Sync Settings screen. This synchronizes changes to your Calendar with the calendar on your computer(s) and any other mobile phones.

⑦ You can add other accounts by repeating Steps 3–6. When you finish, press the Home key to return to the Home screen.

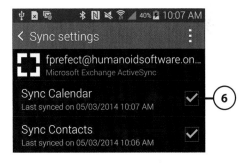

Working in Calendar

Within Calendar, you can create events and tasks, choose a view (Year, Month, Month and Agenda, Week, Day, or Agenda), and edit or delete events and tasks.

Creating Events and Tasks

In addition to events and tasks that are pulled from your Gmail/Google, Facebook, Exchange, and Samsung accounts, you can also create new items within the Calendar app. These new items can be synced with your accounts automatically, manually, or not at all.

Every Calendar item is either an *event* (a scheduled item for a specific date, with or without a start time) or a *task* (an unscheduled item with or without a due date). An event can be an all-day occurrence, such as a vacation day or birthday, or have a defined start and end time.

Create an Event

(1) Launch the Calendar app by tapping Apps, Calendar or by tapping a Home screen shortcut.

(2) *Optional:* On the calendar, select the date or time when you want to schedule the event. (Selecting the start date or time saves you the trouble of specifying this information when you create the event.) To change the Calendar view so that you can pick a start date or time, tap the active view name and choose Month, Week, or Day.

The section "View the Calendar," later in this chapter, shows the different calendar views.

(3) Tap the plus (+) icon to create a new event. The scheduling screen appears.

Be General or Specific

The more specific your selection (start date or date/time), the more information is prefilled for the event. On the other hand, regardless of the currently selected date or start time, you can still set a different date or time when you create the event.

Active view — **3**

≡ Month   Today   **+**   ⋮

<			May, 2014			>
Sun	Mon	Tue	Wed	Thu	Fri	Sat
27	28	29	30	1	2	3
4	5	6	7	8	9	10
11	12	13	14	15	16	17
18	19	20	21	22	23	24
25	26	27	28	29	30	31
1	2	3	4	5	6	7

All day   Memorial Day

2

Another Plus Icon Option

You can also create a new event or task by tapping the plus icon in a Calendar widget.

Calendar (Mini Today) widget

Mini today   Today   + ——— **Create event or task**

<   **Wed, May 14, 2014**   >

9:45 AM   Dr. appointment

(4) Ensure that Add Event is selected.

(5) Select an account to use if you want to associate the event with a different calendar. (My Calendar is the phone-specific calendar and does not appear as an option on Verizon phones.)

Using Multiple Calendars

The calendar you specify for each new item is very important. When you sync calendars, it's the calendar that records the event. If you choose your Google/Gmail calendar, for example, the event will also be available to you from Google's website using any browser and on any other devices running Gmail. On the other hand, if you choose My Calendar, the event will be available only on your Galaxy S5. To use other account calendars with Calendar, see "Adding Calendar Accounts" at the beginning of this chapter.

(6) Enter a title for the event.

4   **5**

Add event ◢   Cancel   Save

editor.ford.prefect@gmail.com

6

Mom's Birthday Party

Home   📍

Start   Mon, 05/26/2014   2:00 PM

End   Mon, 05/26/2014   7:00 PM

All day ☐

View more options

(7) *Optional:* Select a color that signifies something about or helps
classify the event.

(8) *Optional:* Enter the event's location. This can be something simple like "Home" or a real, physical
address. Type in the Location box
or tap the Location icon, perform
a search, and tap Done.

(9) Do one of the following:

- If this is an all-day event or
one with no specific schedule
other than the day on which it
occurs, tap the All Day check
box. The From and To times
are removed, as well as the
time zone. Go to Step 10.

- If the Start or End date or
time is incorrect, tap the date
or time item and correct it.
Tap arrow icons to increment
or decrement a component
(such as the hour) by one unit.
Alternatively, you can select
the item you want to change
and type the new value. If
the other date or time is also
incorrect, tap its button at the
top of the screen (Start or End)
and repeat this process. Tap
Set to accept the corrected
dates and/or times.

(10) Tap View More Options to view
more event options including the
ability to set a reminder, choose a
meeting time zone, and more.

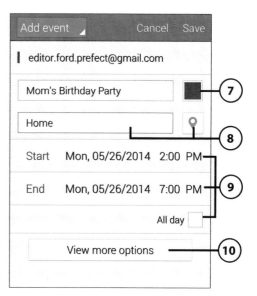

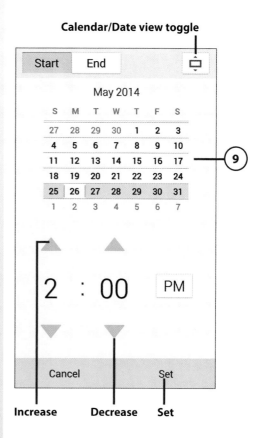

Calendar/Date view toggle

Increase   Decrease   Set

(11) *Optional:* Set a *reminder* (alarm) for the event by tapping the Reminder plus (+) icon. To specify an interval other than the default (15 min before), tap the interval box, and select a new one from the scrolling list. Select Customize if none of the intervals is correct.

More About Reminders

You can optionally set *multiple* reminders for an event. Tap the plus (+) icon to add a new reminder. To remove a reminder, tap the minus (–) icon to its right. If the Calendar account with which this event is associated has an email address (such as your Google/Gmail account), you can elect to be notified via email rather than by the usual methods. Tap the box to the right of the reminder interval and choose Email.

Add event ◢			Cancel	Save

~~Start   Mon, 05/26/2014   2:00 PM~~

End   Mon, 05/26/2014   7:00 PM

All day ☐

Reminder   + **—(11)**

Participants   👤

Show me as
Busy

Privacy
Default

Repeat
One-time event

Description

Empty 😊 🏛 🏫 ⭐ 🎂 •••

Time zone
(GMT-07:00) Mountain Standard Time

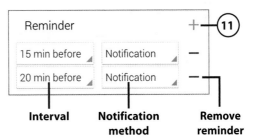

Reminder   + **—(11)**

| 15 min before ◢ | Notification ◢ | — |
| 20 min before ◢ | Notification ◢ | — |

Interval   **Notification method**   **Remove reminder**

(12) *Optional:* Specify an interval for repeating this event (such as a weekly staff meeting on Monday at 1:00 p.m.) by tapping Repeat and selecting a repetition interval. Then specify a duration or end date, and tap OK.

(13) *Optional:* Enter a detailed description of or notes related to the event in the Description box.

(14) *Optional:* Select a sticker to visually identify the event on the calendar and to use as a filtering criterion.

(15) *Optional:* Tap the Time Zone entry to specify a different time zone to use for scheduling this event.

(16) Tap the Save button at the top of the screen to add the event to the calendar or tap Cancel to discard it.

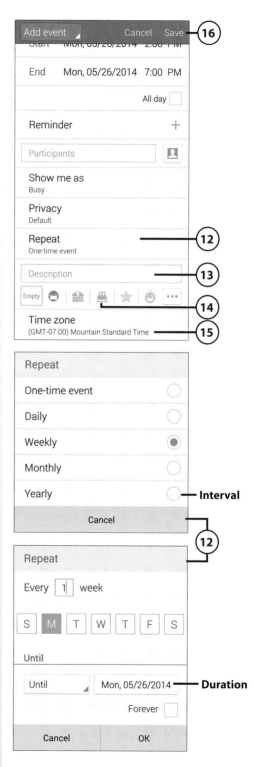

Advanced Calendaring

To maintain compatibility with events created in Google/Gmail and Microsoft Exchange ActiveSync accounts (or created in Calendar and designated as either of these account types), additional fields (Participants, Show Me As, and Privacy) appear when you create, edit, or view such events. The fields are normally used to manage attendance at corporate meetings and can—or should—be skipped when creating standard Calendar events. When you save an item with designated participants, each person is automatically emailed an invitation when you save the event.

Event participants ——— Douglas Schwartz ⊖ ——— Remove participant

Evan Schwartz ⊖

Participants 👤 ——— Add participants

Create a Task

1 Launch the Calendar app by tapping Apps, Calendar or by tapping a Home screen shortcut.

2 *Optional:* Select the due date for the task's completion from the calendar. (Selecting the date saves you the trouble of specifying it when you create the task.) To change the Calendar view so that you can select a due date, tap the active view name and choose Month, Week, or Day.

3 Tap the plus (+) icon. The scheduling screen appears.

(4) Ensure that Add Task is selected.

(5) Select the account to use if you want to associate the new task with a different account. (My Task is the phone-specific account.)

(6) Enter a title for the task.

(7) Do one of the following:

- If there's a particular date on or by which the task must be completed, tap the Due Date entry, specify the date in the Set Date dialog box, and tap the Set button.

- If the task is open-ended, tap the No Due Date check box.

(8) Tap View More Options to see other scheduling options for the task.

(9) *Optional:* Set a *reminder* (alarm) for the task by tapping the plus (+) icon. In the Reminder dialog box, select either On Due Date or Customize (to specify a different date). The selected date and the current time are set as the reminder. To change the time, tap its entry, specify the time in the Set Time dialog box, and tap the Set button.

(10) *Optional:* Enter a detailed description of or notes related to the task in the Description text box.

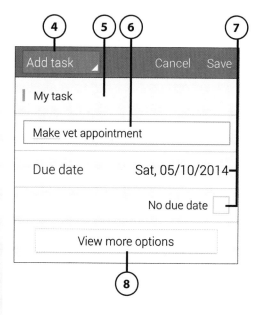

(11) *Optional:* Specify a completion priority (high, medium, or low) by tapping Priority.

(12) Tap the Save button to add the task to the calendar or tap Cancel to discard it. (When added to a calendar, a task is preceded by a check box.)

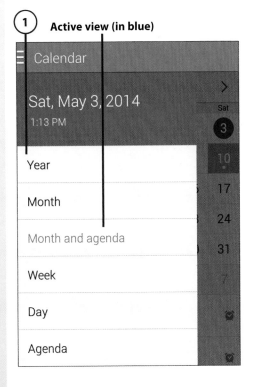

Edit task — Cancel Save **(12)**

| My task

Make vet appointment|

Due date   Sat, 05/10/2014

                   No due date ☐

Reminder   +

Ear infection

Priority
Medium|

(11)

View the Calendar

Calendar has six *views:* Year, Month, Month and Agenda, Week, Day, and Agenda. You interact differently with Calendar in each view.

(1) When you launch Calendar, the last displayed view appears. To change views, tap the active view (such as Month) or swipe from the left edge of the screen, and then select a new view.

(1) **Active view (in blue)**

☰ Calendar

                              >

Sat, May 3, 2014   Sat
1:13 PM   ③

                              10

Year   17

Month   24

Month and agenda   31

Week   7

Day   🔔

Agenda   🔔

(2) *Year view.* You can't view events or tasks in Year view. Its purpose is to enable you to easily select a month for viewing—in this or another year. Scroll to previous or future years by tapping the arrow icons or by swiping the screen horizontally. When the target month and year appear, tap the month to view it in Month view.

Other Year View Options

To immediately return to the current year, tap the Today button. Today's date is encircled in dark blue.

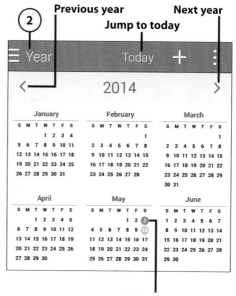

(3) *Month view.* In Month view, event/task text is color-coded to match the calendar account with which the item is associated. For example, bright blue text is used to show My Calendar items, dark blue for Facebook events, purple for Google Calendar items, and green for holidays. (You can select the colors you want to use.) Tap a date to display events and tasks for that date in a pop-up window. To move forward or back one month, tap an arrow icon or flick the screen vertically or horizontally.

Month and Agenda

If you choose the Month and Agenda view, a reduced version of Month view is presented. Scheduled events and tasks for the selected date appear at the bottom of the screen.

4 *Week view.* In Week view, items are colored-coded to match the calendar with which they're associated. Tap an item to view its details in a pop-up. Tap the pop-up to edit or delete the item. Scroll to the previous or next week by tapping an arrow icon or swiping horizontally.

Changing the Magnification

To make it easier to examine scheduled items in Week or Day view, you can change the magnification by pinching two fingers together (decrease) or spreading them apart (increase).

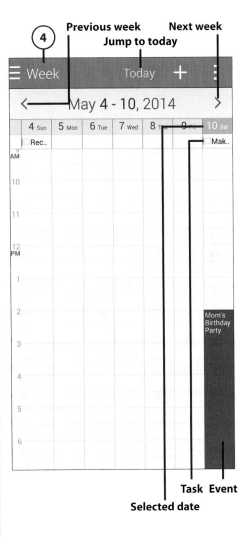

(5) *Day view.* Use Day view to see scheduled items and their duration for a selected date. Items are colored-coded to match the calendar with which they're associated. Tap an item to view its details in a pop-up. Tap the pop-up to edit or delete the item. Press and hold a time slot to create a new item with that start time. You can scroll through the day's time slots by flicking vertically and switch days by tapping arrow icons or swiping horizontally.

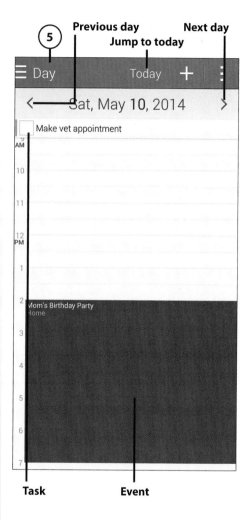

(6) *Agenda view.* Select Agenda view to see a chronological list of events and tasks. Items are color-coded to match the calendar with which they're associated. Tap an item to view its details, edit, or delete it. Scroll through the list by flicking vertically.

Filtering the Agenda

Your Agenda is made up of Events, Tasks, and Anniversary items. Normally the filter for the view is set to All, which means that all Events, Tasks, and Anniversaries are shown. You can limit the view by filtering it to only show certain items. For example, if you choose Events, you only see Event items.

6 Event — Jump to today — Filter view

≡ Agenda   Today **+** ⋮

All

Tap here to view events bef All

Sat, May 10, 2014

2:00 PM   Mom's Birthd   Events

7:00 PM   Home   Tasks

Sun, May 11, 2014

All day   Mothers' Day   Anniversaries

Sat, May 10, 2014   ∧

☐   Make vet appointment   ⏰
    May 10 2014

Mon, May 26, 2014   ∧

All day   Memorial Day

Tap here to view events after **06/09/2014**

Task

Searching in Views

To display the search box, tap the menu icon and choose Search. You can optionally filter a search to display only events to which a particular sticker has been assigned. With the search box displayed, open the menu, choose Filter by Sticker, and select a sticker.

Exit search — ⟨ Q Search   ⋮ — **Menu icon**

Sun, May 4 2014

Search box — Record promo   Filter by sticker — **Filter by sticker**
             May 4 2014

Sat, May 10, 2014   ∧

2:00 PM   Mom's Birthday Party   ☺
7:00 PM   Home

Sun, May 11, 2014   ∧

All day   Mothers' Day

Sat, May 10, 2014   ∧

☐   Make vet appointment   ☺
    May 10 2014

(7) Go to a specific date by tapping the menu icon and choosing Go To. In the Go To dialog box, specify the target date and tap Done.

(8) You can display events and tasks from one or multiple calendar accounts. To select accounts to show, tap the menu icon and choose Calendars. Select the calendar and task accounts to display, and tap the Back icon when done.

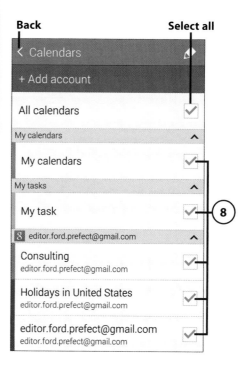

>>>Go Further
CONSIDER CALENDAR WIDGETS

You can do much of your Calendar viewing on the Home screen by installing Calendar widgets. They draw their data from Calendar and let you view upcoming events and tasks, as well as create new ones.

- *Calendar (Mini Today).* This widget displays a day's events and tasks. Tap any item to view, edit, or delete it in Calendar; tap an arrow icon to move one day forward or backward; tap a task's check box to toggle its completion status; and tap the plus (+) icon to create a new event or task.

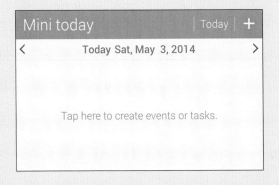

For help with adding, moving, and removing widgets, see "Adding Shortcuts and Widgets" and "Adding, Removing, and Rearranging Home Screen Items" in Chapter 13, "Customizing Your Screen."

Manage Events and Tasks

After creating an event or task, you can delete it or edit any aspect of it, such as the title, start date, start time, description, reminder interval, or completion status.

(1) Open the Calendar app and, in any view, tap the item that you want to delete or edit. If a pop-up window appears, tap the item in the pop-up window to examine it in Detail view. In certain views (such as Agenda), no pop-up appears; the item is immediately displayed in Detail view.

Faster Editing, Deleting, and Rescheduling

In Week and Day views, you can change the date/time or duration of an event by dragging in the Calendar. To reschedule the event, press and hold the event, and drag it to a new date/time slot. To change its duration, drag the event's top or bottom edge (marked by dots) up or down. Note that only events—not tasks—can be rescheduled this way.

(3) (2)

< Detail view ✎ 🗑 ⋮

Mom's Birthday Party
Sat, May 10 2:00 PM - 7:00 PM

editor.ford.prefect@gmail.com

Repeat : Yearly; Until 12/31/2036
Reminder : 15 min before / Notification
Show me as : Busy
Privacy : Default

📍 Location
   Home

👥 Invitee (3)
   Craig Johnston, Derek Johnston, James Johnston

(2) Tap the Trash icon to delete the task or event and confirm by tapping OK.

(3) Tap the edit icon to edit the task or event, and then tap Save to save your edits.

Task Completion

To mark a task complete, tap its check box on the calendar, in its pop-up, or in a widget.

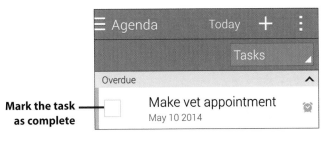

Editing or Deleting a Repeating Event

When you edit a repeating event, a dialog box appears that enables you to change only this occurrence or every occurrence. Similarly, when you try to delete a repeating event, a dialog box asks you to confirm whether to delete all or only a specific occurrence of the event.

Edit a repeating event

Details
Only this event
All events in series

Responding to Reminders

When an event or task reminder is triggered, a message appears briefly in the status bar and is replaced by a number (denoting the number of current alerts) or a separate alert screen appears. A distinctive ringtone may also play. The notification methods used are determined by Event Notification settings, as explained in "Setting Calendar Preferences," later in this chapter. You can respond to a reminder by *snoozing* (requesting that it repeat later), dismissing, or ignoring it.

Simple Alarms

If you just need an alarm to remind you that it's time to wake up or do *something*, you don't need to schedule a Calendar event. You can create alarms in the Clock app.

(1) If the Set Alerts and Notifications setting is *Status Bar Notifications*, an icon showing the number of waiting reminders appears in the status bar. Open the Notification panel to view them.

(2) Tap Snooze to snooze the alert.

(3) Tap the event to open an Event Notifications screen in which you can set a specific snooze duration.

(4) Swipe the alert left or right off the screen to dismiss it.

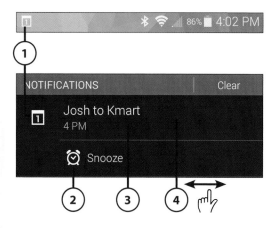

Dismissing a Reminder

Dismissing an event or task's reminder doesn't delete the item from Calendar; it merely eliminates the reminder. To *delete* the event or task, you must perform the procedure described in "Manage Events and Tasks," earlier in this chapter.

Responding to a Lock Screen Reminder

A full-screen notification appears when the screen is dark; that is, when the lock screen is active. To respond, press and drag the Dismiss (X) or Snooze (zZ) icon. If you elect to snooze, the reminder is snoozed for the default duration.

Dismiss — Snooze

Setting Calendar Preferences

You can set options on Calendar's Settings screen to customize the way the app works.

(1) Launch the Calendar app.

(2) Tap the menu icon and choose Settings. Review Steps 3–14 for descriptions of each option that you can set.

(3) *First Day of Week.* Specify whether calendar weeks should start on Saturday, Sunday, Monday, or match local customs.

(4) *Show Week Numbers.* When checked, Week view also displays the week number (1–52).

(5) *Hide Declined Events.* When checked, event invitations that you've declined aren't shown in Calendar.

(6) *Hide Completed Tasks.* When checked, tasks that have been marked as completed aren't shown in Calendar.

(7) *Weather.* When this option is checked and the calendar is in Month view, the weather forecast for the next six days is shown.

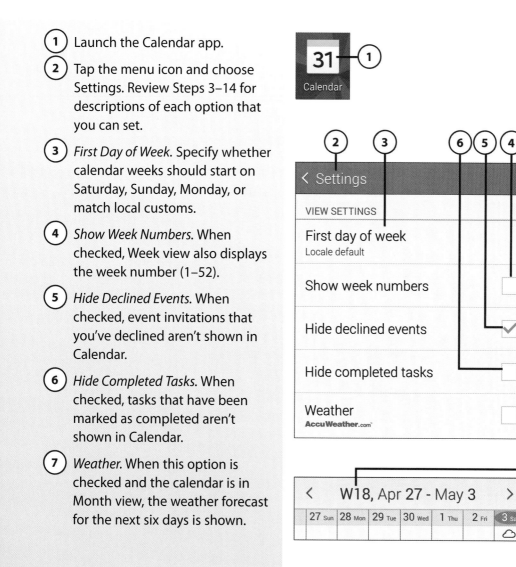

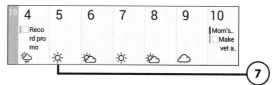

⑧ *Lock Time Zone.* When Lock Time Zone is disabled (unchecked), all event times reflect the phone's current location. When enabled (checked), event times always reflect the time zone specified in Select Time Zone (see Step 10).

A Lock Time Zone Recommendation

This is one of the most confusing aspects of Calendar. In general, the easiest way to use Lock Time Zone is to leave it disabled. When you're home in California, for example, all event times reflect Pacific time. If you travel to New York, the events display Eastern times. Finally, when you return home, events automatically change to show Pacific times again.

⑨ *Select Time Zone.* To force all event times to reflect a particular time zone (when you're traveling or if you want events to always reflect the home office's time zone, for example), enable Lock Time Zone (see Step 8) and tap Select Time Zone to choose a time zone.

⑩ *View Today According To.* If you have chosen to lock the time zone (as described in Step 8), use this option to specify how today's events are displayed. You can elect to use the current local time zone or the one you specified in Step 9.

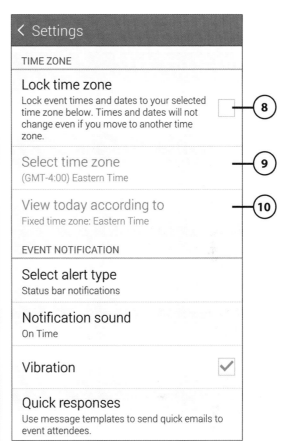

11. *Select Alert Type.* Specify whether a reminder will display as a status bar icon (Status Bar Notification), as a full screen pop-up (Sound Alerts), or not at all (Off).

12. *Notification Sound.* Select a sound to play with each reminder alert. Select Silent if you want to disable this option.

13. *Vibration.* Enable Vibration if you want Calendar reminders to cause the phone to vibrate. Like other notification settings, you can set Vibration as the sole notification method or use it in combination with other methods.

14. *Quick Responses.* View, edit, add, or delete brief email responses that you can send in response to event invitations.

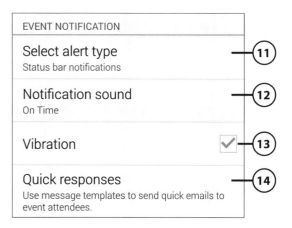

EVENT NOTIFICATION

Select alert type
Status bar notifications — 11

Notification sound
On Time — 12

Vibration ✓ — 13

Quick responses — 14
Use message templates to send quick emails to event attendees.

What Are Quick Responses?

Quick Responses are canned messages that you can send to event attendees. For example, if you are running late, there is a Quick Response that reads "I'm running just a couple of minutes late." As your meeting approaches, your Galaxy S5 alerts you. If you are running late, you will be given the option to send one of the Quick Responses.

Synchronizing Calendar Data

To quickly perform a manual Calendar sync based on your current account settings, tap the menu icon and choose Sync.

In this chapter, you explore the fine points of communicating with others through email, texting, and social media. Topics include the following:

→ Sending and receiving email
→ Attaching files to email
→ Using Messages to send and receive text and multimedia messages
→ Exploring social media

12

Communicating with Others

After mastering the calling features of the Galaxy S5, many users want to explore the world of email and texting. To help you learn about these other ways of communicating with others, this chapter explains the ins and outs of working with email, using Messages—the default messaging app that is probably on your Samsung Galaxy S5—chatting live with other users, and using social media.

Sending Email

You'll spend a lot of time using your Galaxy S5 to send and receive email. In fact, current social trends indicate that once you start using email, you'll probably use the phone for email more than you use it for making phone calls.

Compose and Send Email with the Gmail App

You have two options for composing and sending email on the Galaxy S5: Gmail and any other email app you download. This section uses Gmail for the examples.

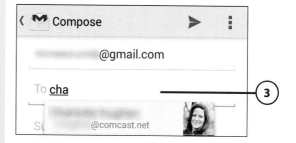

1. Tap the Gmail icon to open the program.

2. Tap the Create Message icon.

Keep Your Inbox Clean

Make it a practice to delete messages after you have read and dealt with them. Some people don't realize that any undeleted messages take up memory on your phone and can contribute to slower performance.

3. Type the recipient's name or email address in the To box. As you type, the app suggests people from your Contacts who might be a match. Either tap one of the suggestions or continue typing. You can enter more than one recipient—just put a space between each name.

Time-Saving Feature

Every time you type a new email address, your phone remembers it and saves the name and email address to your Contacts list. That way you don't have to re-type the email address the next time you want to send email to that person.

>>>Go Further

ADDING CC/BCC RECIPIENTS

You might want to specify that people receive copies of the email without designating them as recipients (if you're sending something to an insurance company, for instance, and you want your lawyer to know about the email). Tap the menu icon and select Add Cc/Bcc, then tap the Cc line and enter a name. Use the same procedure to send someone a blind carbon copy (Bcc).

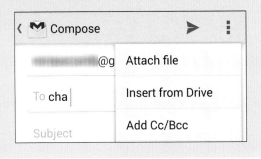

4 Type a subject line for the message.

5 Type the body of your message.

6 Optionally attach a file to an email by tapping the menu icon.

7 Tap Attach File.

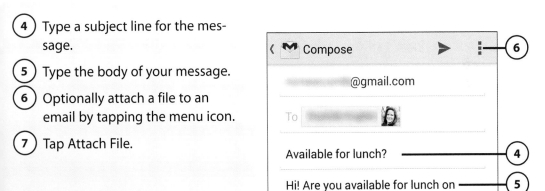

8 Select the location of the file. This example uses the Gallery.

9 Locate the file you want to attach and then tap it.

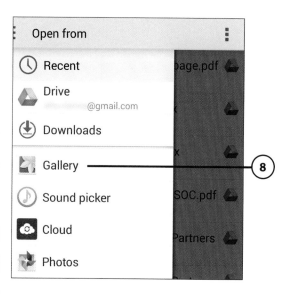

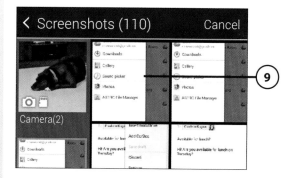

10 The attachment is added to your message. Tap the Send icon to send the email.

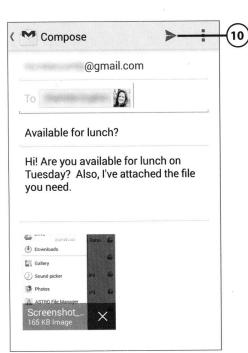

Save a Draft in the Gmail App

You can save a draft of your email without sending it so that you can complete the message and send it at a later time.

1 Follow the steps in the "Compose and Send Email with the Gmail App" task until you get to the point that you want to save a draft to return to later.

2 Tap the menu icon and select Save Draft. (Make sure the last character you typed is not a carriage return, or you won't be able to select the Save Draft option.) The message is saved in your Drafts folder within the email application.

Tap here to delete a draft

Want to Discard a Draft?

From time to time, you might start an email, save a draft, and then think better of sending it. To discard a draft before you've sent it, tap the menu icon and select Discard.

Use the Email App

Not everyone likes to use Gmail, and some carriers might not be equipped to handle all the Gmail options. Instead, you can use the Email app.

1. Tap the Email icon.

2. Tap the composition box near the bottom of the screen.

3. Type the recipient's name.

4. Type a subject.

5. Type the message and tap the Send icon.

Other Features of the Email App

Tap the menu icon if you want to send the email to yourself at another device, schedule it to be sent at a certain date or time, mark it Priority, or secure it with security options. The arrow next to the recipient field lets you add names for Cc or Bcc. The icons at the top let you attach a file, retrieve emails that haven't appeared on this device, and delete this email.

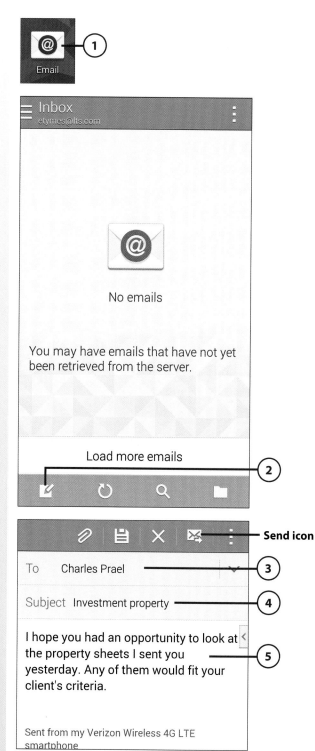

Reading Email with Gmail

(1) Tap the Gmail icon. Your inbox opens.

(2) All unread messages appear in boldface. Messages you have read are in a regular typeface. Tap an unread message. The full message appears on your screen.

(3) Reply to, forward, or print the message by tapping the message's menu icon.

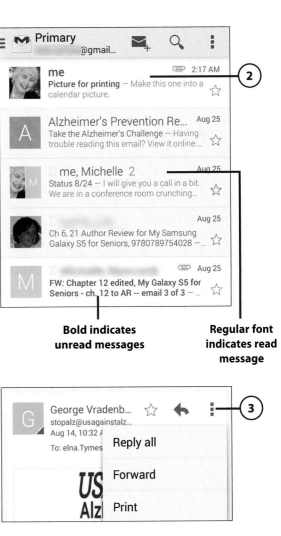

Bold indicates unread messages

Regular font indicates read message

④ Tap the app's menu icon to see the following options:

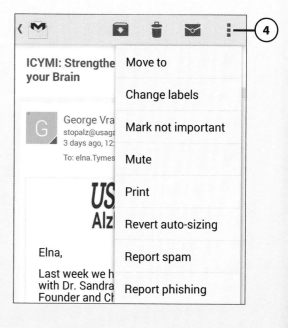

- *Move To* lets you specify the email folder in which you want to save this email. See the "Sorting Your Email" sidebar for more information about folders.

- *Change Labels* lets you change the name of a folder where this message will be stored.

- *Mark Not Important* keeps the email in your inbox but assigns it a check mark, rather than the initial icon.

- *Mute* turns off the sound on any attached audio or video file that has audio as part of it.

- *Print* sends the email to a device you specify that has a printer attached.

- *Revert Auto-sizing* lets you continue to read your email message while an incoming phone call might interrupt. See the Help's User Guide for more information.

- *Report Spam* lets you report to your carrier unsolicited, unwanted, or illegal messages. Your carrier probably has a spam filter that catches and deletes most spam, but sometimes a spam message gets through. Reporting spam lets your carrier know that something new has made it past the filter, which has to be fixed.

- *Report Phishing* is a response to an illegal attempt to acquire personal or sensitive information, such as bank account numbers, Social Security numbers, or other information that could be used to cause damage to you or your computer. Information about the email in question is sent to Google for investigation.

Reply to Email

1. After you have read a message, with a message still open, tap the arrow. The response form appears.

2. Type your message and tap the Send icon.

>>>Go Further
SORTING YOUR EMAIL

By default you have a number of folders where you can save your email. Some messages are automatically saved in some of them; others you have to specify. You can see them by tapping the Gmail app's menu icon as shown in Step 4 of the "Reading Email with Gmail" section. The important folders to remember are the following:

- *Starred*: This folder is for any email where you have tapped the star to mark it as important.

- *Sent*: This tracks all email you have sent. (Very useful to track what you actually said last week, for instance.)

- *Drafts*: This folder contains any email you've composed but not sent.

- *Spam*: The Spam folder is mildly interesting if you want to see what your spam filter prevented from getting to you.

- *Trash*: This folder contains all the email you discarded.

After you have read an email message, decide whether you want to save it, discard it, or do something else with it. Any email you want to save will stay in your Inbox unless you move it somewhere else. Any email you discard (by tapping the garbage can icon) gets automatically saved in the Trash folder. Otherwise, move an email out of your inbox and to a folder by tapping the menu icon and selecting the folder name.

Tap here to choose a folder ———

——— Discard this email

Take the Alzheimer's Challenge

Inbox

A   Alzheimer's Prev...
info@endalznow.org
Yesterday, 4:50 PM

To: me

Having trouble reading this email? View it online.

About Text and Multimedia Messaging

Phone calls can be time-consuming and, depending on the caller's timing, intrusive. To get a quick message to a friend or colleague, you can contact that person by sending a text or multimedia message (MMS).

Texting is strikingly similar to emailing. You specify recipients, compose the message text, and—optionally—add attachments. The main differences are that texting generally occurs between mobile phones, the messages must be short (160 characters or less), and a subject is optional rather than the norm.

Some Differences Among Carriers

Different carriers have slightly different messaging features, determined by their implementation of text and multimedia messaging. Settings options depend on your carrier, too. As a result, not all of the information in this section will apply to every carrier. Additionally, depending on the plan you have with your carrier, you have anywhere from unlimited text messaging to a charge of 20 cents per message, incoming or outgoing.

Composing a Text Message (SMS)

A text message can contain only text and is limited to 160 characters. If a message is longer, it is transmitted as multiple messages but typically recombined on the recipient's screen.

(1) Tap the Messages+ icon at the bottom of any Home screen page. (If you've removed the Messages+ shortcut, tap Apps, Messages+.)

Verizon Texting App

Verizon phones come with two text messaging programs: Messages+ is the Verizon program, and Messages is the Google program.

(2) A screen showing all past conversations appears. Do one of the following:

- To continue a conversation, tap its entry in the conversations list, and then go to Step 9.

- To start a conversation with someone who isn't in the conversations list, tap the Compose Message icon. Each message can have one or more recipients. Use any of the methods described in Steps 3–5 to specify recipients.

(3) The New Message screen appears.

(4) *Manually enter a mobile number.* If you know that the recipient doesn't have a Contacts record, type the person's mobile phone number in the Enter Recipients box and then tap the plus (+) icon.

(5) *Enter partial contact info.* Type any *part* of the person's contact information (such as a first name, area code, or email domain) in the Enter Recipients box and select the person from the match list that appears.

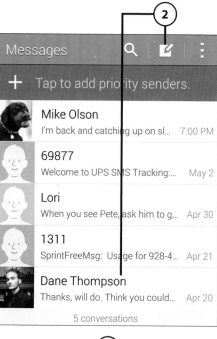

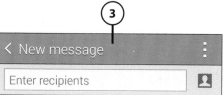

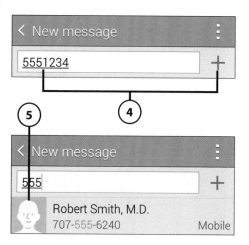

6 *Select recipients from Contacts.* Tap the Contacts icon. Select one or more recipients from the list by tapping each person's check box and then tap Done.

Finding Recipients in Contacts

To find someone in Contacts, you can scroll through the list by flicking up or down, go directly to an alphabetical section of the list by tapping an index letter, or drag down or up in the index letters and release your finger when the first letter of the person's name displays.

You can also filter the list to show only certain people. To view people with whom you've recently spoken, tap the Logs or Recent tab. Tap the Favorites tab to restrict the list to contacts you've marked as *favorites*. To search for a person, select the Contacts tab and type part of the name, email address, or phone number in the Search box; press the Back key to view the results; tap the person's check box; and tap Done.

7 If a recipient selected from Contacts has only one phone number or you've set a default number for him, that number is automatically used. Otherwise, a screen appears that lists the person's contact details. Tap the phone number—normally a *mobile* number—to which you want to send the message.

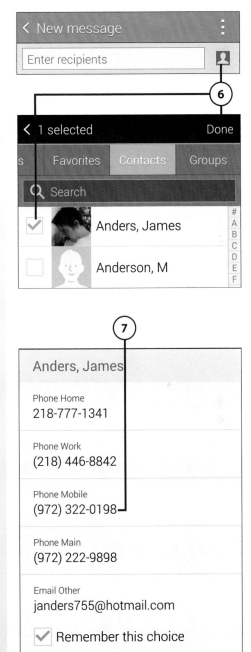

8 *Optional:* Remove a recipient by tapping the minus (–) icon following the person's name. Similarly, you can change or edit a person's phone number by tapping her name and selecting Edit in the dialog box that appears. (If recipients are listed as "Joan Duran and 1 more," tap this text to list them separately and display the minus (–) icon.)

9 Enter your message in the Enter Message box. You can type the message or tap the microphone key to use voice input. (If the microphone isn't shown on the key, press and hold the key, and *then* select the microphone.) As you type or dictate, the number of remaining characters is shown beneath the Send button.

10 Tap the Send button to transmit the message.

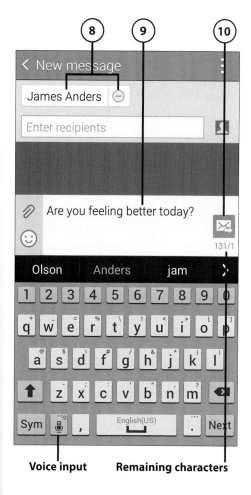

Voice input   Remaining characters

Group Conversations

When you specify multiple individuals or a contact group (see "Working with Contact Groups" in Chapter 6, "Setting Up Your Contacts") as recipients, Messages considers it a *group conversation*. Each message is treated as a multimedia message even if it contains only text, is transmitted only once to the message server, and then is delivered to all recipients.

To treat this as a normal conversation, remove the check mark from Group Conversation. Each text message is transmitted repeatedly to the message server (once per recipient), but retains its normal text message (SMS) form.

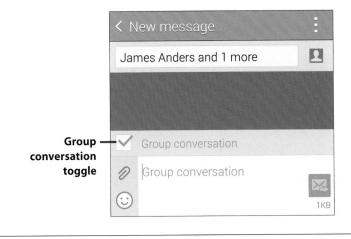

Group conversation toggle

Saving a Message as a Draft

If you aren't ready to send the message, you can save it as a draft by pressing the Back key. To later open the message, select it in the conversations list. You can then edit, send, or delete it. (To delete a draft message that you're viewing, open the menu and choose Discard.)

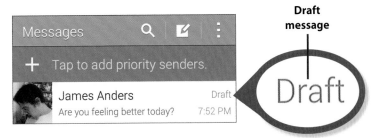

Draft message

>>>Go Further

MORE WAYS TO START A CONVERSATION

Choosing a contact record is only one of the ways to start a texting conversation. Others include these:

- Immediately after completing a call, you can begin a conversation with the person by tapping the Message icon.

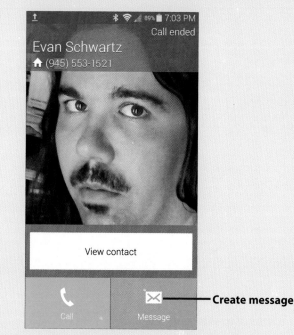

Create message

- To text someone to whom you've recently spoken, launch Phone and then tap the Logs or Recent tab. Find the person in any log and then swipe his entry to the left. You can use this swipe technique on the Contacts and Favorites tabs, too—as long as items are displayed in List View rather than Grid View.

- Open the person's record in Contacts and tap the envelope icon.

Smith, Robert, M.D.

Create message

Mobile
707-555-6240

- You can also send a message to a *group* you've defined (see "Working with Contact Groups" in Chapter 6). Tap the Contacts icon, the Groups tab, and the group's name. Select the specific members whom you want to message and then tap Done.

>>>Go Further
LAZY MESSAGING

If you text frequently, many of your messages are short, simple phrases that you use regularly, such as "When will you be home?", "Where are you?", or "Can't talk now. I'm in a meeting." Rather than laboriously typing such messages whenever one's needed, you can pick it from a list.

Quick Responses

Quick responses

Can't talk right now. Send me a message.

Call me.

Where are you?

Many phrases aren't complete; they're the beginnings of messages that you must finish, such as "Don't forget to...", "Meet me at...", and "I'll be there at..." In addition, Quick Responses don't have to be the sole message content. When you select one, it's inserted at the text insertion mark—so it can be added to the beginning, middle, or end of a message.

To modify the Quick Responses phrases, go to the main Messages screen and tap the menu icon. Choose Quick Responses or Settings, Quick Responses—depending on your carrier. You can do any of the following:

- To delete unwanted phrases, tap the Trash icon, select phrases to delete, and tap Done.

- To add a new phrase, tap the plus (+) icon, enter the phrase, and tap Save.

- To edit an existing phrase, tap the phrase to open it for editing, make the necessary changes, and tap Save.

Quick Responses (in Messages Settings)

Delete phrases

Create a new phrase

Tap to edit this phrase

>>>Go Further

MORE MESSAGE-COMPOSITION OPTIONS

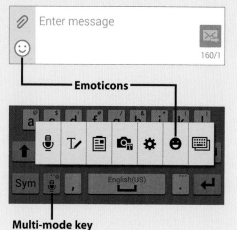

Emoticons

Multi-mode key

Although somewhat unusual, the following composition options can sometimes be very useful:

- *Adding a Subject.* Unlike email messages, text messages generally don't have a Subject. If you'd like to add one, tap the menu icon and choose Add Subject.

- *Inserting Smileys.* If you want to insert a *smiley* (also called an *emoticon*) into a message you're creating, tap the menu icon, choose Insert Smiley, and select the smiley to insert. It appears at the text insertion mark. To insert more elaborately drawn emoticons, switch to Emoticons input. Tap the emoticon icon to the left of the Enter Message box or long-press the multi-mode key and select Emoticons.

- *Embedded links in messages.* If a message contains a web address, email address, or phone number shown as underlined text, you can tap the embedded text and choose Open Link, Send Email, or Call to visit the page using the phone's browser, address a new email message to the person, or dial the phone number, respectively.

- *Texting to email or a landline.* If a recipient doesn't have a mobile phone, you can send text messages to an email address. Some carriers, such as Sprint, even allow you to send texts to a landline phone. (Check with your carrier to see if it offers this feature.) Create the message as you normally would, but specify an email address or landline number in the Enter Recipients box. As appropriate, the text message is emailed, or the service calls the landline and a computer voice reads the text when the phone is answered. (Emoticons are read, too!)

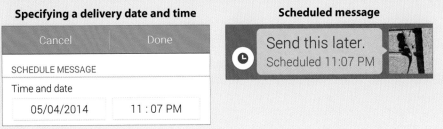

Specifying a delivery date and time   **Scheduled message**

Composing a Multimedia Message (MMS)

A *multimedia message* (*MMS*) is any message that has one or more attachments, such as a picture, video, audio recording, Contacts record, or Calendar item.

Some Attachments Are Just Text

Material that you add to a message from Maps, My Location, or Memo is text and does not result in a text message becoming a multimedia message.

(1) Perform Steps 1–9 of the "Composing a Text Message (SMS)" task—that is, every step other than tapping Send.

(2) Tap the paper clip icon at any time during the message-creation process.

(3) Select the item type that you want to attach to the message. If you're attaching a file that's already on your phone, continue with Step 4. If you want to create a *new* file, skip to Step 5.

(4) *Attach an existing file.* Select the item(s) to attach, opening enclosing folders if necessary. For most item types, you complete the attachment process by making the selection or by tapping Done. Go to Step 6.

Size Matters

Existing video clips and audio recordings such as songs may be too large to transmit as part of an MMS message. Depending on the file type, Messages may either reject the item as an attachment, ask you to trim the item, or compress it for you. Photos, on the other hand, are automatically compressed to meet MMS size limits.

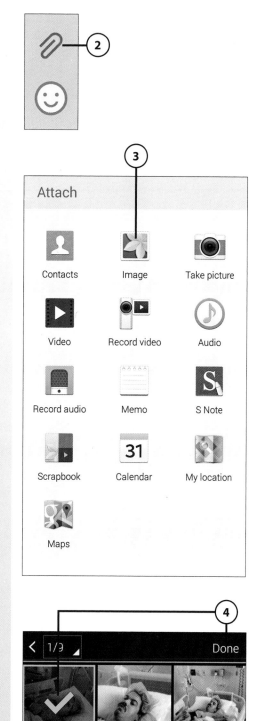

(5) *Create an attachment (Take Picture, Record Video, or Record Audio).* Take a new picture or capture a video. Tap Save to add it to the message or tap Discard to try again. When you finish recording an audio clip, tap the Stop button to save it, listen to the clip, and tap Done.

Shooting a photo

Discard   Save

Recording an audio clip

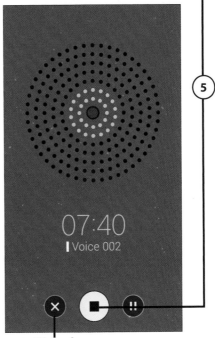

07:40
▌Voice 002

Discard

6 A thumbnail representing the media is inserted into the message or the item is shown as a file attachment. As you add items, the total size of the message and attachments updates.

7 If you want to view/play, replace, or remove a multimedia item, press and hold its thumbnail and then select the appropriate option. (If you remove *all* attachments from a message, it reverts to a text message.)

Another Removal Option

You can also remove a multimedia item by selecting it and tapping the Delete key.

8 Tap Send when the message is complete.

Invite22.vcs

Here's a quick shot of my gear.   87KB

Total size

Message options

View

Replace

Remove

It's Not All Good

Your Mileage May Vary

When it works, nothing is cooler than having a photo, video, or other MMS attachment appear on your screen during a texting session. Unfortunately, MMS transmissions aren't 100% reliable. Each message must pass through multiple servers and conversions. As a result, multimedia messages sometimes arrive late, vanish altogether, or are dramatically compressed. The moral? MMS messages are more appropriate for fun than for mission-critical transmissions. When sending important data (especially when it needs to be delivered quickly and uncompressed), stick with computer-to-computer email. For lengthy back-and-forth text conversations, you might also consider trying one of the many chat apps, such as the ones mentioned at the end of this chapter.

Managing Conversations

There's more to participating in a conversation than just creating messages. The following tasks explain how to respond to new message notifications; continue, review, and delete conversations; and search for messages.

Responding to a New Message Notification

If you're in Messages and a message for the current conversation arrives, it simply appears onscreen as a new message balloon. If you're doing something else with the phone, the phone is resting quietly on your desk, or you're viewing a different conversation, a new message notification appears.

Depending on your Messages settings and what you're currently doing, you may be notified of a new message in one of several ways:

- The message text appears briefly in the status bar and is replaced by an envelope icon. The Messages shortcut on the Home screen shows the number of new messages.

- A pop-up notification with options may appear. Tap Call to initiate a phone call to the person, tap Reply to type your reply in the pop-up—without leaving the current screen, tap View to open the message and its conversation in Messages, or tap the X to dismiss the pop-up window.

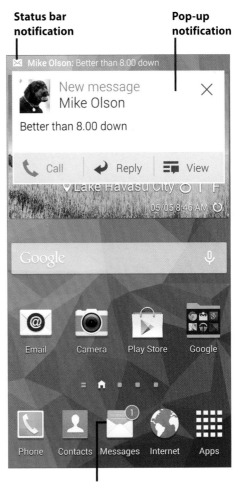

Status bar notification

Pop-up notification

1 new message

- You can view a preview of the new message in the Notification panel. Tap the message notification to view the complete message or respond to it in Messages.

- You can launch Messages (if it isn't currently running) and open the conversation that contains the new message.

- Finally, if the screen is dark when a message arrives, press the Power button to see a preview of the message on your lock screen. To remove the message from the lock screen, tap Clear.

Notification panel

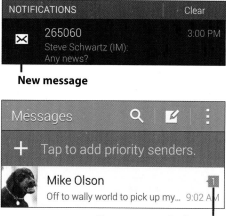

New message

New message indicator

Lock screen

New message   **Clear the notification**

Continue a Conversation

The default length for a conversation on your phone is 200 text or 20 multimedia messages—whichever occurs first. As long as the length limit hasn't been exceeded, a conversation can be continued immediately or whenever either participant wants—days, weeks, or even months after it was begun.

Creating a New Message

Don't worry if you mistakenly create a new message to someone already in the conversations list. Messages automatically treats the message as a continuation of the existing conversation rather than generating a second conversation with the person.

(1) If Messages+ isn't running, launch it by tapping its Home screen shortcut or by tapping Apps, Messages+.

2 Select the conversation that you want to continue. The conversation appears.

3 Tap in the Enter Message box to display the onscreen keyboard.

4 Create a text or multimedia message as described in "Composing a Text Message (SMS)" or "Composing a Multimedia Message (MMS)," earlier in this chapter.

5 Tap the Send button to transmit the message. It is appended to the end of the conversation.

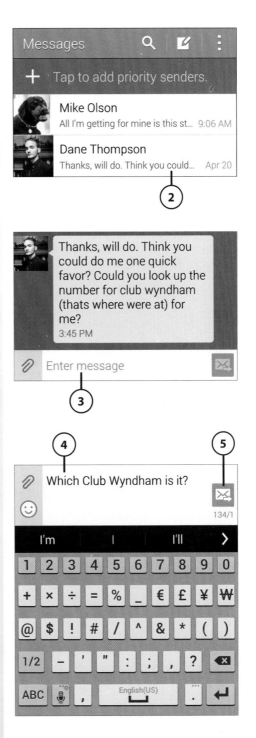

Reviewing a Conversation

As long as you haven't deleted a conversation, you can reread it whenever you like. This is especially useful when a conversation contains important information, such as the time of an upcoming meeting, a phone number, a web address (URL), or driving directions. To review a conversation, select it from the conversations list on the Messages+ main screen (as described in the previous task) and scroll through the messages by flicking or dragging up and down.

Reviewing a conversation

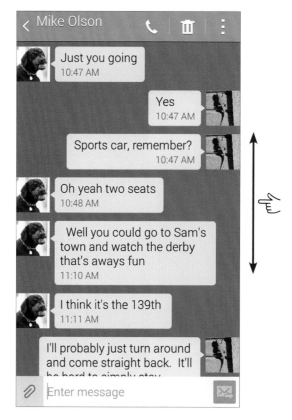

Delete Conversations

For the sake of privacy, saving storage space, or eliminating clutter in the conversations list, you can delete entire conversations.

(**1**) Launch Messages by tapping its Home screen shortcut. (If you're currently in a conversation, press the Back key until the conversations list appears.)

(**2**) Tap the menu icon and choose Delete.

(**3**) Select the conversations that you want to delete, or tap Select All to select all conversations.

(**4**) Tap Done.

(**5**) Confirm the conversation deletion(s) by tapping OK.

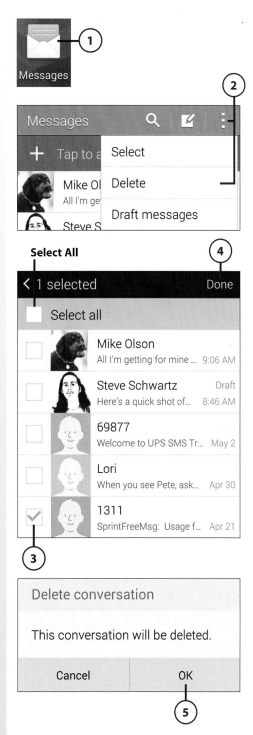

Delete Messages

In addition to deleting entire conversations, you can selectively delete individual messages from a conversation.

① In Messages+, open the conversation from which you want to delete messages.

② Tap the Delete icon.

③ Scroll through the conversation, and select each message that you want to delete.

④ Tap the Delete button.

⑤ Tap OK to confirm the deletion(s).

Deleting a Single Message

To delete a *single* message in a conversation, you can press and hold the message, tap Delete in the Message Options dialog box, and confirm the deletion by tapping OK.

Other Options for Individual Messages

In addition to deleting individual messages, you can copy message text to the Clipboard for pasting elsewhere, lock a message to prevent it from being deleted, save the multimedia elements in an MMS message, forward a message to others, or view a message's properties.

SMS (text) message

Message options
Delete
Copy text
Forward
Lock
Share
View message details
Translate

MMS (multimedia) message

Message options
Delete
View slideshow
Copy text
Forward
Lock
Save attachment
Share
View message details
Translate

(1) Within a conversation, press and hold a message for which you want to display options. The Message Options dialog box appears. SMS and MMS messages offer slightly different options, as explained in Step 2.

(2) Tap an option to perform one of the following actions:

- *Delete.* Delete the current message.

- *View Slideshow (MMS messages only).* Display message text and certain types of attachments (such as photos) as a slideshow.

- *Copy Text.* Copy the message text to the Clipboard, making it eligible for pasting into another message or app, such as an email message.

- *Forward.* Send the message to another recipient—passing along a picture, phone number, address, or driving directions, for example.

- *Lock.* Prevent an important message from being inadvertently deleted—even if you delete the conversation that contains the message. After a message has been locked, the Lock command is replaced by Unlock. You can optionally override the lock while attempting to delete the message or its conversation.

- *Share.* Share the message by posting it to a social networking site, emailing it, transferring it to a computer or another phone, and so on.

- *Save Attachment (MMS messages only).* Save an attached item, such as a picture or video, to the Download folder.

- *View Message Details.* Examine the message properties, such as who sent it and when, the date and time it was received, and its total size including attachments.

- *Translate.* Translate the message text from its current language to another. (Verizon does not have a Translate option.)

Search for Messages

You can search all conversations for specific text.

(1) On the Messages+ main screen, tap the Search icon. A Search text box appears.

(2) Enter the search text; matches appear as you type. Continue typing until the desired message is shown.

(3) Do one of the following:

- Tap a message to display the match. The conversation appears and displays the selected message. The matching text is shown in blue anywhere that it appears in the conversation.

- Tap the search key on the keyboard to display a list of *all* matches. The matches are shown in blue. Tap a match to display the message in the context of its conversation.

Match in context

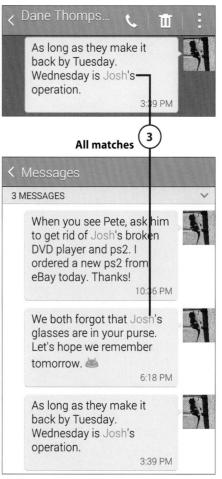

All matches

>>>Go Further
MESSAGING CONSIDERATIONS

Here are a few practical and etiquette considerations for texting:

- *Know your service plan*. Although your Galaxy S5 can create and receive text and multimedia messages, your plan determines how you're charged—whether messages are unlimited, limited to a certain number per month, or there's a per-message charge. Received messages generally count, too—including unsolicited ones. Review your plan before you leap into texting.

- *Check with the recipient before texting*. Whether you *should* text someone depends on many factors, such as the recipient's phone (not all phones can display multimedia messages and many older phones can't even accept text messages) and the recipient's data plan. Unless someone has texted you first, it's a good idea to ask before initiating a conversation.

- *You can refuse all incoming messages*. If your plan doesn't allow for texting or it's expensive and you have no interest in receiving messages, contact your plan provider to see if there's a way to block incoming messages. Incoming messages typically cost the same as those you initiate, so you might prefer to refuse them.

Other Messaging Apps and Alternatives

There are other ways to send and receive messages on your Galaxy S5. This section discusses some of them.

Text Chat

One of the great things about messaging is that it's platform- and device-independent. That is, you can exchange text messages with anyone who has a mobile phone and a messaging plan—regardless of the manufacturer and model of phone or their carrier. Apps you use can be different, too. (Note, however, that some *features* aren't universal, such as the availability of certain emoticons and the ability to exchange some types of multimedia data.) Most carriers ship their Galaxy S5 with *multiple* messaging apps: Messages and Hangouts, for example.

After you get your feet wet with Messages+, you should check out the others to see if their approach and feature sets better suit your needs. When you decide on a favorite, you can set it as your default messaging app.

Before texting became popular, people relied on dedicated chat programs to conduct online conversations. Many of those same programs are now available as Android apps you can use on your Galaxy S5. Unlike texting, chat messages carry no per-message surcharge, and there's no limit to the number of messages that can be exchanged in a billing cycle. In addition, some go further than chat, enabling you to exchange files—considerably larger ones than those allowed in multimedia messages. Some social networking apps—Facebook, for example—also have a chat feature, in addition to making it possible for you to post updates and share items.

Many chat programs only allow you to chat with other users of the program (although the app may be available on multiple devices and platforms). In some cases, you must be using the same type of device; that is, Galaxy S5 owners may not be able to chat with iPhone owners. If you already have chat friends who use many different chat programs, you have a few options:

- Install a dedicated app for each chat program and hop among them as you attempt to find friends who are online and available to chat. Most of the major chat services, such as Yahoo! Messenger, AIM, and ICQ, have a free Android app that you can download from Google Play.

- Convince your friends to switch to a specific chat service to chat with you. For example, previous Galaxy S phones shipped with ChatON, a Samsung chat app/service. Note, however, that not all chat services are platform-independent or device-independent.

- Search Google Play for an app that can aggregate your chats and chat buddies from multiple services.

Audio and Video Chat

The logical step up from text chat is audio or video chat. Rather than type, you can say—or say and show. Note that audio and video chat apps are good options in two situations: when you're at home using Wi-Fi (avoids hits to your data plan and assures you of a high-speed connection) or when you have an unlimited data plan and are in a 4G/LTE area with a solid cellular connection. Some popular apps for video and voice chat are ooVoo Video Call, Skype, and Yahoo! Messenger with plug-in for voice and video calls. Another is SnapChat, which combines text and video chatting with photo sharing.

Staying Connected with Social Media

Social media is the term for websites where people form communities to do things like discuss issues, organize events or group actions, post pictures, rate and review restaurants, share music, ask for help, or raise money for particular causes.

Social media groups can be as small as two or three people or as large as Facebook, which had more than 1 billion users as of mid-2014. (Read more about Facebook in Chapter 17, "Connecting with Family and Friends on Facebook.")

The websites associated with social media can be as simple as a bulletin board-style forum, where people comment and respond to one another in topical threads, or as multifaceted as collaborative projects like Wikipedia. They include blogs (short for "web log," where an individual or team regularly post columns and articles), social news networking sites (for example, Leakernet), content communities (such as YouTube), virtual game-worlds (such as World of Warcraft), and virtual social worlds (such as Second Life).

Watch a YouTube Video

YouTube is a video-sharing service where users can upload, view, and share videos for free. Both private individuals and large production companies have used YouTube to grow audiences. Independent content creators have built grassroots followings numbering in the thousands at very little cost or effort. Some celebrities, such as Beyoncé, have launched new releases on YouTube. The widely used independent learning environment Khan Academy has based its lessons on YouTube videos.

Anyone can watch the videos posted on YouTube, but you must be a registered user in order to post one. The YouTube app is already on your Galaxy S5 when you purchase it.

1. Tap the Apps icon, and then tap the YouTube icon.

2. YouTube immediately opens and shows you a sampling of content. Tap the icon to the left of the YouTube icon to select a category.

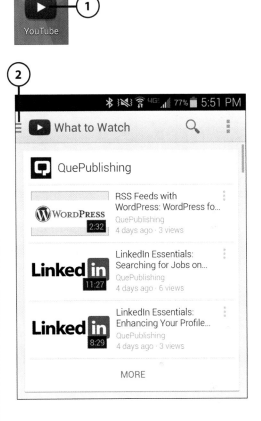

(3) Tap a category. Alternatively, you can tap the Search icon to find a specific person, video title, or keyword. A list of videos displays.

(4) Tap a video to start playing it.

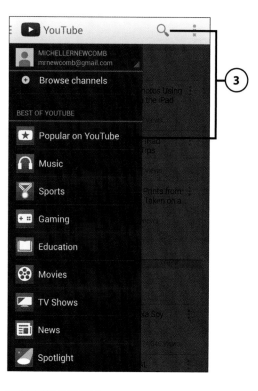

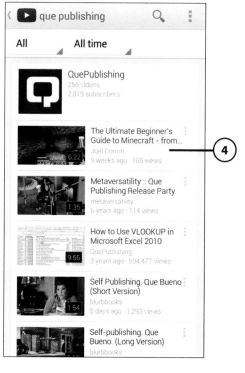

>>>Go Further
OTHER SOCIAL MEDIA APPS

There are a couple of social media apps that might be of particular interest to you:

- *Pinterest* is like an online bulletin board, where people share collections of pictures (actually visual bookmarks, or "pins"). Readers use these pictures to plan trips, outline projects, store ideas for different interests, organize events, save recipes, or plan purchases.

  Pinterest is a free app, but to participate you must register. In addition, Pinterest is not one of the default apps on your Galaxy S5, so you have to download the app from the Play Store if you want to use it.

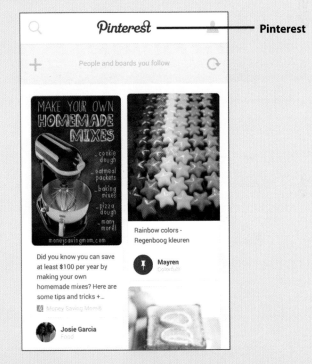

Pinterest

- *Yelp* is an online guide and review site. Users post reviews of various businesses—especially restaurants and merchandisers. Note, however, that it has been estimated that about 20% of its reviews are fake—in other words, many reviews are posted by someone who's been hired to post positive or negative things about a particular business. Even so, if you want to know what the dim sum is like in a particular Chinese restaurant, Yelp is one place to find out. You can download the Yelp app from the Play Store.

Select wallpaper image ————

In this chapter, you become familiar with the basics of setting up and operating your new phone. Topics include the following:

→ Selecting wallpaper
→ Adding and removing Home screen items
→ Adding shortcuts and widgets
→ Creating folders

13

Customizing Your Screen

One of the main reasons for buying a smartphone such as the Galaxy S5 is that you can do considerably more with it than you can with an ordinary telephone or cell phone. Much as you can do with a computer, you can customize your phone by populating the Home screen with custom arrangements of widgets and app icons, change the Home and lock screens' background (*wallpaper*), install additional useful apps, and set preferences (*settings*) for the system software and installed apps.

>>>*Go Further*

CHANGING SYSTEM SETTINGS

To change certain operating system features (such as choosing a new Wi-Fi network or adjusting the screen timeout interval), you need to access the Settings screen by tapping the Apps icon and then tapping the Settings icon.

Settings icon

Because there are now so many icons in Settings, you can elect to display them in several different ways. To change their display, open Settings, tap the menu icon, and choose Grid View, List View, or Tab View.

Setting the Wallpaper

The simplest way to customize the phone is to change its Home screen background (wallpaper) by selecting an image that represents you and your tastes. Wallpaper can be a static image or a moving image. The image you choose is applied to all Home screen pages.

(**1**) Tap the Apps icon and then tap the Settings icon.

(**2**) Tap Wallpaper.

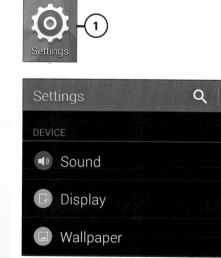

(**3**) Tap Home Screen, Lock Screen, or Home and Lock Screens—depending on the screen(s) you want to customize. The same screen appears for any selection.

(**4**) Scroll through the provided images and tap one to use it, and then tap Set Wallpaper to immediately start using it as the wallpaper. Alternatively, you can tap More Images to select a custom image for your wallpaper. Continue to Step 5 if you want to use a custom image.

(**5**) Select the source for the image you want to use. Tap Always if you want to pull your image from this source every time you change your wallpaper, or tap Just Once if you want to use this source only this time. This example shows you how to use a figure from the Gallery.

(**6**) Tap the album that contains the photo you want to use.

(**7**) Tap the image you want to use as the wallpaper.

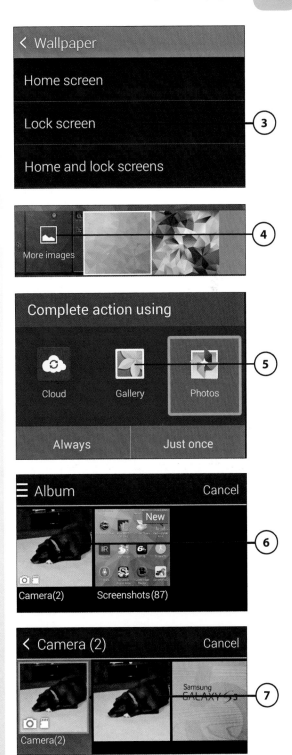

8. Tap Done.

9. The image is set as your wallpaper.

Wallpaper Considerations

If you want to crop the image you've chosen so that you're only using a portion of it as the wallpaper, use the blue cropping guidelines on the figure shown for Step 8 of the "Setting the Wallpaper" section to trim the image.

Also, as you pick an image for your wallpaper, consider how easy it will be to see the app icons against the background. An image that provides good contrast will be easier to use than a very busy background.

:

Adding, Removing, and Rearranging Home Screen Pages

There are five horizontally scrolling pages that together comprise your Home screens. The main Home screen is represented by the little house icon; the other Home screens are represented by dots, which turn white when you are on a particular screen. You can add new Home screens (up to a maximum of seven), remove ones that you don't need, and rearrange the pages.

Main Home screen indicator ———

——— **Dot indicators for other Home screens**

Add a Home Screen Page

1. From a Home screen, pinch the screen with two fingers. The Home screens reduce in size so you can manipulate them.

2. Scroll through the screens to find one with a + on it. Tap the screen to add a new Home screen at the end of the existing screens. Another Home screen dot indicator will be added.

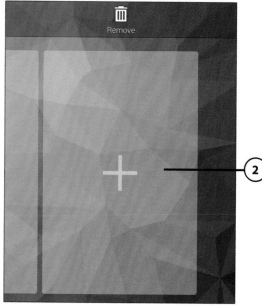

>>>Go Further

CHANGING THE MAIN HOME SCREEN

If you want to change the main Home screen, pinch with two fingers on any Home screen to see a screen that looks like the one for Step 1 of the "Add a Home Screen Page" task. Scroll through the pages to find the Home screen that you want to be the main screen, and then tap the gray house icon at the top of the page.

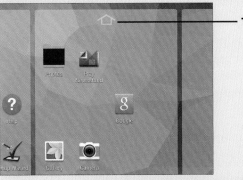

Tap the house icon

Remove a Home Screen Page

1. From a Home screen, pinch the screen with two fingers.

2 Drag the screen you want to delete onto the Remove icon at the top of the screen. There will be a red glow around the icon when you're in the right place. If the page contains any items, you see a confirmation box.

3 Tap OK to confirm the deletion or Cancel if you change your mind.

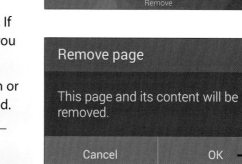

Effects of Deleting a Page

As indicated by the confirmation box, deleting a page also removes the items on that page, such as widgets and shortcuts, but it does not actually delete those items from your Galaxy S5. (Uninstalling an app is covered in Chapter 16, "Adding, Removing, and Using Apps.")

Rearrange Home Screen Pages

You can rearrange the order of your Home screen pages.

1 From a Home screen, pinch the screen with two fingers.

2 Find the screen you want to move, and then tap and hold it. You feel a vibration, which indicates you've grabbed the page. Drag the screen left or right to its new position.

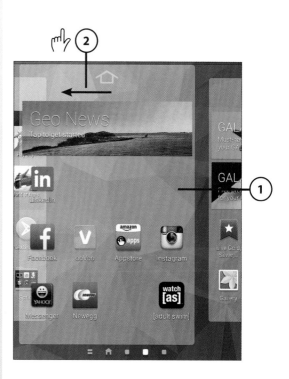

Adding Shortcuts and Widgets

Shortcuts are icons that let you go immediately to the app you want, rather than going through a series of menus to reach the app. Widgets are like mini-apps that let you have apps running on your Home screens. You can add shortcuts and widgets to any of your home pages.

Add Shortcuts

You can place shortcuts to your favorite apps on any Home screen. When you tap an app shortcut, the app that it represents launches. An Android shortcut is the equivalent of a Mac alias or a Windows shortcut.

(1) Tap the Apps icon to find the app that you want to add to a Home screen as a shortcut.

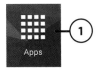

(2) Tap and hold the icon for the app for which you want to create a shortcut.

(3) A group of small shadowboxes appears near the bottom of the screen. Note that the shaded areas correspond to placement of existing app icons. Some shadowboxes will have open spaces, meaning that there is space on the page for that icon. Drag the icon into an open spot onto one of the shadowbox pages and release the icon.

(4) The icon appears on the home screen.

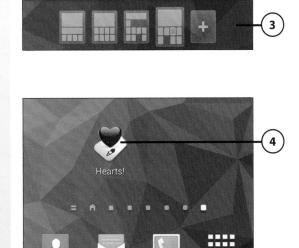

Creating a Bookmark Shortcut

You can also create shortcuts to your favorite web pages. In your favorite Internet app (Chrome, Firefox, Internet Explorer, Opera, Safari or any other browser app you use), open the page or site for viewing, press the Menu key, and tap Add Shortcut. The bookmark is added to a Home screen page, and you can move it around the same way you move the app icons.

Add Widgets

A *widget* is an application that runs on the Home Screen. Many, such as Weather, aren't interactive or are only minimally so. For example, you can tap the refresh icon on the Weather widget to force an update of the weather information. Otherwise, such widgets simply provide continuously updated information. Other widgets, such as the Music widget, are designed for interaction. By tapping its buttons, you can pause or restart playback, and skip to the next or previous song.

You can add a widget in any free space on a Home screen page, as long as there's room for it. Widgets come in a variety of sizes, from one- or two-section widgets to full-screen ones.

(1) To add a widget to a Home screen page, press and hold an empty space on a home screen. Tap the Widgets option at the bottom of the screen.

(**2**) Scroll through the options and tap and hold the desired widget to add it to the screen.

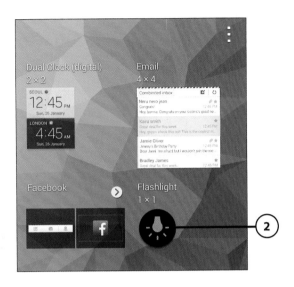

Moving a Widget

To move a widget from one screen to another, touch and hold the widget until it releases from the grid, then drag it toward the edge of the current screen into the frame of the next screen. You also use this method to move widgets from one position to another on the same screen. (The process also works for moving shortcuts.)

>>>Go Further

WIDGET SHORTCUTS

Shortcuts in an Android system give you lots of flexibility because they can provide direct links to a variety of things: files, records, or operating system elements. For instance, you can create a Direct Dial shortcut that, when tapped, automatically dials a person's phone number. After adding the Direct Dial widget to a Home Screen page, you tap the person's contact record to link it to the shortcut.

Here are some other widget-based shortcuts you might want to add:

- *Book.* Links to a favorite downloaded ebook that you can read with the Play Books app.

- *Bookmark.* Links to a web page selected from your stored bookmarks.

- *Contact.* Links to a person's record in Contacts, letting you easily call, message, email, or locate the person.

- *Direct Message.* Lets you create a new text or multimedia message to a specific person in Contacts.

- *Settings Shortcut.* Opens a Settings category that you frequently access.

Creating Folders

To help organize your items, you can add folders in which you store them.

(1) Tap the Apps icon.

(2) Navigate to the page where you want to add a folder, tap the menu icon, and select Create Folder.

(3) Type a name for the folder and then tap the plus (+) icon.

(4) Tap the checkboxes of the items you'd like to include in the folder. You can swipe right and left to see other screens.

(5) Tap Done after you've selected all the items you want in the folder.

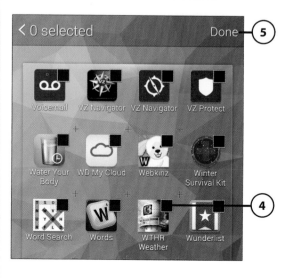

(6) The new folder with items in it
appears on the page.

>>>*Go Further*

WORKING WITH FOLDERS

Of course, creating a folder is just the first step. Adding and organizing shortcuts within the folders is what makes them useful.

To insert an item into a folder, press and hold the item's icon, then drag it into the folder. Tap the folder to access its items. In the pop-out contents list that appears, tap an item to launch or open it.

To remove an item from a folder, tap the folder to open it, press and hold the item's icon, and then drag it to any location outside of the folder. To delete an app shortcut that's in the folder, drag the shortcut out of the folder. Then press and hold the shortcut and drag it into the Remove icon.

Finally, like any other Home screen items, you can reposition a folder by pressing and holding its icon and dragging it to its destination on a current or different page.

Repositioning and Removing Home Screen Items

Part of the fun of setting up your Home screen pages is that you can freely rearrange items. And because many items are shortcuts, removing items from the Home screen has no effect on the actual items they represent.

① On the Home screen page, press and hold the item that you want to reposition or remove.

② Remove the item by dragging it onto the Remove (trash can) icon at the top of the screen. When you release the item, it is removed. If it's an app, you will be asked if you want to uninstall the app. Confirm your action.

③ Reposition an item by dragging it to an empty or occupied spot on the current or another Home screen page. (If the destination is currently occupied, items will shift to make room—if possible.) When you release the item, the move is completed.

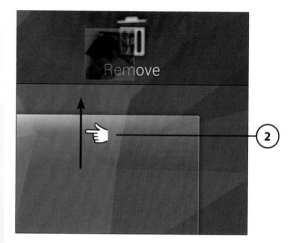

Moving Items Between Pages

When moving an item between Home screen pages, don't let up on the finger pressure until the destination page appears. If you inadvertently release the item on the wrong page or in the wrong space, press and hold the item again and finish the move.

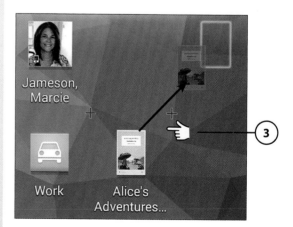

>>>Go Further

REARRANGING AND REPLACING PRIMARY SHORTCUTS

At the bottom of every Home Page screen are the five primary shortcuts: Phone, Contacts, Messaging, Chrome (the Internet browser), and Apps. If you want, you can rearrange, remove, or replace any of the first four.

To rearrange the primary shortcuts, press and hold the one that you want to move. Drag it left or right and release it when it's in the position you want.

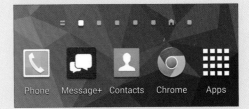

Original shortcut order   **Rearranged shortcuts**

To remove a primary shortcut, press and hold it, then drag it to the Remove icon at the top of the Home screen page. (Refer to the figure for Step 2 of the "Repositioning and Removing Home Screen Items.") If you want to remove the primary shortcut from the bottom of the screen but keep it on the page, drag it to any blank spot on the current Home screen page.

To replace a primary shortcut (or add one, if you currently have fewer than five), find the replacement shortcut on a Home screen page and drag it onto the primary shortcut you want to replace. If the desired app shortcut isn't already on a Home screen page, you must first create a shortcut for it as described earlier in the "Add Shortcuts" task.

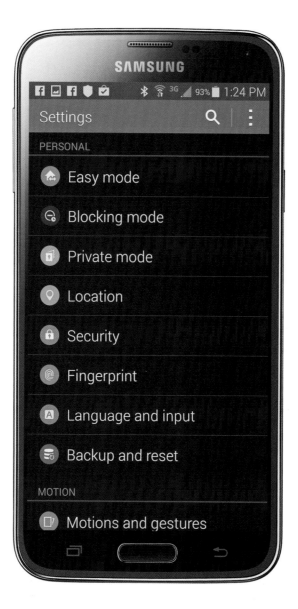

In this chapter, you become familiar with the security features of your phone, all of which are in the Personal section in Settings. Topics include the following:

→ Exploring your Galaxy S5's built-in security features
→ Using the Fingerprint App
→ Locking your screen
→ Using Blocking and Private mode
→ Setting up Safety Assistance

14

Securing Your Cell Phone

Mobile phone theft has become a frequent crime in many places. As of this publication date, Samsung has not yet released a "kill switch" app that would make your phone inaccessible—and hence undesirable—to a thief, but there are other built-in security features that can make your Galaxy S5 useless to a thief. This chapter discusses these features.

Locking the Screen

Do you occasionally leave your phone unattended? If you don't like the idea that someone might use your phone and see everything you've stored on it, you can secure it using Lock screen and security settings.

Whenever you turn on the phone or restore it from a darkened state, you normally see the lock screen. Its purpose is twofold. First, when the phone is idle, the lock screen appears to provide a bit of privacy from casual observers. Second, you can secure the phone by requiring that a pattern, PIN, password, or fingerprint be supplied to clear the lock screen, rather than simply swiping it away.

Change the Screen Locking Method

① On the Home screen, tap Apps and then tap Settings.

② Tap Lock Screen.

③ Under Screen Lock, you can see the currently selected locking method. Tap Screen Lock to change the lock type or confirm the method you have.

④ Tap one of the locking options and then use the instructions in one of the following tasks to customize the locking mechanism.

- Swipe means just swipe your finger across the security area.

- Pattern means you use your finger to draw a pattern on the screen.

- Fingerprint means draw your finger across the registration area on the back of your phone. (See "Use Your Fingerprint" later in this chapter.)

- PIN is a four-digit Personal Identification Number.

- Password is an 8-character (or longer) sequence of letters and numbers.

Currently selected locking method

Encrypt the Phone

Encryption means that your Galaxy S5 requires a private decryption entry (a password) in order to translate the contents into something readable. Using encryption makes the contents useless to anyone else. You may want to use encryption if you're travelling to a country where smartphone security is a problem. As with any of the security options, if you try it and don't like it, you can always turn it off.

1. On the Settings screen, tap Security (in the Personal section).

2. Tap Encrypt Device.

Location

Security — 1

Fingerprint

< Security

ENCRYPTION

Encrypt device — 2
Password required to decrypt device each time you turn it on.

Encrypt external SD card

Heed the Warning!

Read the warning notes on the screen. Note that the encryption process takes time—an hour or more—to complete.

It's Not All Good

Word to the Wise

Encrypting your device means that you will be required to enter your password each time you turn on your S5. Think about a meaningful password *that you will remember* before entering it. Also think about the fact that you'll be required to use the password *each time* you turn on your Galaxy S5—you might decide that you don't want to use encryption after all. If you try encryption but you don't like using it, you can turn it off and try something else.

3 Scroll down and tap Set Screen Lock Type.

4 Tap Password.

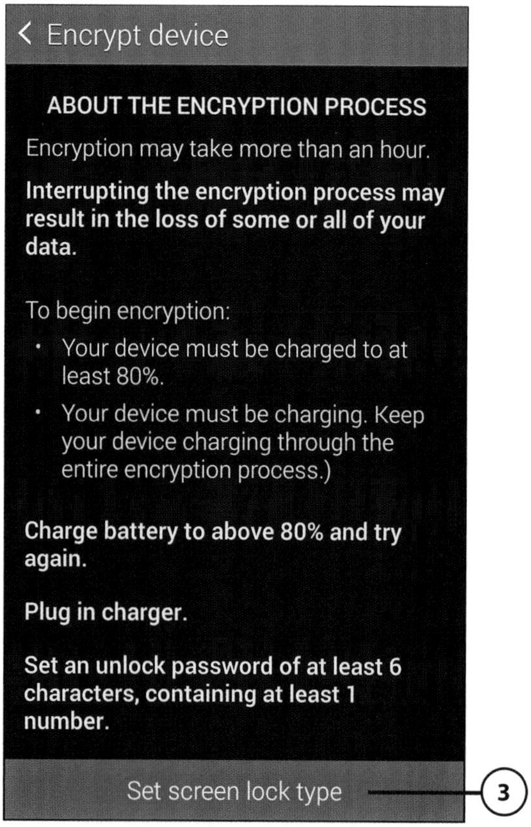

< Encrypt device

ABOUT THE ENCRYPTION PROCESS

Encryption may take more than an hour.

Interrupting the encryption process may result in the loss of some or all of your data.

To begin encryption:

- Your device must be charged to at least 80%.
- Your device must be charging. Keep your device charging through the entire encryption process.)

Charge battery to above 80% and try again.

Plug in charger.

Set an unlock password of at least 6 characters, containing at least 1 number.

Set screen lock type ———— **3**

PIN
Turned off by administrator, encryption policy or credential storage.

Password ——— **4**
High security

5 Type a password (preferably containing letters, numbers, and at least one symbol) on both the Select Password and Confirm Password screens. The minimum number of characters you can use is 4; it's better to use 6 to 10. Tap Continue after you've typed the password for the second time.

6 After you have set an encryption password, every time your screen times out (goes black), you have to tap Alternative password, retype your password, and tap Done.

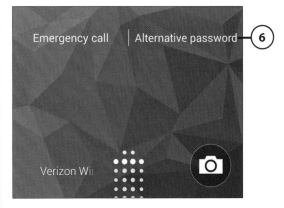

Use Your Fingerprint

A new feature in the Galaxy S5 is fingerprint recognition, which you can use as an alternative to using passwords. Unless a password is specifically requested, swiping a fingerprint across the recording device on the back of your Galaxy S5 unlocks your phone.

1 On the Settings screen, tap Fingerprint. The Fingerprint options appear.

2 Tap Fingerprint Manager, read the next screen, and tap OK.

3 The next screen shows a moving finger entering a fingerprint on the Galaxy S5. If you have already registered an alternative password, that prompt will also appear. Ignore it.

4 Swipe your finger over the blinking dots as shown eight times. Each time your fingerprint is collected, a green dot appears at the bottom of the screen and one of the squares above the swipe area turns green. If the box doesn't turn green, your fingerprint didn't register; swipe again, perhaps with a different angle.

5 Choose the type of unlock mechanism you want to use. To use your fingerprint instead of a password, tap Fingerprint.

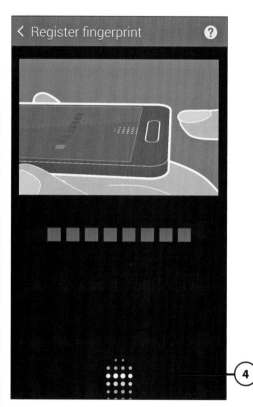

< Fingerprint

Use fingerprint recognition as an alternative to entering passwords.

SETTINGS

Fingerprint manager
1 fingerprint is registered. — **2**

< Register fingerprint

— **4**

< Select screen lock

Swipe
No security

Pattern
Medium security

Fingerprint
Medium to high security — **5**

(6) Tap Screen Lock to make your fingerprint the default lock for your Galaxy S5, rather than a password. This takes you back to the previous screen.

FEATURES

Screen lock
Secured with fingerprint lock   (6)

Verify Samsung account
Off

>>>Go Further
PASSWORD SAFETY

It's important to select appropriate passwords—in particular passwords that you will remember. It might help you to keep a separate file of the passwords you use and the programs that use them. Some people write them down on a piece of paper; unfortunately, though, if you can find the piece of paper, so could someone who's breaking into your house and stealing your Galaxy S5.

By default, passwords are invisible when you're entering them. If you have trouble correctly typing a password, it might help to turn on the feature that makes them visible.

On the Security screen, tap Make Passwords Visible. This toggles on or off this feature. The green check mark means that passwords will be visible as you type them.

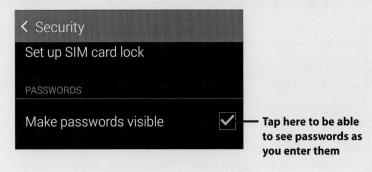

‹ Security

Set up SIM card lock

PASSWORDS

Make passwords visible   ☑ — Tap here to be able to see passwords as you enter them

Security

There are seven sections to the Security screen, each covering a different aspect of securing your Galaxy S5. You can find the security options covered in this section by tapping the Settings icon, scrolling to the Personal section, and then tapping Security.

Protecting and Locating a Lost Phone

The Galaxy S5 has several ways of helping you protect and find your phone should you misplace it.

Lock Your Phone with Remote Controls

If your phone disappears, you can use the Remote Control app to lock your Galaxy S5, which reduces the risk of your information being stolen.

1. Tap Security.

2. Tap Remote Controls. On the next screen, read the information and tap OK.

3. You must register your Galaxy S5 with Samsung. Tap Add Account.

4. Tap Sign In. Fill in the requested information and tap Done when you're finished. After you have registered, there is a small plus (+) sign next to Add Account.

Indicates an account has been added

Find Your Galaxy S5 with the Find My Mobile Website

If you misplace your Galaxy S5 or it is stolen, you can use the Find My Mobile website to help you find it. You can use a computer to visit the Samsung website to locate your Galaxy S5. You have to have created a Samsung account to take advantage of this feature. If you don't already have a Samsung account, see Chapter 7, "Setting Up Accounts."

(1) From a desktop or laptop computer, go to http://findmymobile.samsung.com/login. do. Enter the email address and password you use for your Samsung account and then click Sign In.

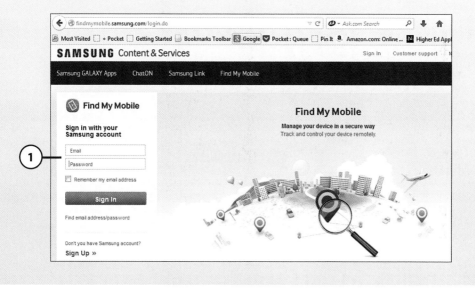

(2) A map showing the current location of your Galaxy S5 displays.

(3) Click Ring My Device if the phone is in the same location where you are and you want to have an audible clue for finding it.

(4) Click Lock My Device if you want to put a lock on the Galaxy S5 so that no one else may use it until you can retrieve it.

(5) Click Wipe My Device if the phone seems to be irretrievably lost and you want to clear it of all personal data.

SIM Card Lock

A *Subscriber Identity Module* (SIM) card is included on your Galaxy S5. If the SIM card wasn't preinstalled when you purchased the phone, you can install one by turning off the phone, opening the case, and inserting the SIM card into its slot (beneath the memory card slot). Ensure that the notched edge goes into the slot first and that the card's gold contacts face down. (You can do an Internet search to get detailed instructions.)

To replace an existing SIM card with a new one, remove the battery and then slide out the SIM card. Slide the new SIM card into the slot—notch first, gold contacts down—until it clicks into place. Finish by replacing the battery and the phone's back cover.

You can lock the SIM card to prevent anyone else from being able to remove it. You might want to do this because someone else who has access to your phone might want to modify it to meet his or her needs. Locking the SIM card means they won't be able to change your phone's configuration.

(1) Tap Security.

(2) Tap Set Up SIM Card Lock.

(3) Tap Lock SIM Card to put a check mark in the box on the right. Please refer to earlier sections of this chapter for instructions on how to create a password.

Location

Security — (1)

SIM CARD LOCK

Set up SIM card lock — (2)

‹ SIM card lock settings

Lock SIM card
Enter PIN to use device.   ☐ — (3)

Change SIM PIN

Security Update Service

Two options let you manage your security information.

Manage Security Policy Updates

By default, your security policies (installed by Samsung during the manufacturing process) are automatically updated to reflect current procedures. This happens any time you are connected to a network; you don't have to do anything to make it happen.

You might want to turn off this feature because you don't want to send security reports every time an application misbehaves, or if you're tired of getting security reports from Samsung.

(1) Tap Security.

(2) Tap Security Policy Updates.

Sending Security Reports

You can tap Send Security Reports to turn on or off the feature that enables your Galaxy S5 to send periodic security reports to Samsung so that the company can update its threat analysis software.

(3) Tap the green check mark next to Automatic Updates to turn off the feature.

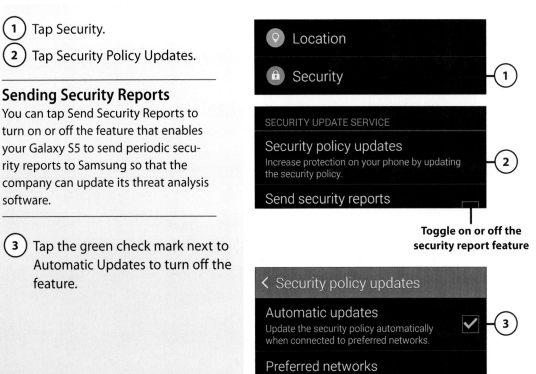

Toggle on or off the
security report feature

Specify what type of network
to use for security updates

Choose a Network Type

To specify the type of network from which you will receive security updates, tap Preferred Networks and then select either Wi-Fi or Mobile Networks or Wi-Fi Networks Only. By choosing Wi-Fi Networks Only, you will avoid an unexpected data hits to your plan.

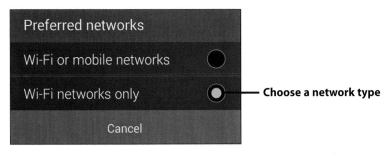

Choose a network type

Using Blocking Mode and Private Mode

You can set your phone's security options so that you receive only those calls you want.

- *Blocking mode* lets you turn off the notifications for functions that you select, and you will receive notifications about calls only from those people whose names are on a special list.

- *Private mode* lets you specify that data for apps you select is unavailable for viewing by anybody else. This mode is particularly useful to guard personal data such as a stored list of passwords, your banking information, your Social Security number, and any music, photos, video, or recordings of your voice.

Turn On Blocking Mode

Blocking Mode means that your phone prevents any incoming phone calls from reaching you during the time you set, such as between 9:00 p.m. and 6:00 a.m. Any calls to you during that time will be treated as missed calls, with an icon in the status bar showing that you missed the call.

1. Tap Blocking Mode on the Settings screen.

2. Swipe the Blocking Mode button in the upper-right corner to the left to turn it on; notice that the options on the screen are no longer grayed out. Make sure there's a green check mark next to the features you want to use.

3. Set the time period during which Blocking Mode will be active.

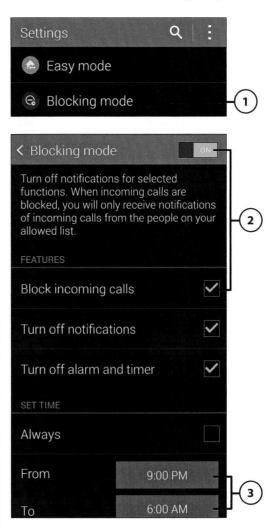

4 Scroll down the screen to see the Allowed Contacts area and tap Allowed Contacts.

5 Specify which contacts are allowed to bypass the blocking feature.

- None is the default. With this option set, your phone will not notify you when you receive a call or message.

- If you select All Contacts, the blocking does not apply to any of the individuals in your Contacts.

- If you select Favorites, the blocking does not apply to any of the individuals on your Favorites list. You have to already have specified a Favorites list in Contacts for this option to work.

- If you select Custom, you see another screen from which you choose specific individuals who will not be blocked. Tap the plus (+) icon to display your entire Contacts list, and put check marks next to the names you want to allow past your block.

6 When you're finished, tap Done. Your list of exceptions appears. Tap + to add more names, or tap the menu icon and Delete to remove one or more names.

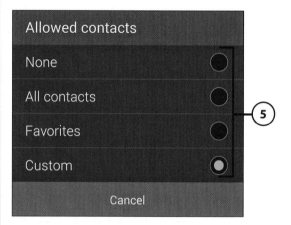

Turn On Private Mode

(1) In the Settings, tap Private Mode to prevent anyone else from seeing some of your data.

(2) Swipe the Private Mode button to On and read the informational screen.

(3) Enter your password and tap Done. Every time you return to the Galaxy S5 after it has timed out or turned off, you are asked for your password. Any time you want to stop this, slide the Private Mode button to Off.

And for Serious Privacy...

You can use a different password for Private mode than the one you normally use for security, but you run the risk of trying to remember too many different passwords.

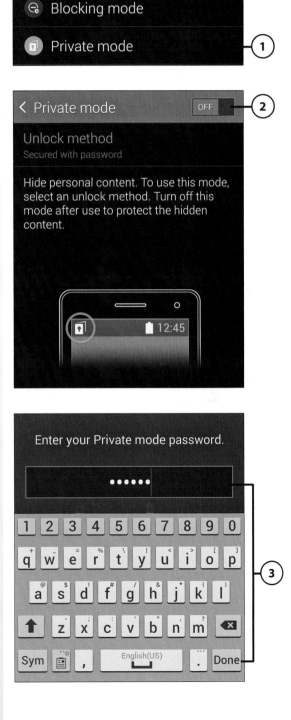

Setting Up Safety Assistance

The Galaxy S5 has several features that let you get help in emergencies. Some let you notify other people that you need assistance; some other features let you use your Galaxy S5 as an emergency tool.

Create an Emergency Contacts List

You can use the Galaxy S5 to maintain a list of people who should be called, messaged, or emailed in case of an emergency.

1. Tap the Settings icon and tap Safety Assistance.

2. Tap Manage Emergency Contacts.

3. The first time you do this, you're told that you have no emergency contacts set up. Tap Create Emergency Contact.

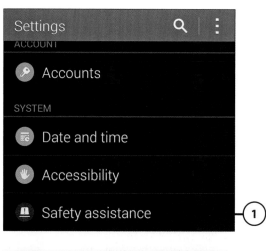

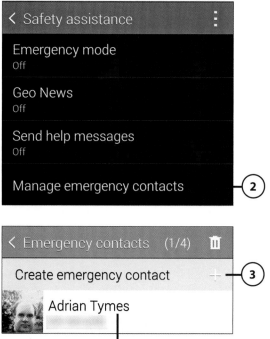

An emergency contact

4 Tap either Create New Contact if the name isn't already in your Contact list, or tap Select from Contacts to choose someone on your Contact list.

5 Tap to select one or more names of people you want contacted if there is an emergency.

6 Tap Done when you're finished.

7 Your current emergency contact list appears. You can add to this list any time by tapping the plus (+) sign.

Deleting Emergency Contacts

To delete someone from your emergency contact list, tap the Trash icon. On the selection screen, put a check mark next to the name of the person you want to delete and then tap the Trash icon. Confirm the deletion to finish removing the person from your emergency contacts.

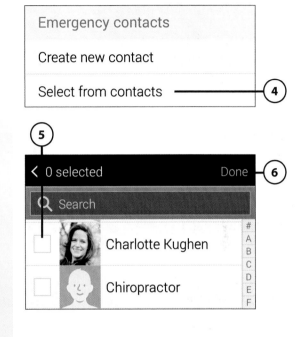

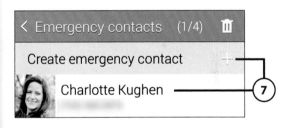

Trash icon

Tap to delete an emergency contact

Turn On Emergency Mode

Emergency mode is for when you are low on power and you're not sure when you will be able to recharge the Galaxy S5.

1. In the Settings, tap Safety Assistance.

2. Tap Emergency Mode.

3. Swipe the Emergency Mode button to On to use Emergency Mode.

Turning Off Emergency Mode

When you no longer need to use Emergency Mode, tap the menu icon, select Turn Off Emergency Mode, and tap OK.

Extend battery power by applying a grayscale theme to your home screen. You will be able to use Messages, Contacts, and emergency calls, but many other apps and functions will be restricted.

Turn On Geo News

Geo News provides weather, flood, earthquake, slides, and other environmental news that may be useful in an emergency.

1. In the Settings, Tap Safety Assistance.

2. Tap Geo News.

3. Read the information on the next screen and move the Off button to On. There will be a few seconds while your device is electronically registered.

4. To receive notifications about any potentially dangerous environmental conditions, tap the button next to Notification Pop-ups.

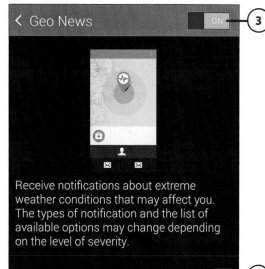

Send Help Messages

When you turn on the Send Help Messages feature of your Galaxy S5, you enable your Galaxy S5 to send a message to your emergency contacts when you need assistance.

1. In Settings, tap Safety Assistance.

(2) Tap Send Help Messages.

(3) Swipe the Send Help Messages button to On.

(4) Turn on the features you want to use when a help message is sent:

- *Send Pictures* enables the Galaxy S5 to take a picture that will be attached to the help message.

- *Send Sound Recording* enables the Galaxy S5 to create an audio file (such as a voice message or a recording of the ambient noise that might help identify where you are) and attach it to the help message.

(5) When you are in an emergency situation, press the Power button three times quickly. This sends a message to those on your emergency contact list.

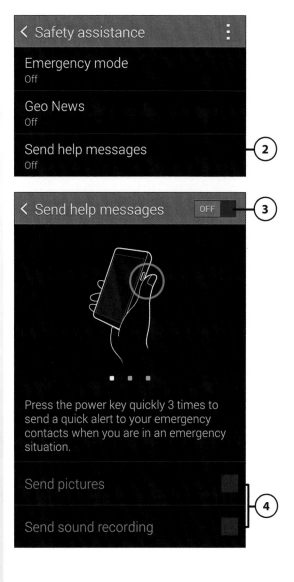

< Safety assistance

Emergency mode
Off

Geo News
Off

Send help messages — (2)
Off

< Send help messages   OFF — (3)

Press the power key quickly 3 times to send a quick alert to your emergency contacts when you are in an emergency situation.

Send pictures

Send sound recording — (4)

>>>Go Further

GETTING HELP QUICKLY

If you have enabled Emergency mode as described earlier in the chapter in the "Turn on Emergency Mode" task, you can extend the battery life of your Galaxy S5 by reducing power to unessential applications. You might use this in a traffic accident in a remote area where it could take some time to find emergency help.

Once enabled, the Emergency screen shows you several options:

- Flashlight: Your Galaxy S5 beams enough light to help guide you.

- Emergency Alarm: Your Galaxy S5 sounds an emergency tone.

- Share My Location: Your location is sent to those on your Contact list.

- Phone: Dials, in order, the people in your Emergency Contact list.

- Emergency alerts: You will receive emergency alerts as discussed in Chapter 10, "System Functions and Tools."

Open in Reader

Windows Menu

Back Forward Home Saved Bookmarks
Pages

In this chapter, you find out how to use the Internet app and Google Chrome to browse the Web. Topics include the following:

→ Launching Internet
→ Configuring the browser
→ Viewing web pages
→ Creating and organizing bookmarks
→ Using other menu commands
→ Learning about Google Chrome

Browsing the Web

You're probably already familiar with the basics of using a web browser. Making the transition from browsing on a computer to browsing on your phone is relatively easy. As with a desktop browser, you can enter page addresses by typing, tapping links, and selecting bookmarks for your favorite sites.

The Galaxy S5 generally ships with a pair of browsers: Internet and Google Chrome. Although this chapter focuses on using Internet (the default browser for most carriers), you should check out Chrome, too. You can use whichever browser app you prefer, as well as switch between them whenever you like. See "Google Chrome Essentials," at the end of this chapter, for information on getting started with Chrome and how it differs from Internet.

Verizon Users and the Internet App

At its launch, the Verizon Galaxy S5 included Google Chrome as its *only* web browser.

Launching Internet

You can launch the Internet app in several ways. The most common are as follows:

- On the Home screen, tap the Internet icon at the bottom of the screen.

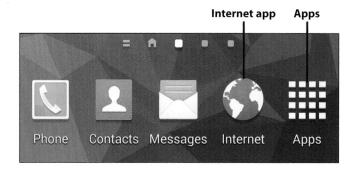

- On the Home screen, tap Apps, followed by Internet.
- Tap a web link in an email message. Links can be blue underlined text, images, or other objects. If the item you tap is indeed a link, the linked page appears in the browser.

Link in an email message

Complete Action Using

Because there *are* two browser apps installed on the phone (and you may have installed others), whenever you perform an indirect action that requires a browser (such as tapping a link), a Complete Action Using dialog box appears that asks which browser to launch. Select a browser (Internet or Chrome), and then tap Just Once. After familiarizing yourself with both browsers, you can specify a *default browser* to use for all future indirect launches by tapping Always.

If you ever want to reverse your decision, open Settings, scroll to the Applications section, and tap Default Applications. In the Clear Defaults area, find the browser that you previously set as the default and tap its Clear button.

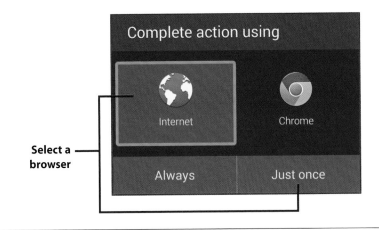

Select a browser

- Tap a blue underlined link in a text or multimedia message. In the dialog box that appears, tap Open Link to open the link in the browser or tap Cancel if you change your mind.

Link in a text message

Open in browser

Unexpected Web Redirections

Apps and certain documents can contain links that automatically redirect you to web pages, causing the browser to launch if it isn't currently running. For example, if you tap text, an icon, or a button in some apps when searching for instructions, a help file or manual might open in the browser.

Configuring the Browser

As is the case with a Mac or PC browser, you can configure the Internet app to match your preferred way of working and perform common browser actions, such as clearing the cache and managing cookies.

(1) With any web page displayed, tap the menu icon (the three dots) and choose Settings. (You may have to scroll the menu to see the Settings command.)

Another Path to Settings

Regardless of whether the Internet app is currently running, you can also configure it by opening Settings, scrolling to the Applications section, and tapping the Internet app icon. The same screen appears.

2 The Settings screen appears, divided into two sections: Basics and Advanced.

- *Account.* Specify the types of data that you want to sync with your Samsung account.
- *Set Homepage.* Specify a new home page by setting it to the carrier's default, the current page, your Quick Access links, Most Visited Sites, or Other—a URL that you manually enter.
- *Auto Fill Forms.* Enable forms on web pages to be automatically filled in with stored text for your name, address, phone number, and email address.
- *Privacy.* Propose common search terms when performing finds and popular websites when entering addresses; remember form data and site passwords; delete a variety of cached data types.
- *Screen and Text.* Adjust zoom control and full-screen mode, text size and scaling.
- *Content Settings.* Accept cookies; enable/disable location information access and JavaScript; block pop-ups; specify the default storage location (device or memory card); clear all data stored by selected websites; enable or disable website notifications; and reset browser settings to defaults.
- *Bandwidth Management.* Preload pages; disable image downloads.

To view or modify any of these settings, tap a category and make the necessary changes. When you're done, press the Back key or tap the Back icon.

Back **2**

< Settings

BASICS

Account
Select the type of data you want to sync.

Set homepage
http://mobile.nytimes.com/

Auto fill forms
Manage your text for automatically filling out Web forms.

ADVANCED

Privacy

Screen and text

Content settings

Bandwidth management

Privacy settings

Delete personal data

Browsing history ☐

Cache ☐

Cookies and site data ☐

Passwords ☐

Auto fill data ☐

Location access ☐

Cancel   Done

Visiting Web Pages

You can go to a particular web page (called an *address* or *URL*) using the same methods that you use with Internet Explorer, Safari, Firefox, and other popular desktop web browsers. The most common methods are typing the address, tapping a link on the current page, choosing a bookmarked or recently visited (History) site or page, and searching for a site or page with one of the popular search engines.

Immersion Mode

In this new version of Internet, web pages are normally displayed in a full-screen *immersion* mode, enabling you to see as much of every page as possible without the distraction of the address box. Regardless of where you are in the current page, you can reveal the address box and status bar by slightly dragging down.

Type the Address

(1) If the browser isn't currently running, go to the Home screen and
tap the Internet icon.

(2) Tap the address box. The current
page's address is selected.

3 Enter the new address and tap Go. (Because the current address is already selected, typing anything immediately replaces the old address.) The web page loads.

Fast Address Selection

As you type, a list of possible addresses appears. If you see the one you want, you can tap it instead of completing the address. You can also select a search suggestion if the site's actual URL isn't in the list.

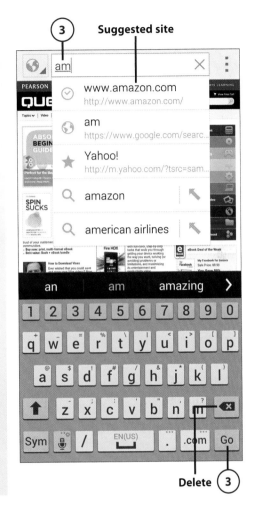

3

Suggested site

Delete 3

Following a Link

In the browser, if you tap an object, graphic, or text that represents a web link, the link briefly flashes blue and then the linked page loads.

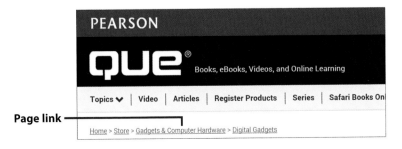

Page link

Not Every Link Leads to a Page

Other than special *mobile* versions of web pages (designed for viewing on cell phones), pages displayed in the Internet app are identical to those you see in Internet Explorer, Safari, and other desktop browsers. That means that they also contain links designed to download PC and Mac applications, device drivers, and the like. Of course, such programs and drivers can't be used by your phone, but you might not be prevented from downloading them.

To remove these downloads, go to the Home screen and tap Apps, My Files, Download History. Select any listed item by pressing and holding its entry. Then tap the check box of every additional inappropriate download and tap Delete.

You can also delete files directly from the Download folder. In the Local Storage section of My Files, tap Device Storage or SD Card, and then open the Download folder. Select any listed item by pressing and holding its entry. Tap the check box for every additional inappropriate download, and then tap the Delete icon.

Visit a Bookmarked, Recent, or Saved Page

(1) Drag or flick down until the Address box appears, and then tap the Bookmarks (star) icon at the bottom of the screen.

Lumen Toolbar handle (Sprint only)

(2) To visit a *bookmarked* page (one whose address you stored), tap its thumbnail or name. (For information about creating and managing bookmarks, see "Working with Bookmarks," later in this chapter.)

Bookmark Display Options

You can view bookmarks as a thumbnail grid or scrolling list. To switch views, tap the menu icon, and choose List View or Thumbnail View.

You can change the order of your bookmarks by tapping the menu icon and choosing Change Order. (If you've created folders, open the folder whose bookmarks you want to reorganize *before* choosing Change Order.) To move a bookmark, press and hold the bookmark's dot grid to select it and then drag it to the new position. When you're satisfied with the changes, tap Done—or tap Cancel to ignore the changes.

(3) To open a *saved* page (one that you saved for later or offline reading), drag or flick down until the Address box appears, and tap the Saved Pages icon on the bar at the bottom of the screen. Locate the page in the scrolling list, and tap its thumbnail.

Saving a Page

To store a copy of the current page in Saved Pages, tap the menu icon and choose Save Page. Use this command for any page that you want to read later or that might not be readily available online, such as a receipt for an online purchase.

Back **Menu**

History folder **(2)**

Rearranging bookmarks

Select and drag

(3)

(4) Internet stores the list of recently viewed pages in History, a folder at the top of the Bookmarks screen. To revisit a recently viewed page, drag or flick down until the Address box appears, and tap the Bookmarks icon on the bar at the bottom of the screen. Open the History folder, scroll to locate the desired page, and tap its name. To make it easier to find the page, you can *expand* (show) or *collapse* (hide) page-view periods (Today, Last 7 Days, and so on) by tapping section heads.

It's Not All Good

Configuring or Removing the Lumen Toolbar (Sprint)

If you have a Sprint S5, an additional toolbar (called Lumen Toolbar) that presents links to social media, other popular sites, and added favorites can be displayed at the bottom of the current page. To reveal it, tap its handle; to hide it, tap any spot in the current page.

Unfortunately, even when the toolbar is hidden, its handle can make it difficult to tap the Bookmarks icon (see the Step 1 figure). If you find that it interferes, you can reposition the handle or eliminate the toolbar altogether. To remove, restore, or configure the toolbar, go to the Home screen and tap Apps, Lumen Toolbar, Settings.

Lumen Toolbar (Sprint)

Facebook   eBay   Twitter   Games   Big Fish

Search for a Site or Page

1. The address box doubles as a search box. Enter your search phrase, such as "exercise machines" or "trim a parrot's beak." As you type, the search engine builds a list of possible search topics.

2. You can do any of the following:

   - Tap a suggestion to immediately perform that search in the default search engine.

   - Tap the arrow at the end of a suggestion to transfer the text into the address box—enabling you to add to or edit the search text before performing the search.

   - Tap a direct link in the suggestion list to load that specific page—rather than performing a search.

   - Tap the Go key on the keyboard to perform the search using the text that's in the address box.

Changing Search Engines

The active search engine's icon is shown to the left of the address box. To change search engines, tap the icon and choose a different one.

Current search engine

1

Google search

Direct links

Search phrases

2

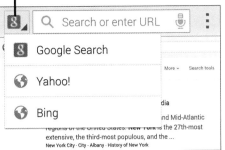

Tap to choose a search engine

Using the History List

You can see which pages you've visited lately with the History List. Tap the menu icon in the location bar near the top of the screen, and select History from the list.

Tap History to see a list of your recently visited sites

The history list lets you return to frequently visited pages without using the Back button.

Viewing Pages

Similar to your computer's browser, the Internet app provides several ways for you to view pages, such as viewing in portrait or landscape mode, scrolling the page, changing the magnification, reloading the page, and displaying multiple pages in separate windows.

Portrait or Landscape View

Depending on the direction that you rotate the phone, you can view any page in *portrait* (normal) or *landscape* (sideways) mode. You can change the phone's orientation whenever you want; the page adjusts automatically. (If the orientation doesn't change when you rotate the phone, launch Settings; tap Display, Screen Rotation; and set the Rotate Screen slider to On. By default, there's also a Screen Rotation button in the Quick Setting buttons at the top of the Notification panel.)

Portrait   **Landscape**

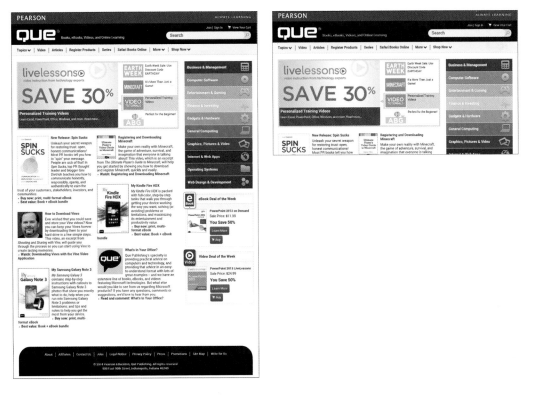

Scrolling the Page

Many pages don't fit entirely onscreen. To view parts that are off-screen, flick or drag up, down, right, or left, depending on the direction you want the page's material to scroll. If you want to take advantage of some tricks, you can scroll by tilting your head or the phone up and down *(Smart Scroll)* or by waving your hand up and down over the sensor at the top of the phone *(Air Browse)*.

- To activate Smart Scroll, open Settings and tap Accessibility, Dexterity and Interaction, Smart Scroll. Drag the Smart Scroll slider to the On position, and select Tilting Head or Tilting Device.

- To activate Air Browse, open Settings and tap Motions and Gestures, Air Browse. Drag the Air Browse slider to the On position, and ensure that Internet is one of the checked options.

Magnification (Zoom)

You can increase the magnification of the current page to make it easier to read *(zoom in)* or reduce it to get a bird's-eye view of the entire page *(zoom out)*.

Zoomed in

Zoomed out

- To *zoom in* (making everything on the page larger), put your thumb and forefinger on the page and spread them apart.

- To *zoom out* (making everything on the page smaller), put your thumb and forefinger on the page and pinch them together.

Other Zoom Options

You can quickly zoom in or out by double-tapping the screen. Repeat to reverse the zoom. If Magnification Gestures (an Accessibility setting) is enabled, you can triple-tap to zoom. To enable or disable Magnification Gestures, open Settings and then tap Accessibility, Vision, Magnification Gestures.

Reader View

To make it easier to read certain pages (such as articles), tap the Reader icon—if it's present—to the left of the address box. When reading an article in Reader view, you can increase or decrease the size of text by tapping an icon. To view the text as white on a black background, tap the menu icon and choose Night Mode. To return to the original web page, tap the Back icon or press the Back key.

Reader icon · Back · Increase font size · Decrease font size · Menu

Original web page · Page in Reader

Refreshing the Page

If the current page didn't load correctly or you think the content might have changed while you were viewing it, you can refresh the page by tapping the Reload icon in the address box. If a page is loading slowly, you can stop it by tapping the X icon.

Working with Windows

The tabbed interface of current desktop browsers enables you to keep several web pages open simultaneously and easily switch among them. The Internet app mimics this feature by enabling you to open multiple *windows*. Each window is the equivalent of a new browser and operates independently of other windows.

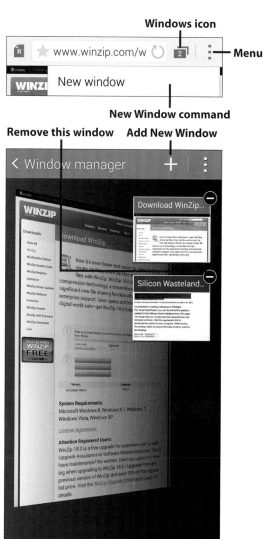

- To create a new window, tap the menu icon and choose New Window. You can also tap the Windows icon to the right of the address box and then tap the plus (+) icon in Window Manager. A new browser window opens.

- To navigate among or manage the open windows, tap the Windows icon to open the Window Manager. To switch to a window, tap its thumbnail. To remove a window that you no longer need, tap its minus (–) icon or swipe its thumbnail horizontally off the screen.

Create a New Window from a Bookmark or History Item

You can press and hold a site's name in Bookmarks or History to select it, and then tap the Add New Window icon in the toolbar. Doing so opens the website or page in a new window.

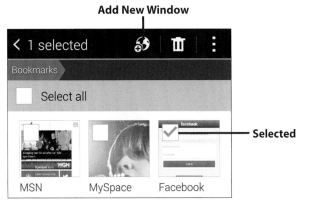

Page Navigation

As you replace the current page with new ones by entering addresses, tapping links, and selecting bookmarks, you can move back or forward through the stack of pages. (Note that each window has its own stack.) To return to the previous page, tap the Back icon at the bottom of the screen or press the Back key. You'll go back one page for each tap or key press. If you've gone back one or more pages, you can move forward through the stack by tapping the Forward icon.

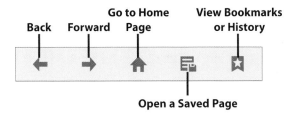

One Too Many

If you use the Back key to move back through the pages in the current window and press it when you're on the *first* page, you'll exit Internet.

Incognito Browsing

The Internet app supports *incognito browsing* in which entries aren't recorded in History, searches aren't recorded, and cookies aren't stored. Rather than make this a general browser setting, Internet enables it only for pages loaded into a designated incognito window.

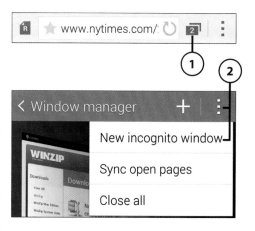

(1) Tap the Windows icon at the top of any browser page.

(2) In Window Manager, tap the menu icon and choose New Incognito Window.

(3) Review the text in the Incognito Mode dialog box, and tap OK to dismiss it.

(4) A new browser window appears. Specify the first page to display by tapping a Quick Access icon, entering an address in the address box, performing a search, selecting from bookmarks or History items, or using another method. Web activities performed in this window are secure; activities performed in *other* Internet windows are recorded normally.

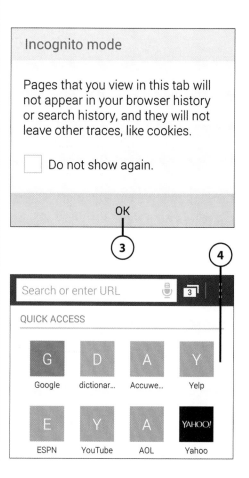

Quickly Switching to Incognito Mode

In addition to creating a new window for Incognito mode, you can apply Incognito mode to the *current* window by tapping the menu icon and choosing Incognito Mode.

5 To remove an incognito window and its pages, open the Window Manager, find the incognito window, and delete it by tapping the minus (–) icon in its upper-right corner.

Incognito icon **5**

Working with Bookmarks

As explained earlier in this chapter, *bookmarks* are stored addresses of websites and pages that you regularly visit. The purpose of creating a bookmark is to enable you to view the site or page again by simply tapping its entry in the Bookmarks grid or list rather than having to reenter the address.

Create a Bookmark from the Current Page

It's common to decide to bookmark a page while you're viewing it.

1 Do either of the following:

- Tap the star icon at the left end of the address bar.

- Tap the Bookmarks icon at the bottom of the screen and then tap the plus (+) icon on the Bookmarks toolbar.

2 Edit the bookmark name, if necessary.

3 By default, new bookmarks are stored in the Bookmarks folder. To select a different folder or subfolder, tap the current folder name and select a destination folder.

4 Tap Save to store the new bookmark.

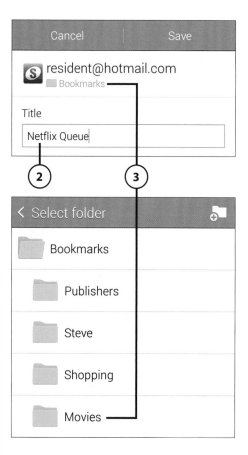

Bookmark title   Folder

Create a Bookmark from the History List

If you've recently visited a page, the quickest way to add it as a new bookmark is to locate it in the History list.

1. With any web page displayed, tap the Bookmarks icon at the bottom of the screen.

2. Open the History folder at the top of the Bookmarks list or grid by tapping its icon.

3. In the History list, locate the page that you want to bookmark. Press and hold its entry to select it.

4. Tap the menu icon, and choose Add Bookmark.

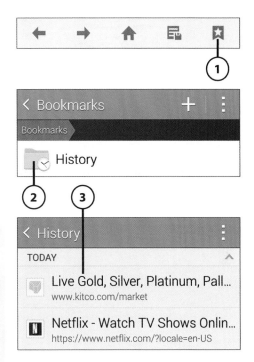

Selected bookmark (List View)

Menu

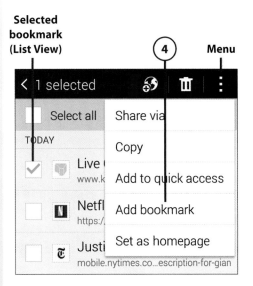

5 Perform Steps 2–4 from the previous task, "Create a Bookmark from the Current Page": editing the name, selecting a storage location, and saving the new bookmark.

5

Cancel | Save

S resident@hotmail.com
Bookmarks

Title

Kitco metals quotes

Bookmark title

Folder

Edit Bookmarks

You can edit a bookmark's title, its address (setting it for a site's main page or another specific page), or the folder in which it's stored.

1 In the Bookmarks list, find the bookmark that you want to edit—opening folders, if necessary. Press and hold the bookmark to select it.

2 Tap the menu icon and choose Edit.

Other Options

The menu also enables you to set the selected bookmark as your home page, share it with a friend, create a Home screen shortcut to it, or delete it.

Selecting a bookmark (Thumbnail View)

< 1 selected

Bookmarks > Shopping

Select all

General   Amazon.co...   Newegg.com

2   **1**

< 1 selected

Bookmar

Share via

Edit

Move to folder

Add to quick access

Add shortcut to home screen

Set as homepage

(3) Make any desired changes to the title, address, and/or its folder, and then tap Save.

Editing the Address

Although you normally won't want to edit a page's address if it requires a lot of typing, it's relatively simple to change a page-specific address to one that goes to the site's main page. Just delete the extraneous material to the right of the main part of the address, such as http://m.newegg.com/.

(3)

| Cancel | | Save |

(S) resident@hotmail.com
📁 Shopping

Title

Newegg.com home page

Web address

http://m.newegg.com/

URL   **Bookmark**   **Folder**
(address)   **title**

Using Bookmark Folders

After amassing more than a handful of bookmarks, you can optionally create folders in which to organize your bookmarks—rather than storing them all in Bookmarks, the main folder. When creating a new bookmark or editing an existing one, you can move it into the most appropriate folder.

Navigating Among Bookmark Folders

When viewing items in a bookmark folder, don't press the Back key or tap the Back icon if you want to move up a level. Either action exits Bookmarks and returns you to the browser screen. If you want to continue working in Bookmarks, tap the appropriate path element (such as Bookmarks or the name of a higher folder in the hierarchy) at the top of the screen.

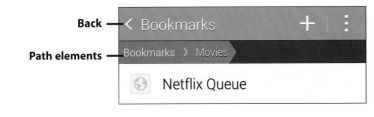

Back ⟶ ‹ Bookmarks ＋ ⋮

Path elements ⟶ Bookmarks › Movies

🌐 Netflix Queue

Create a Bookmark Folder

(1) With any web page onscreen, tap the Bookmarks icon at the bottom of the screen.

(2) Tap the menu icon and choose Create Folder.

(3) Name the new folder.

(4) Select a *parent* (containing) folder for this new folder.

(5) Tap Done. The new folder is created within the selected folder and added to the Bookmarks list.

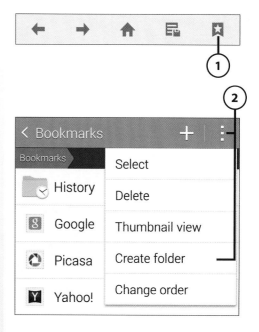

Move Bookmarks into Folders

(1) With any web page onscreen, tap the Bookmarks icon at the bottom of the screen.

(2) As necessary, open folders to expose the bookmarks that you want to move. (Bookmarks to be moved must all have the same destination folder.) Tap the menu icon and choose Select.

(3) Select each bookmark by tapping its check box (in List View as shown here) or its thumbnail (in Thumbnail View).

(4) Tap the menu icon and choose Move to Folder.

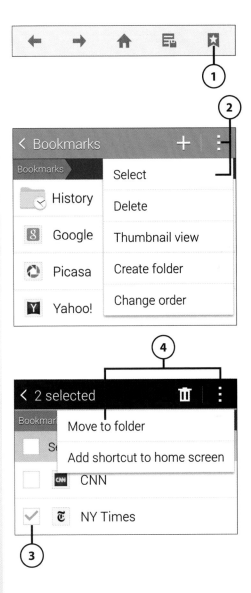

5 Tap the destination folder. The selected bookmarks move into the folder.

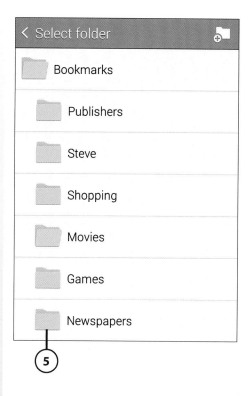

Delete Bookmarks

You can delete bookmarks that you no longer use.

1 With any web page onscreen, tap the Bookmarks icon at the bottom of the screen.

2 Opening folders as necessary, press and hold one of the bookmarks that you want to delete. (When deleting more than one, they must all be in the same folder.)

(3) *Optional:* Tap the check boxes of additional bookmarks that you want to delete. If desired, you can mark entire bookmark folders—and their contents—for deletion.

(4) Tap the Delete icon. The selected bookmarks are immediately deleted.

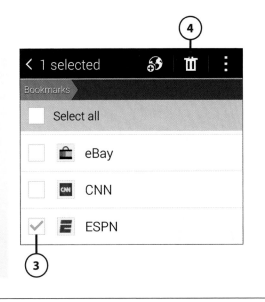

Another Approach

In Bookmarks, display the list of items from which you want to delete, tap the menu icon, and choose Delete. Tap the check box of each bookmark and folder that you want to delete. When you finish selecting, tap Done.

Deletions performed in this manner are also immediate. However, if you realize that you made a mistake, quickly tap the Undo bar that briefly appears near the bottom of the screen.

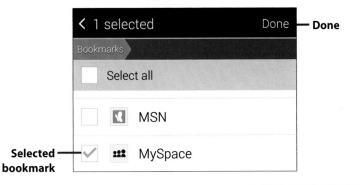

More Menu Commands

The main menu of the Internet app contains additional useful commands that haven't been discussed. Here's an explanation of what the remaining commands do.

1. With any web page displayed, tap the menu icon. (To see all the commands, you have to scroll the menu.) Brightness and Settings apply to all pages; the other commands apply only to the current page.

2. *Add to Quick Access.* When you create a new window, your list of Quick Access icons appears. Choose this command to add the current page to the Quick Access roster.

3. *Add Shortcut to Home Screen.* Create a Home screen shortcut for the current page. When you tap the shortcut, the Internet app launches and displays the web page.

4. *Share Via.* Share the page with another person or device using a variety of methods.

www.kitco.com/ma

New window

Add to quick access

Add shortcut to home screen

Save page

Share via

Live Gold, Silver,...

Share via

Add to Dropbox

Bluetooth

Copy to clipboard

Drive

Email

Flipboard

Gmail

Google+

Hangouts

LinkedIn

Memo

Messages

Wi-Fi Direct

(5) *Find on Page.* Search the current page for a text string. Each match (if there are any) is highlighted. To move between matches, tap an arrow icon. The page scrolls as needed to display each match.

(6) *Desktop View.* By default, if a mobile version of a site is available, it is displayed; otherwise, the desktop version is shown. Enable this option to automatically display *all* sites as though they were being viewed in a desktop browser—ignoring a mobile version, if one is available.

(7) *Brightness.* Enables you to specify a browser-specific brightness setting.

(8) *Print.* Print the current page on a supported Wi-Fi printer.

(9) *Settings.* View and modify Internet app preferences (see the previous section, "Configuring the Browser").

Find on page

Incognito mode

Desktop view

Brightness

Print

Settings

(5) (9) (8) (7) (6)   **Previous   Next**
                        match   match

Match   **End search**

Google Chrome Essentials

Although most carriers treat the Internet app as the Galaxy S5's primary browser, you might want to give Chrome a whirl, too. As you experiment with Chrome, you'll note that many of the instructions provided in this chapter for Internet also apply to Chrome. The two apps have similar menu commands, Settings options, and display options, for example. This section contains a rundown of some Chrome features that differ substantially from those of Internet.

Launching Chrome. Go to the Home screen and tap Apps, Chrome. Or tap a Home screen shortcut for Chrome, if you have one.

Specifying a Default Browser. If you tap a web link in an email or text message, a Complete Action Using dialog box appears. If you decide that you prefer Chrome to Internet (or vice versa), select the desired browser and tap Always. From that point forward, the selected browser will automatically launch whenever you open a link. For more information on setting or changing the default browser, see "Launching Internet," at the beginning of this chapter. Note that you aren't *required* to specify a default browser.

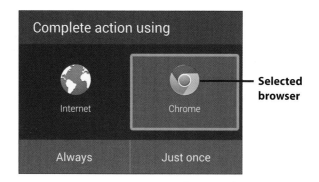

Tabs versus windows. Like Internet's windows, Chrome's *tabs* enable you to keep multiple web pages open simultaneously and switch among them as desired.

- To create a new tab, tap the menu icon and choose New Tab, or tap the Tabs icon and tap New Tab. The tabs icon always shows the number of open tabs.

- To switch among tabs, you can swipe horizontally across the address box area. You can also tap the Tabs icon, and then tap the tab that you want to make active.

- To remove a tab, tap the Tabs icon. Then tap the X in the tab's name or swipe the tab off either side of the screen. To simultaneously remove all tabs, tap the menu icon and choose Close All Tabs.

Search engine. Google is Chrome's default search engine. To use a different one, tap the menu icon and choose Settings, Search Engine.

Working with bookmarks. You can create, open, delete, and organize bookmarks for frequently visited pages.

- To create a bookmark for the current page, open the menu; tap the star icon; specify the bookmark's name, address, and containing folder; and tap Save.

Creating a bookmark

Add bookmark

Name

Silicon Wasteland - Steve Schwartz

URL

http://www.siliconwasteland.com/

Folder

Desktop bookmarks

| Cancel | Save |

- To remove a bookmark or edit its details, open the menu and tap the star icon. Then tap Remove or make the desired edits, respectively, and tap Save.
- To open a bookmark, tap the menu icon and choose Bookmarks. Open folders as necessary, and then tap the thumbnail of the bookmark to open.

History. To open the list of recently viewed pages (History), tap the menu icon and choose History. Tap any page name to view it, search History for a particular page, delete an entry by tapping its X, or quickly delete the stored browsing history and other data, such as cookies.

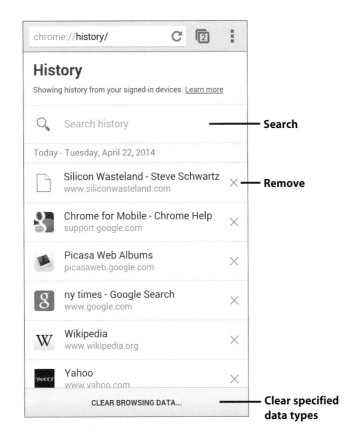

In this chapter, you become familiar with using the apps that come with your Galaxy S5 and getting new apps through Google Play and the Amazon Appstore. Topics include the following:

→ Exploring the Google Play Apps
→ Exploring the Amazon Apps
→ Using the Applications Manager
→ Adding an App
→ Removing an App

Adding, Removing, and Using Apps

Applications (or apps, as they're called when referring to smartphone software) are programs that run on your phone. They add new functionality to the phone, such as enabling you to stream video, manipulate databases, play video games, and do almost anything else you can imagine.

The Galaxy S5 comes with dozens of apps preinstalled, ready for you to use. In addition, you can download and install other apps from Google Play and the Amazon Appstore.

Using the Google Apps

Your Galaxy S5 comes with a large number of apps already installed, as you can see when you tap the Apps icon on the Home Screen. Some of the preinstalled apps are the apps that Google provides so you can enjoy various types of media on your Galaxy S5.

Add an App with the Play Store

1. On the Home Screen, tap the Apps icon, and then tap the Play Store icon.

2. Tap the Apps button.

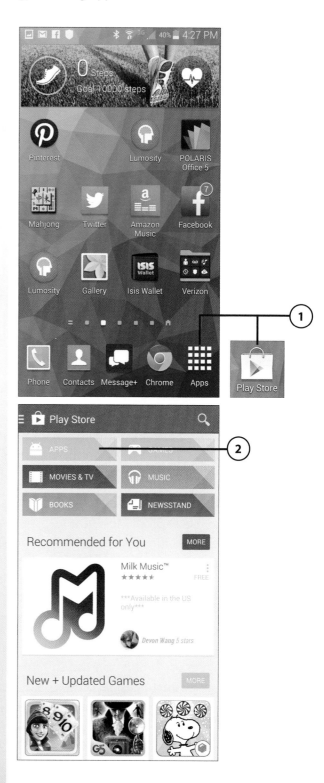

(**3**) Scroll through the screen to find an app you want to install. Alternatively, if you know the name of the app you're looking for, you can tap the Search icon and type the name. Tap the app to go to its main screen.

(**4**) Tap Install.

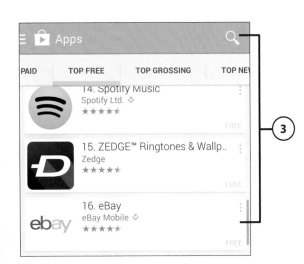

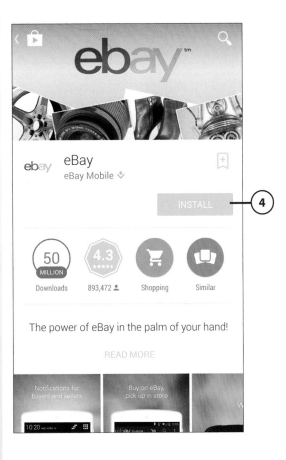

(5) You see a screen that tells you what parts of your Galaxy S5 the app would like to access. Tap Accept and the app downloads to your phone.

(6) Tap Open to launch the newly downloaded app.

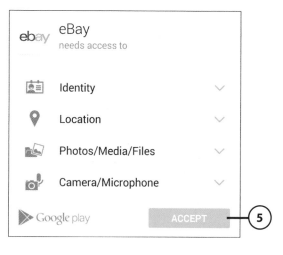

Be Permissions-Savvy

Most apps request permission to access features of your Galaxy S5, such as access to your photos or your location. In some cases, those permissions are appropriate; a map app works better if it knows your current location. Make sure to read the list of requested permissions closely to verify that the requested access seems appropriate for the type of app you're downloading—for example, a to-do list app probably doesn't need to access all your contacts. If something seems suspicious, try searching for another app that has the same functionality but doesn't require access to things you don't want to share.

>>>Go Further
INSTALLING PAID APPS

If you're installing an app for which there is a charge, you will be asked how you want to pay for it. Select the option you want and fill in the appropriate information.

Most applications that have a charge have a secure website, so unless you specify that you want your information saved, it will not be available for anyone else to see.

Some apps have no cost initially, but you have to make in-app purchases to enjoy the full functionality of the app or to be able to use an ad-free version of it. You can always download a free app to try and then remove it from your Galaxy S5 if you decide you don't want to incur the cost of the in-app purchases.

Get eBooks with Play Books

You can download and read books on your Galaxy S5 with the Play Books app.

Play Books

1. Tap the Apps icon and then tap the Play Books icon.

2. Scroll through the books offered and choose one or more. Note that some are free and some have a minimal cost. Tap a book you'd like to investigate.

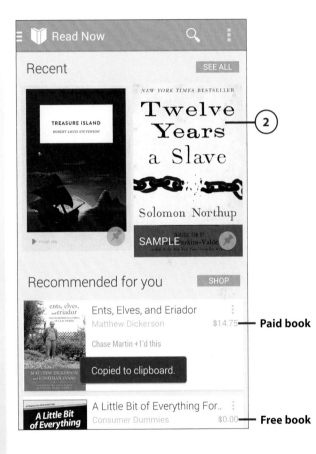

Paid book

Free book

3 Tap the Free Sample button if you'd like to read a sample from the book. (Not all books offer free samples.) Tap the Buy button if you want to purchase the book.

Make Sure You're Connected

You need a Wi-Fi or cellular connection to download a book. After you have the book on your Galaxy S5, though, you don't need to be connected to be able to read.

4 Your book will be downloaded to your Galaxy S5.

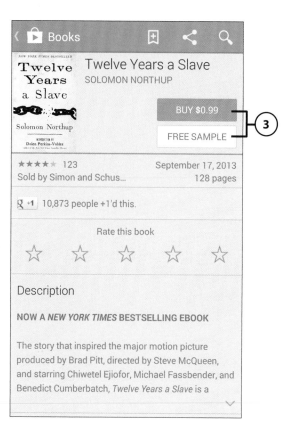

Have Fun with Play Games

1 Tap the Play Games icon to start the Play Games app.

2. You see a menu of options. Until you've added at least one game, the Play Now option won't work. Tap Explore to see the list of games offered by Google.

3. Explore the categories of games by scrolling through and tapping the menu options at the top of the page.

4. Tap the Search icon and type the name of the game you want.

5. Tap a game you'd like to learn more about.

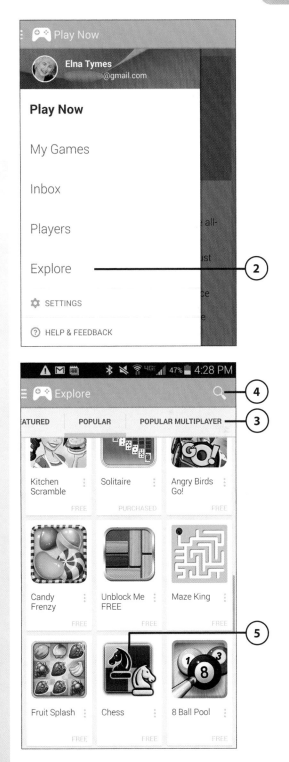

(6) Tap the Free button, tap the Install button, then the Accept button to install the app on your Galaxy S5. The game takes a few seconds to install.

(7) Tap the Play button to begin playing.

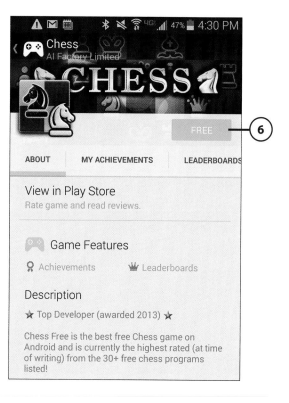

Purchase Movies and TV Shows

(1) Tap the Play Movies & TV icon to start this app.

Try Before You Buy

You might be asked if you want to watch a sample movie for free. Add the sample to your movie library by tapping Add to Library or bypass it by tapping No, Thanks.

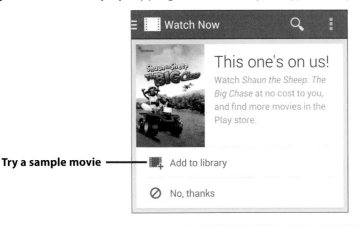

Try a sample movie ——— Add to library

---

2 Scroll through the tabs at the top of the screen to pick a category of TV or movies, and then scroll through the options that are offered in that category.

3 Tap a thumbnail of a movie or TV show.

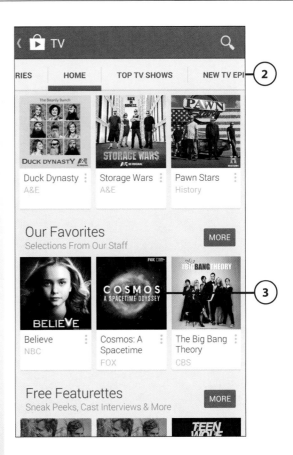

(4) The prices per episode, show, or movie will be shown with each offering. If you want to buy it, tap the price.

(5) Complete the purchase. (It's much like the process for installing an app as described in the "Add an App with the Play Store" task earlier in this chapter.) The movie or TV show is now stored on your Galaxy S5. You can play it any time, and for as many times as you want.

Play Music

(1) Tap the Play Music icon. The first time you launch Play Music, the only thumbnail you see is for Samsung brand music.

(2) Tap the icon in the upper-left corner and select Shop.

3 Tap the Search icon (the magnifying glass) and enter one or more words of the song or artist you want to hear. In the example, I entered "neil diamond."

4 Tap the menu icon for an album or a song you want to hear and then tap the price. Follow the steps to complete the download and purchase process, which are much like the steps used to download an app as described in the "Add an App with the Play Store" task earlier in this chapter.

5 Tap the icon in the upper-left corner and select My Library. You see thumbnails of the music on your Galaxy S5.

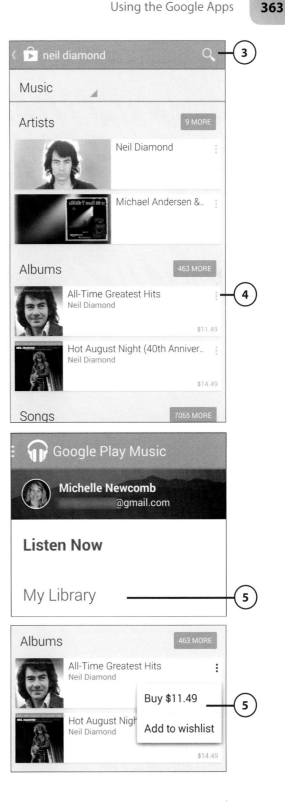

6 Tap a category at the top of the screen to sort the music by genre, artist, album, or song and then tap a thumbnail to see music related to that item. Keep tapping the thumbnail until you get to a song list.

7 Tap the title of a song you'd like to hear. The song begins to play.

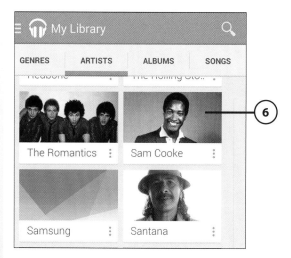

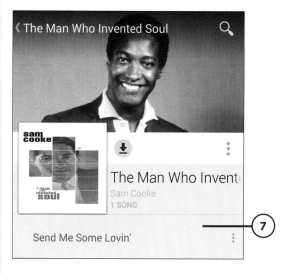

(8) Use the controls at the bottom of the screen to control playback of the song.

Using Play Newsstand

Play Newsstand works much like the Play Games and Play Music apps. You can read more about Play Newsstand in Chapter 22, "Getting the News."

Using the Amazon Apps

You need an Amazon.com account to use anything offered in any of the Amazon apps. When you first enter the Appstore or any of the other Amazon apps, you need to provide your Amazon account username and password.

Using the Appstore

Amazon.com has provided a number of apps for the Galaxy S5, which you can manage via the Appstore.

① Tap Apps and then tap the Appstore icon. When the app opens, you see a set of thumb-nails describing the apps available on the Appstore.

② Scroll through the list of apps to find one you want, and tap on its thumbnail. Alternatively, if you know the name of the app you want, tap the Search icon to type the name.

3 The screen displays a description of the app you're after. If there is a price, it's shown in the upper-right corner; otherwise, the app is identified as being free. Tap the price/Free button if you want to purchase the app.

4 Tap the Get App button to download it. Most Amazon apps begin running immediately after downloading is complete.

Use Amazon.com

Perusing Amazon.com is like walking through the biggest department store you've ever seen. It carries hundreds of thousands of items for sale; you can buy any of them from your Galaxy S5 fairly simply using the dedicated Amazon.com app.

1 Tap the Amazon.com icon.

(2) The opening screen shows you some samples of items for sale.

(3) Tap Shop by Department to see a list of categories of merchandise. Alternatively, enter the name of the item you're looking for in the Search box.

(4) In the list of search results, tap an item to see more information.

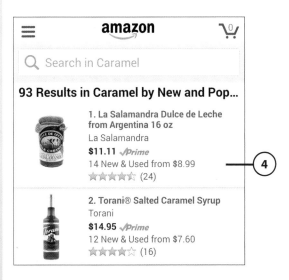

5 If you have previously set up account information, you can tap Buy now with 1-Click. If you haven't, tap on Add to Cart. You can then resume shopping and deal with what's in your cart later.

Buy now with 1-Click — **5**

Order within 2hr 10min to get it:

| Tue +3.99 | Wed Free |

Using Amazon for Comparison Shopping

When you're in a local store and want to know if Amazon.com might have the same item for a lower price, you can tap the small bar code icon in the Amazon.com search bar and take a picture of the UPC code on the item. If Amazon.com carries the item, you'll see the price of the item.

Changed Your Mind?

You can always cancel an Amazon.com transaction. Each purchase generates an automatic confirmation email. Follow the links in the email to remove the transaction from your account. You'll receive a second confirmation email for the cancellation.

Read with the Kindle App

If you have an Amazon Kindle, you can connect to the books you've downloaded to it. This can be particularly useful if you have some time to kill and don't happen to have your Kindle with you.

1 Tap the Amazon Kindle icon to open the Kindle store. When the app first opens you have the opportunity to explore recommended titles or the Kindle Select 25 list.

 — **1**

Automatic Account Access

If you have previously logged in to your Amazon.com account with one of the other Amazon apps, the Kindle app will automatically sync to your account. If you haven't used one of the other Amazon apps, you need to log in to your account.

2 Download items that you have previously purchased by tapping the icon in the upper-left corner and selecting All Items. You see thumbnails of the books you have purchased.

3 Tap a thumbnail to download a book to your Galaxy S5. After the book has downloaded, a check mark is displayed in the lower-right corner. Tap the thumbnail again to open the book.

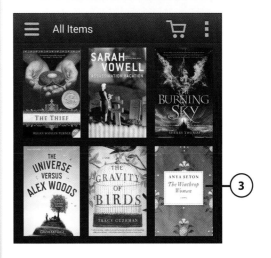

4 Swipe left or right to move forward or back through the book.

Change text size, spacing, and background color

‹ kindle   A*a*   🔍   ⋮   — **Search the book**

THIS book is built on a solid framework of fact; from these facts I have never knowingly deviated, nor changed a date or circumstance.

I have hoped that readers would be interested in following the story as it emerged for me in the original documents, and I have included excerpts from some of these documents, *verbatim*, except that for clarity I have occasionally modernized the spelling a bit.

I have also incorporated my characters' own written words into the dialogue whenever possible. All these characters are real; even Peyto and Telaka (though nameless in the references) are based on fact. —— **4**

My determination to present authentic history has necessitated a scrupulous adherence to the findings of research. And I felt that this woman, with her passionate loves, dangers, tragedies, and courage, lived

Location 32 of 10114   **1%**

Using Amazon Music

You can purchase and download music from Amazon Music on your Galaxy S5.

1 Tap the Apps icon and then tap the Amazon Music icon.

The Amazon Prime Option

When you initially tap on the Amazon Music icon, you see an advertisement for Amazon Prime, a subscription-based service that gives you special benefits, such as accessing and ordering items prior to official release and getting free two-day shipping. Because Prime is a for-pay service, you may not want to purchase it at first. After you've been using your Galaxy S5, you might decide that it's worth the money.

1

(2) Navigate to the Music Store screen. Tap the Search icon to look for a specific song, album, or artist. Or you could tap one of the albums or songs that's featured on the Music Store screen as done for this example.

Where Do I Make My Purchase?

You might need to tap the album or song title a couple of times to get to the screen where you actually make your purchase.

(3) Tap a price button to buy either the whole album or a particular song. If you want to buy one of the songs listed, tap it. If you have already set up a Buy with 1-Click account on Amazon, the purchase will be made immediately and the song will be stored in your music library. It may take a few minutes for the song to show up in your music library.

Try a Sample

You can also listen to samples from the album by tapping Sample This Album in the middle of the album thumbnail.

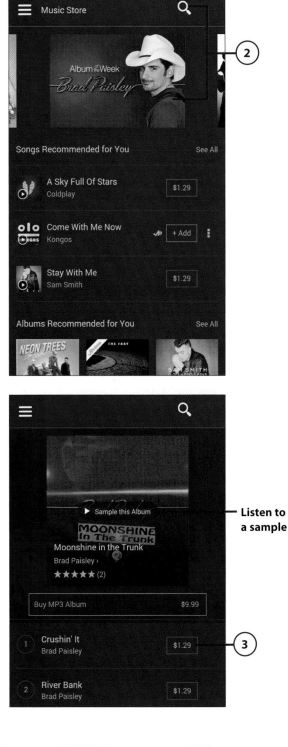

Listen to a sample

(4) Tap See Track in Library to open your Amazon music library and play the song.

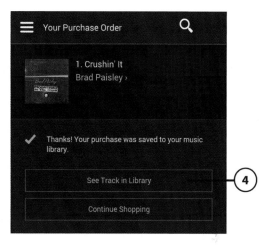

>>>Go Further
KEEP YOUR MUSIC IN THE CLOUD

If you have already copied some or all of your music library to the Amazon.com cloud, you can listen to those songs from your Galaxy S5 without downloading them as long as you can connect to the Internet with a Wi-Fi or cellular connection. Any time you order music from Amazon.com, the music is automatically stored in the cloud. If you're connected to the Internet with a cellular connection, be careful about streaming your music directly from the cloud, though; it can really eat through your data allowance.

Managing Your Apps

With the Applications Manager, you can sort apps, reset app preferences, and do bulk uninstallations of apps.

Installing Apps

To add an app, use the Google Play Store, the Amazon Appstore, or the install feature on an app you want to add, such as Twitter or Yelp.

(**1**) Tap the Settings icon.

(**2**) Tap Applications.

(**3**) Tap Application Manager to see an alphabetical list of your installed applications.

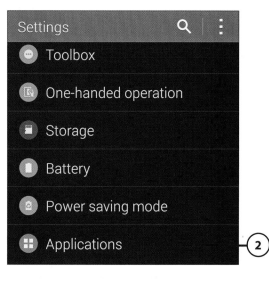

4 Tap the menu icon to change the sort order of the list of apps. You can choose Sort by Date or Sort by Size.

5 Tap Reset App Preferences to reset all apps' preferences to their default values.

6 Tap Reset Apps to reset your app preferences to default values as noted. Tap Cancel if you've changed your mind about resetting the preferences.

7 To remove an individual app, tap its name to open the detail page for that app.

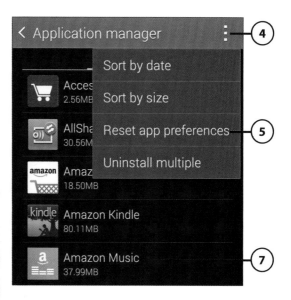

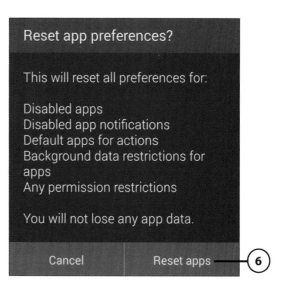

8 The information on this screen shows how much memory this app is using in total, how much memory is for the app software, and how much memory is for the data. You can also see whether any space on the SD card is being used by it, and how much cache memory is reserved for this app. If you scroll down, it also lists any defaults that have been set for this app, and shows you a list of function permissions this app has that might affect other apps.

9 If the app seems to be causing a problem (for example, if the Galaxy S5 has frozen) and you want to shut it down, turn off the app by tapping the Force Stop button.

10 If you want to remove the data for this app, tap the Clear Data button.

11 Tap the Clear Cache button to disable the app's operation.

12 If you are unhappy with recent updates to this app, you can remove them by tapping Uninstall Updates.

13 To remove the app from your Galaxy S5, tap the Uninstall button. This removes it, and any data that's associated with it, from memory. You can reinstall it later if you choose.

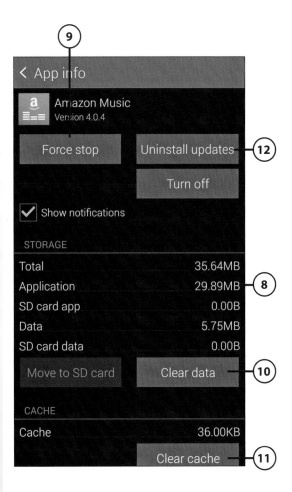

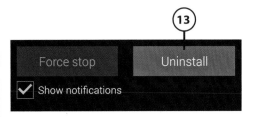

In this chapter, you learn about using Facebook, the biggest online community in the world. Topics include the following:

→ Installing Facebook
→ Creating a Facebook account
→ Finding friends
→ Managing your status, photos, and videos

Connecting with Family and Friends on Facebook

Facebook is the largest single example of social media, a topic briefly touched on in Chapter 12, "Communicating with Others." With Facebook you can post messages, pictures, and videos about what's going on in your life, and you can see and comment on the same from others you select (or *friend*).

Why Use Facebook?

Although Facebook started out as a means of socializing between college students, it has grown tremendously. Today it has more than one billion users.

Facebook is all about a broad concept of "friends." Facebook friends can be a neighbor, someone across the country (or in a different country), someone you used to work with, someone you met recently, a family member, or just about anyone. The idea is that you get to stay in touch with what your friends are doing by reading what they post, and posting your own updates and comments. Some people use Facebook to help gather support for a political issue, such as climate change; some use it to publicize events, such as a street carnival; and some simply use it to show people what they're doing.

In addition to seeing your friends' posts in your News Feed, you can use Facebook to hold live text chats or host video chats with friends who are online.

Installing the Facebook App

Facebook is not one of the default apps already installed on your Galaxy S5. But downloading it from the Play Store and installing it is easy.

(1) Tap the Play Store icon.

(2) Tap the Apps button.

(3) Tap the Top Free category.

(4) Scroll until you find the Facebook item, and then tap it.

Check App Names Carefully
Be sure you tap on the Facebook app and not the Facebook Messenger app. They're two different things.

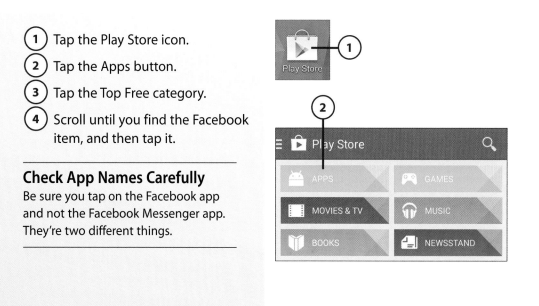

5 Tap the Install button. A list of conditions for the app appears.

6 Read the list and tap Accept. The Facebook app installs by itself and creates an icon you see when you tap the Apps icon.

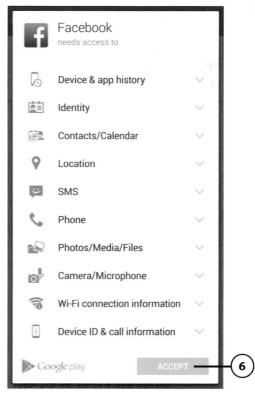

⑦ Tap the Open button.

⑧ Enter your email address and a password if you already have an account with Facebook, and then tap the Log In button. If this is your first time using Facebook, tap the Sign Up for Facebook link. The app walks you through the sign-up process.

Making Signup Easy

You have to do some typing to sign up for a Facebook account, so you might find it easier to use a desktop or laptop computer. To sign up for a Facebook account through your computer's Internet browser, go to www.facebook.com and fill in the sign-up form.

The Home Page

After you log in, you see a page with what Facebook calls your News Feed. This is where your friends have posted things for you to see.

Posts in a News Feed

The Toolbar

The toolbar has handy buttons that enable you to accept friend requests, create a post for your News Feed, or search Facebook for people, places, or things.

1. Tap the Friend Requests button to see requests from others who would like to be your Facebook friend.

2. Tap the Message icon to start a message thread with another Facebook user.

3. Tap the Notification icon to see a comment someone has posted or to find out who liked a post you created.

4. Tap the Menu icon to see your profile, nearby friends, nearby places and events, your friends list, things you've saved, Games, and Groups.

5. Tap the News Feed icon to go back to your News Feed after you've been exploring other areas.

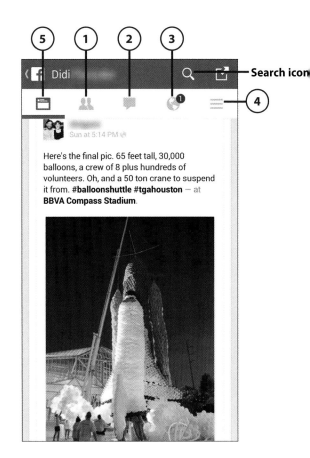

Completing Your Profile

Facebook offers you the opportunity to add information to your profile, listing members of your family, places you've worked, places you went to school, and so on. Although privacy is a concern, the more you put in your profile, the easier it will be for friends to find you.

(1) Tap the Menu icon.

(2) Tap your name.

(3) Tap the About panel.

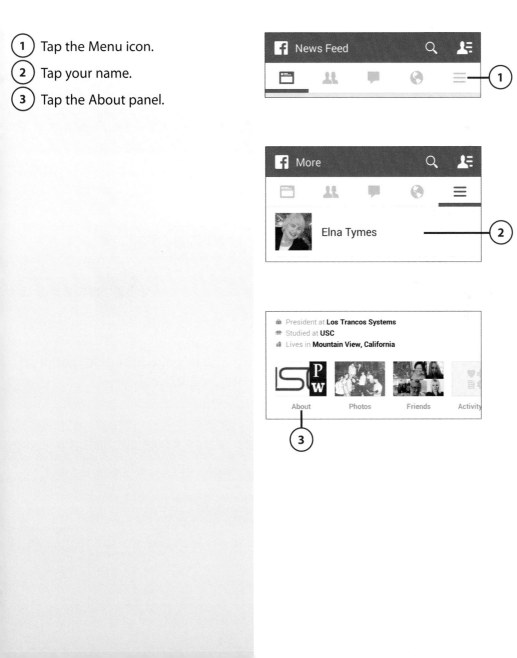

4 Tap the right-pointing arrows next to each category to enter or change the information for that item. Scroll down the page to see all the categories.

Do As Much As You Want

Remember, with the exception of the information you had to give when you first signed up for Facebook, you don't have to share any information about yourself. Only complete the sections you feel comfortable sharing with other people.

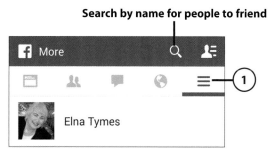

Finding Friends

One of the benefits of Facebook is the ability to connect with family and friends. You can accept friend requests that other people send you, or you can seek out people and send them invitations to be friends. You can also "unfriend" people if you decide you no longer want to see their posts in your News Feed.

Add Friends

Facebook can help you find people to friend. It does this based on the information in your profile, such as places you've worked and schools you've attended, as well as the list of people with whom you're already friends.

1 Tap the three bars in the right end of the Notification bar.

Search by name for people to friend

Searching for Friends

If you have a specific person you'd like to try to find, you can use the Search icon to type in the person's name. Tap the Add Friend button on that person's profile to send a friend request.

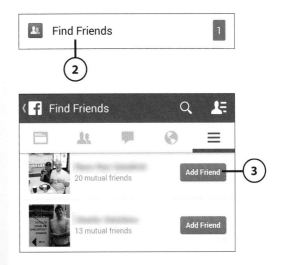

2) Scroll through the menu and tap Find Friends. Facebook presents a list of people you might know.

3) Tap the Add Friend button to the right of a person's name. Request Sent will appear under the person's name. The person will receive a notification that you want to be a Facebook friend, and he or she can accept or ignore the request.

>>>Go Further

ACCEPTING FRIEND REQUESTS

When someone sends you an invitation to be friends, you see a notification next to the Friend Request icon in the Facebook notification bar. Tap the notification to see who wants to be friends with you and then tap Accept or Ignore. Posts and notifications from any friends you accept will begin to appear in your News Feed.

Unfriend a Person

You might decide later that you want to unfriend a person.

(1) Go to the Timeline of the person you want to unfriend and tap the Friends button.

(2) Tap Unfriend.

Unfriending Happens Quietly

Your friend will not receive a notification that you have unfriended him or her, although he or she might notice that posts from you are no longer in the News Feed or see that you are not listed in the Friends list.

Block a Friend

When you still want to be Facebook friends with someone but you don't want to regularly see posts from them in your News Feed, you can block that person.

(1) Tap the Menu icon.

(2) Scroll down and tap Account Settings.

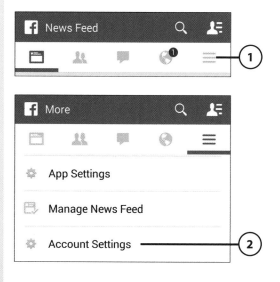

(3) Tap Blocking.

(4) Enter the person's name and tap Block.

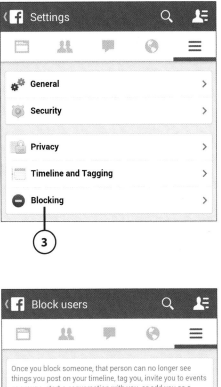

⑤ Locate the person's name on the search results page and tap Block again.

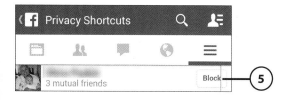

What Does Blocking Mean?
A person that you have blocked can't see things you post, can't tag you in pictures, can't send you invitations to groups or events, and can't send you a message.

Reading Your News Feed

Your News Feed is an up-to-the-minute group of postings from your friends and others. You can get to your News Feed by tapping the icon at the left of the toolbar.

News Feed icon

Post in the News Feed

When you come back to Facebook after having done other things or been away from your phone, you will find a lot of new postings have been added, and there will be a red indicator next to the News Feed icon that tells you how many new stories are in the News Feed.

Updating Your Status Updates, Photos, and Videos

When you post something to your timeline, your friends can see the post in their News Feeds.

1 Tap here to post a photo

To: 🌐 Public **3**

What's on your mind? **2**

(**1**) Tap Status in the bottom-left corner of your Facebook screen. You see a blank screen where you type your post.

Posting Photos

To post a photo to your timeline, tap Photo instead of Status.

(**2**) Tap the What's on Your Mind? area and type your status.

(**3**) Adjust the privacy settings for the post by tapping the right-pointing arrow in the To bar. The privacy settings determine who will be able to see this post.

Location and Privacy

When updating with your location, keep in mind that you're letting people know when you're not home.

(4) Tap Public (which means any-one on Facebook can see the post), Friends (meaning all your Facebook friends), or More to designate specific Facebook friends who will be able to see the post. Tap the left-pointing arrow next to Share With to go back to the Write Post screen.

(5) Tap the Camera icon to add a photo to your post.

(6) Tap the Tag icon to say who you are with or to include a specific person as part of the post.

(7) Tap the Emoticon icon to add a smiley or some other emoticon to your post.

(8) Tap the Location icon to indicate a specific location (a geographic area or a business name) for your post. This is sometimes referred to as "checking in" at a location.

(9) Tap Post when you're ready to send your post to your Timeline and to your friends' News Feeds.

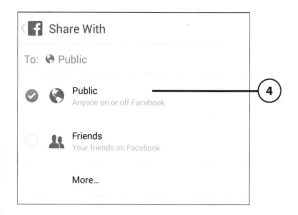

Safety First

Be cautious when using the Location icon to specify your location as part of your status update. Anyone who can see your status knows when you're not home. This probably isn't a problem if you've set your Facebook privacy settings so that only your friends can see your statuses; but if you allow friends of friends or all of Facebook to see your status, then someone with bad intentions can see your "Having a great time in Hawaii" status and know that you're away on vacation while your house is unintended. You can learn more about the Facebook privacy settings in *My Facebook for Seniors* by Michael Miller.

Creating a Facebook Group

You can create groups on Facebook so that you and a particular set of friends or family can share posts with one another without the rest of your Facebook world seeing them. For example, you could create a group that includes all your grandchildren so that you can carry on family-only discussions with them without their friends seeing everything you post.

 Tap the Menu icon.

 Scroll down to the Groups section and tap Create Group.

 Type a group name (such as Grandchildren) in the Group Name box, and then tap the Go button on the keyboard.

 Select a Privacy setting for the group: Open (anyone can see who's in the group and all the posts), Closed (anyone can see the group and who's in it, but they cannot see the posts), or Secret (only members can see the group).

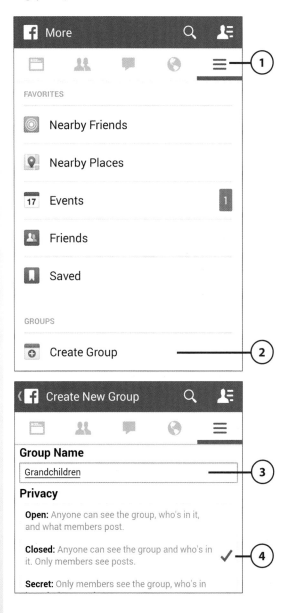

5 Choose an icon to represent the group.

6 Type the name of a Facebook friend that you'd like to add to the group. Facebook finds the person's name in your list of friends and fills it in. Tap the Add Selected button.

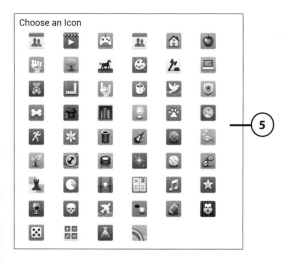

7 You see the timeline screen for the group. Members' profile pictures are displayed across the top of the screen.

8 Tap the arrow to add another person to the group.

9 Facebook suggests a list of potential group members. Tap the Add button next to a person's name to add that person. Alternatively, you can use the Search field to find someone by their name.

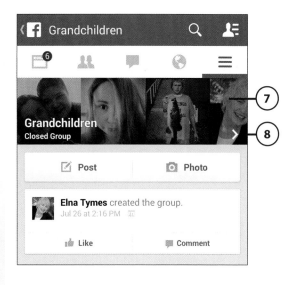

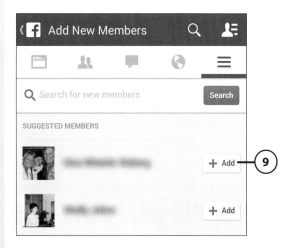

In this chapter, you learn to use the phone's cameras to shoot, edit, share, and manage photos of yourself and other subjects. Topics include the following:

→ Using the front and rear cameras to shoot self-portraits and photos of other subjects
→ Viewing, managing, and sharing the current photo
→ Viewing stored photos in Gallery
→ Using Photo Studio to edit your shots
→ Generating a slideshow from selected folders or photos
→ Posting a picture on Facebook

Shooting, Editing, and Sharing Photos

If you keep your phone handy, there's no excuse for missing an unexpected photo opportunity. Using the built-in cameras on your Galaxy S5, you can easily shoot posed and candid high-resolution photos of friends, family, yourself, and anything else that catches your eye.

Setting a Storage Location for Photos and Videos

If you've added a memory card to the phone, be sure to set the Storage setting to Memory Card (as explained in "Using the Settings Palette," later in this chapter).

Shooting Photos

You can shoot photos of subjects in front of you using the 16MP (*megapixel*) rear camera or take self-portraits with the 2MP front camera.

What's the Deal with MP?

MP indicates the density of pixels in a photo, and to some extent reflects the quality of the photo. The higher the MP number, the more you can increase the dimensions of the photo; however, the higher the MP number, the larger the file—meaning it could be difficult to email.

Shoot Self-Portraits with the Front Camera

Use the front camera to take pictures of yourself—or yourself and a friend or two. Note that you can't use the flash or zoom in this mode.

(1) From the Home screen, launch Camera by tapping its shortcut (if you haven't removed it) or by tapping Apps, Camera.

Other Launch Options

You can launch Camera from the lock screen by sliding the Camera icon upward (if it's present). For instructions on configuring the lock screen in this manner, see Chapter 14, "Securing Your Cell Phone."

You can also launch Camera from within Gallery by tapping the Camera toolbar icon.

Lock screen icon

2 Determine whether the rear or front camera is active. If the rear camera is active, change to the front camera by tapping the Switch Camera icon.

3 *Optional:* Review or adjust the camera settings that will be used for the shot by tapping the Settings icon. After you change the settings, your icons might not be in the same order, and you might have to scroll up or down to see them all. For additional information about Settings, see "Changing the Camera Settings," later in this section.

Shortcut Icons

As described later in "Changing the Camera Settings," you can customize the Camera toolbar by adding shortcuts to frequently used settings. You can tap a shortcut icon rather than opening Settings.

4 *Optional:* Tap the Mode button to set a shooting mode. The default setting is Auto. The current mode is displayed near the top of the viewfinder screen. To learn more about modes, see "Selecting a Shooting Mode" later in this chapter.

5 When you're ready to take the picture, tap the Camera button. (The Volume key can also be used as a shutter button.)

Shortcuts   Adjust the mode

Beauty face

Most recent photo   **5**   Video

Where's the Photo?

To review all photos taken with the cameras, launch the Gallery app, select Album view, and open the Camera folder. (If you have an add-in memory card, there may be *two* Camera folders.) To go straight from the Camera app to the most recent photo you've taken, tap its thumbnail in the lower-left corner of the viewfinder screen.

Shoot Photos with the Rear Camera

Of course, most of the photos you'll shoot with the Galaxy S5 will be of other people and subjects. Shooting photos of others is similar to shooting self-portraits, but it uses the higher-resolution rear camera and has many additional options. Note that virtually every step in the following task is optional, and you can perform Steps 2–5 in any order that's convenient.

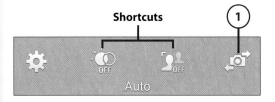

(1) Launch the Camera app and determine whether the rear or front camera is active. If the front camera is active, switch to the rear camera by tapping the Switch Camera icon.

Portrait or Landscape

Whether you use the front or rear camera, you can take any photo in *portrait* (right-side up) or *landscape* (sideways) mode. To shoot in landscape mode, turn the phone sideways.

(2) *Optional:* Frame your subject by zooming in or out. (The Galaxy S5 has a digital zoom.) Touch the viewfinder screen with two fingers and spread them apart to zoom in or pinch them together to zoom out.

3 *Optional:* To review or adjust the camera settings that will be used for the shot, tap the Settings icon. Make any desired changes in the vertically scrolling palette, and then dismiss it by tapping the Settings icon again, tapping elsewhere on the screen, or pressing the Back key. For additional information about Settings, see "Changing the Camera Settings" later in this chapter.

Shortcut Icons

As described later in "Changing the Camera Settings," you can customize the Camera toolbar by adding shortcuts to frequently used settings. You can tap a shortcut icon rather than opening Settings.

4 *Optional:* Tap the Mode button at the bottom of the screen to set a shooting mode. The default setting is Auto. The currently selected mode is displayed near the top of the viewfinder screen. To learn more about modes, see "Selecting a Shooting Mode," later in this chapter.

5 *Optional:* To set the focus to a particular area, tap that spot on the viewfinder screen. The focus area turns green when the lighting and focus are sufficient to snap the photo.

6 When you're ready to take the picture, tap the Camera button. (Turning the Volume up or down can also be used as a shutter button.)

Avoid Odd Angles for Faces

When shooting portraits, you can avoid misshapen faces by holding the camera at the same angle as that of your subject. If your results are subpar, try another shot while ensuring that the phone isn't tilted—even a little.

Changing the Camera Settings

Before taking a photo, you can apply optional settings to enable or disable the flash and adjust the exposure, resolution, ISO, and so on. Note that some settings are available only for the rear-facing camera, others only for self-portraits, and still others apply only to video recordings. Also, certain automated settings can interact with and prevent you from altering manual settings. For example, when Picture Stabilization is enabled, you cannot set ISO.

You can change settings in three places: the shortcuts, the Settings palette, and by selecting a shooting mode.

Configure and Use the Shortcuts

The *shortcuts* are user-selected icons that appear at the top of the viewfinder screen between the ever-present Settings and Switch Camera icons. You can tap them to make the settings adjustments that they represent without opening the Settings palette. You can replace the default shortcuts (HDR and Selective Focus) with up to three shortcuts of your choosing.

(1) Tap the Settings icon to open the Settings palette.

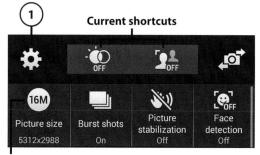

(**2**) In the Settings palette, press and hold the icon that you want to use as a shortcut, and drag it into the shortcuts. If you currently have fewer than three shortcuts, you can drag it into any position. If you already have three short-cuts, drag it onto the shortcut that you want to replace.

Removing Shortcuts

You can remove a shortcut by long-pressing it, and—when the Settings palette appears—dragging the shortcut into the palette.

Display-Only Icons

In the lower-right corner of the screen, one or more settings icons may be displayed, such as the current Flash setting and a Storage icon (indicating that the shot will be saved to an installed memory card). Settings icons in this area are for informational purposes only; you can't interact with them.

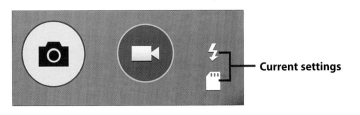

Current settings

Using the Settings Palette

To modify most settings, you must first open the Settings palette by tapping the Settings icon. Here's what the photo-related settings do:

Settings icon ——

- *Picture Size.* To shoot at the camera's highest resolution, select 16M: 5312×2988 (16:9). If you're running out of storage space or intend to share the photo on the Web or in email, you can select a lower resolution.

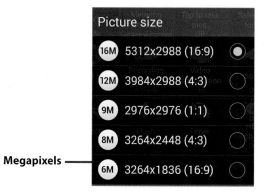

Megapixels ——

Alter the Resolution After the Shot

Using almost any image-editing program, you can reduce the resolution *after* shooting the photo.

- *Burst Shots.* When enabled, you can quickly take up to 30 shots by holding down the Camera button or Volume key. Burst Shot photos are stored in Device memory, regardless of your Storage setting.

- *Picture Stabilization.* This anti-shake setting adjusts shots for unintended blur caused by camera movement.

- *Face Detection.* Enable Face Detection when you want the camera to search for a face in the shot and optimize the focus for the face.

- *ISO.* The ISO setting is for film speed or sensitivity to light. You can use a lower ISO for shots taken on a bright, sunny day and use a higher ISO for dimly lit shots or ones taken in dark settings. Options include Auto (allows the camera to set the ISO), 100, 200, 400, and 800.

- *Metering Modes.* Specify the method used to perform light metering: Center-Weighted, Matrix, or Spot.

- *Tap to Take Pics.* When enabled, you can tap anywhere on the screen to take a picture.

- *Selective Focus.* In general, everything is in sharp focus in photos taken with a fixed-lens digital phone or camera. When Selective Focus is enabled, Camera simulates an effect similar to that of focusing a 35mm camera lens. That is, a nearby object on which you're focusing (less than 1.5 feet away) is in sharp focus, and background objects are out of focus or blurred.

- *Effects.* Select an effect that will be applied as you frame and take the photo. Tap Manage Effects to specify the effects that will be included in the scrolling list. Tap the Download icon to acquire additional effects from Samsung Apps. Select No Effect to cancel the selected effect. (You can't apply an effect when shooting in HDR mode.)

Oil Pastel effect

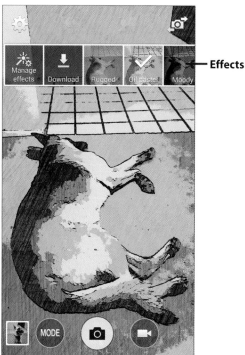

Effects

- *Flash.* Tap Flash repeatedly to cycle through its three states: On, Off, and Auto. When set to Auto, the camera fires the flash when current lighting dictates that it's needed. To avoid blinding you, Flash is automatically disabled when you're taking self-portraits.

- *Timer.* To instruct the camera to snap the upcoming picture after a preset delay, select a 2-, 5-, or 10-second delay.

Timer Shots

With a 35mm camera, you'd use its timer to give yourself a few seconds to dash into a photo. With your Galaxy S5, however, using the timer assumes that you have some way to make the phone stand on its own. Prop it up or mount it in a tripod designed for smartphones.

- *HDR (Rich Tone).* Takes photos in *High Dynamic Range (HDR)* mode, increasing the amount of detail. When shooting in HDR mode, some other settings— Effects, for example—cannot be enabled.

- *Location Tags.* When enabled, the photo file's metadata contains information that shows where the shots were taken, based on the GPS.

- *Save as Flipped.* This setting is available only when shooting a self-portrait with the front-facing camera. Enable it to automatically flip each shot horizontally.

- *Storage.* Specify where photos are stored as they're shot: *Device* (internal memory) or *Memory Card* (add-in memory card). If Camera detects a need for speedier storage (when shooting Burst Shots, for example), Device is automatically used.

- *Review Pics/Videos.* When set to On, each new photo immediately opens in Gallery, enabling you to examine, delete, or edit it. (To *manually* review the most recent camera pic, tap the thumbnail in the lower-left corner of the screen.)

- *Remote Viewfinder.* When enabled, you can use the viewfinder of a compatible device that's connected via Wi-Fi Direct to take pictures.

- *White Balance.* To adjust shots for current lighting "temperature" and how white will be displayed, select Auto (allow the camera to determine the best setting), Daylight, Cloudy, Incandescent, or Fluorescent.

- *Exposure Value.* Drag the Exposure value slider to the right to adjust for a dark scene or to the left for an overly bright scene.

Exposure value

Exposure slider

- *Guide Lines.* When enabled, white guidelines divide the screen into a 3×3 grid to make it easier to center and frame the subject matter.

- *Voice Control.* When enabled, you can optionally use voice commands (Smile, Cheese, Capture, or Shoot) to snap photos.

- *Help.* View elementary Help information about using Camera to take pictures and record videos.

- *Reset.* Select this option and tap OK to reset all settings in the Settings palette to their default values. Remove the check mark if you want to leave modified shortcuts intact.

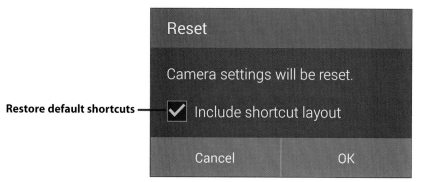

Restore default shortcuts —

Selecting a Shooting Mode

When you're in a rush—but not *that* much of a rush—you can select a shooting mode that automatically specifies a combination of camera settings or enables a special feature to use for the upcoming shot(s). Tap the Mode button and select one of these options:

Shooting modes

- *Auto.* This default mode snaps a single normal photo.

- *Beauty Face.* Smooths the subject's facial features, reducing simple wrinkles, hiding pores and small blemishes, and so on. (People might accuse you of having these shots professionally retouched.) Tap the Beauty Face icon on the right edge of the screen to specify the amount of smoothing.

- *Shot & More.* The camera rapidly takes eight shots in portrait or landscape orientation. (Zooming isn't allowed.) After taking the photo, you can immediately apply one of five modes or do so when it's opened for editing. See the "Using Shot & More" sidebar for an explanation of its modes.

- *Panorama.* Takes multiple shots as you pan across a scene and stitches them together into a single photo. Tap the Camera button to start the shot, slowly pan the camera, and then tap the Stop button to conclude the process. When viewed in Gallery, you can optionally tap the Play icon to pan slowly across the entire scene.

Panorama

Play

- *Virtual Tour.* By automatically taking multiple pictures as you walk around and follow the onscreen turn directions (left, straight, right), this mode creates a "virtual tour" video that's similar to what you see in online advertisements for homes.

- *Dual Camera.* Simultaneously activates both cameras when shooting photos or videos, enabling you to achieve a picture-in-picture effect. To select an effect for the inset picture, such as Cubism, Instant Pic, or Heart Shape, tap the greater than (>) symbol on the viewfinder's left edge. Either the rear or front camera can be dominant when using this mode.

- *Download.* Links to a Samsung Apps page where you can download addition-al Camera modes—including some that came with the Galaxy S 4, such as Animated Photo and Sound & Shot.

Downloadable modes

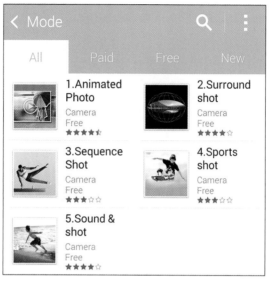

Reset the Shooting Mode

Be sure to always check the onscreen mode indicator before you take the next shot. The most recent shooting mode is sometimes retained. Other settings may also be retained and should be reset as needed.

>>>Go Further

USING SHOT & MORE

Immediately after taking a photo in Shot & More mode, a mode-selection arc appears. Modes appropriate to the shot are highlighted; ineligible ones are grayed out. Select a mode by tapping its button, or you can wait until you're reviewing the photo in Gallery. Shot & More images are identified in Gallery by a star icon in the upper-left corner. To apply a mode to the shot, tap the Edit icon.

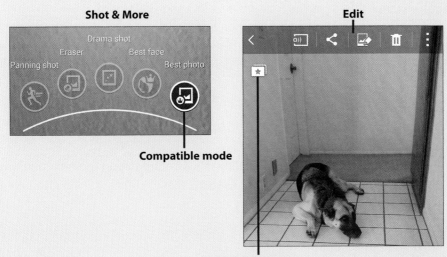

Shot & More

Drama shot

Eraser   Best face

Panning shot   Best photo

Compatible mode

Edit

Shot & More icon

The following modes are supported:

- *Panning Shot.* Enables you to simulate action by selecting the subject and blurring the background.

- *Eraser.* Creates a composite photo that eliminates any person, animal, or object that wandered into the shot.

- *Drama Shot.* Combines multiple shots of a moving person or object into a single photo. Tap thumbnails of the images you want to include, and tap the disk icon to store the composite photo in the Studio folder. Drama Shot works best when the subject moves *through* the shot—from one side of the frame to the other—rather than toward or away from you.

- *Best Face.* Enables you to pick the best expression for each person in a group and then merge them into a single shot. When editing the shot, the camera identifies each face by surrounding it with a rectangle. One person at a time, tap the individual's selection rectangle, review their facial expression thumbnails, and tap the one you like best. Repeat this process for each person in the photo, and tap the disk icon to save the composite photo.

- *Best Photo.* Asks you to pick the shots you want to keep. The photo judged by Camera to be the best is marked with a crown. Review the shots, tap thumbnails of photos you want to save, and tap the disk icon. Selected photos are stored in the Studio folder, while the editable original remains in the Camera folder.

Reviewing Photos

After taking a photograph, you can immediately examine and perform various actions on it, such as sharing, deleting, or renaming the shot. Read about additional options when viewing *any* stored photo or video in "Using Gallery to View and Edit Photos," later in this chapter.

Automatic Review

If you find that you typically review each photo before taking the next one, you can automate the switch to Gallery. In Camera, tap the Settings icon and enable Review Pics/Videos.

(1) To review the most recent shot in Gallery, tap the photo's thumbnail on the viewfinder screen.

(2) In Gallery, if the toolbar isn't visible across the top of the screen, you can make it appear by tapping anywhere onscreen. From left to right, tapping icons enables you to do the following:

- Select a different folder to open.

- Use screen mirroring to share the image with a compatible device.

- Share the image using a variety of methods, such as sending by Email, enclosing in a multimedia message, or posting to Facebook.

- Edit the photo with Photo Studio.

- Delete the photo.

- Open Gallery's menu.

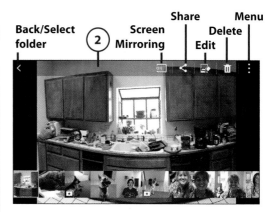

(3) While examining the photo, you can also do the following:

- Review the photo in portrait or landscape orientation by rotating the phone.

- Zoom in or out by double-tapping the photo, spreading your fingers apart, or pinching your fingers together.

- View a different image by tapping a thumbnail at the bottom of the screen or swiping horizontally across the screen.

- Tap the menu icon and choose commands to perform other operations on the photo, such as rename, rotate, crop, or use it as wallpaper (Set As).

(4) When you're ready to return to Camera, press the Back key. (If you're on a Gallery screen that has a camera icon in the toolbar, you can tap the icon to return to Camera.)

Menu

More info —————— **(3)**

Copy to clipboard

Rotate left

Rotate right

Crop

Rename

Detect text

Slideshow

Set as

Print

Settings

Using Gallery to View and Edit Photos

All photos and videos stored on your phone—regardless of whether you took them with Camera—can be viewed, edited, and managed in the Gallery app.

View and Edit Photos

1 From the Home screen, launch Gallery by tapping Apps, Gallery.

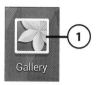

2 *Optional:* Tap the icon in the upper-left corner and choose a view that makes it easy for you to find the images you want to examine, edit, share, or delete. By default, your most recent view is used. Choose Album to work with images arranged in folders or choose Time to see them organized by when the images were taken or created. This example uses Album view. (To learn more about views, see the "Choosing a Gallery View" sidebar later in this chapter.)

Panel icon

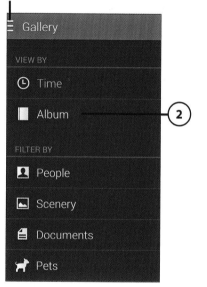

A Time View Trick

You can change the size of thumbnails in Time view by spreading your fingers apart or pinching them together.

---

3 On the main Album view screen, tap the album/folder that holds the pictures you want to view. The Camera folder, for example, contains photos you've taken with the phone's cameras. (Note that *all* folders that contain photos or videos are automatically listed in Gallery, regardless of the files' sources or whether they're in device memory or on an add-in memory card.)

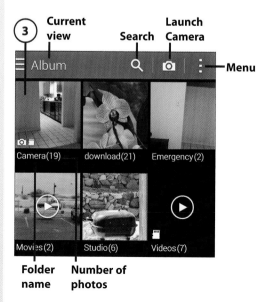

Current view · Search · Launch Camera · Menu

Folder name · Number of photos

4 Thumbnails of the photos or videos contained in the folder appear. Tap a thumbnail to view its photo.

Back

4

Pop-Out Folder List

To enable you to quickly change folders without having to tap the Back icon or press the Back key, a pop-out scrolling list of image folders can optionally be displayed on the left side of the screen. Swipe in from the left edge to reveal the folder list; swipe back to the left to dismiss it.

Selected folder

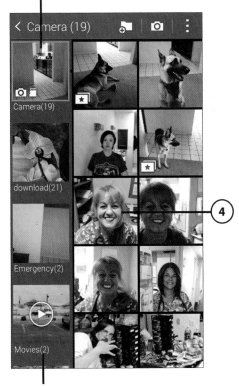

4

Pop-out folder list

5 You can view photos in portrait or landscape mode by rotating the phone. (Note that you must have Settings, Display, Screen Rotation enabled.)

Portrait

5

Landscape

6 You can change the magnification by doing any of the following:

- Double-tap the image to double the current magnification. Repeat to shrink it to its previous size.

- Touch the screen and pinch your fingers together (zoom out) or spread them apart (zoom in).

7 To share the current photo via Email, Messaging, Facebook, or another means, tap the Share Via icon and choose a sharing method from the scrolling palette. Options vary according to your installed apps, registered accounts, and carrier, but typically include the following:

- *Add to Dropbox, Drive.* Upload the photo to one of your cloud accounts.

- *Bluetooth.* To transmit the photo to a Bluetooth-paired device (such as an iMac or a Bluetooth-equipped laptop), tap the Bluetooth icon and then tap the destination in the list of paired devices.

- *Email, Gmail.* Send the image file as an email attachment using one of your email accounts or Gmail.

- *Flipboard.* Post the photo as a status update to your Facebook, Twitter, or similar account using the Flipboard app.

- *Google+, Twitter, Facebook.* Post the photo as a status update to your account.

- *Memo.* Create a new memo that includes the photo.

Open other folders

Selected thumbnail

- *Messages, Messaging+, Hangouts.* Transmit the photo as part of a multimedia message.

- *Picasa.* Upload the photo to Picasa Web Albums (associated with your Google account). To view the uploaded photo, visit https://picasaweb.google.com.

  - *Wi-Fi Direct.* Send the photo to another cell phone within range of yours that supports Wi-Fi Direct.

8 To delete the photo, tap the Delete icon. Tap OK in the confirmation dialog box.

9 To launch the Camera app to shoot a photo or video, tap the Camera icon.

10 Tap the menu icon to see the following additional options:

- *Edit.* Open the image for editing in Photo Studio, an image editor that's integrated with Gallery. See "Image-Editing with Photo Studio," later in this chapter, for instructions.

- *More Info.* Tap the Edit icon to change or set categories and tags. Tap Details to view the image's title, dimensions, file size, storage location, and other properties.

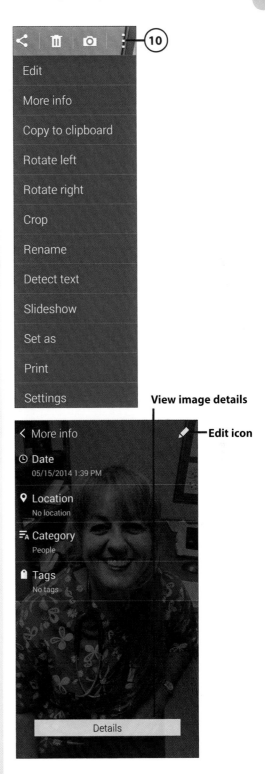

- *Copy to Clipboard.* Copy the image so you can paste it elsewhere—into an email message, for instance.

- *Rotate Left, Rotate Right.* Rotate the image 90° in the specified direction.

- *Crop.* By dragging the selection rectangle and its handles, specify the portion of the image that you want to retain and tap Done. The cropped image is saved *in addition* to the original image—not as a replacement for it.

- *Rename.* Change the default name assigned to the photo to something meaningful. In the Rename dialog box, enter a new filename and tap OK.

- *Detect Text.* If the photo contains a clear shot of some text, this command attempts to extract the text. Although there's no option to save the text, you can use various sharing methods (such as Email or Gmail) to send the text to yourself or others.

- *Slideshow.* Generate a slideshow from all images in the current folder, selected folders, or selected images. See "Running a Slideshow," later in this chapter, for instructions.

- *Set As.* Use the photo as a person's Contacts image, the Home screen wallpaper, the Lock screen wallpaper, or both types of wallpaper.

- *Print.* Print the photo on a compatible wireless printer.

- *Settings.* Open Google/Gmail Settings in which you can enable/disable tagging in your photos and select Filter options.

Crop selection

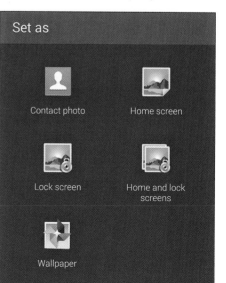

11 To view additional images, do one of the following:

- *Images in the current folder.* Swipe the screen to the left or right. As an alternative, you can tap the thumbnail of the specific image that you want to view. (If the thumbnails aren't visible, tap the current image once to reveal them.)

- *Images in a different folder.* Press the Back key or tap the Back icon repeatedly until the main screen appears, and then go to Step 3.

Back

11

Selected thumb-
nail

>>>*Go Further*

CHOOSING A GALLERY VIEW

Time and Album are the main Gallery views. Choose Time to arrange images by date. Album organizes images by folder, based on the images' source or use. For instance, Camera contains photos taken with the phone, Download holds images that you've transferred to the phone, and Studio has photos that you've edited with Studio. The number in parentheses shows the number of files in the folder.

Finally, you can choose a Filter By option to restrict images to those of a type, such as pets or people. Note, however, that image classification is based on assigned *categories*. Although I have dozens of dog photos on my Galaxy S5, only a small number—those downloaded from my Picasa and Facebook accounts—appear when filtering by Pets. To assign categories to a selected photo, tap the menu icon and choose More Info, tap the Edit icon, tap the + (plus) icon to the right of Category, select one or more categories and tap OK, and then tap Done.

>>>*Go Further*

FOLDER AND IMAGE SELECTION

In addition to operating on one folder or photo at a time, you can apply some commands to multiple selected folders or images.

- *Folder-selection screen (Album view).* You can delete an entire folder or transmit all of its files with a single command. Firmly press the folder and release; a green check mark appears on the folder to show it's selected. Then tap the Share Via or Delete icon. If you want to transmit or delete multiple folders, tap to select the additional folders before tapping a command icon. (To simultaneously select all folders, tap the Selection menu and choose Select All.) The Share Via or Delete command is performed on all selected folders. You can also tap the menu icon and choose Slideshow to create a slideshow based on only images in the selected folder(s)—or choose Studio, Collage Studio to create a collage from the photos.

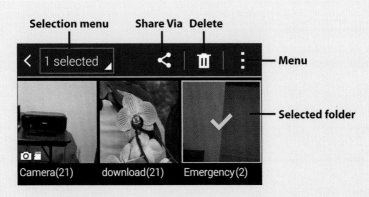

Folder-selection screen (Album view)

- *Image-selection screen.* Similarly, after opening a folder (or with Time view selected), you can select one or more files on which to perform a command. Firmly press and release an image thumbnail to select it; a green check mark appears on the image to show it's selected. To select additional images, tap their thumbnails or choose Select All from the Selection menu. Then tap the Share Via or Delete icon.

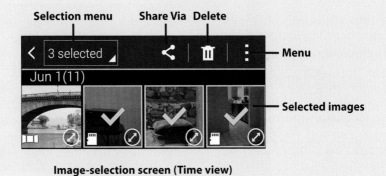

Image-selection screen (Time view)

Different Options for Different Image Sources

Not all actions can be performed on every folder. For example, Picasa and Facebook images can be shared, downloaded, or used to generate slideshows, but you can't delete them.

Image-Editing with Photo Studio

If you don't need the feature set of a dedicated Mac or PC image-editing program, you can use Photo Studio (a Samsung tool that's integrated with Gallery) to perform essential edits on any image stored on your phone. Note the following important tidbits while using Photo Studio:

- You can reverse the most recent edit by tapping Undo or tap Undo repeatedly to step backward through multiple edits. To reverse an Undo, tap Redo.

- If you tap Cancel while applying an edit, changes made with the current editing tool are removed.

- You complete most edits by tapping Done. Before you tap Done, you can compare the edit's effect to the image prior to the edit by pressing and holding anywhere onscreen.

- If you tap Discard (X), *all* edits are discarded.

(1) From within Gallery, do one of the following to open an image for editing:

- Edit the photo you're currently viewing by opening the menu and choosing Edit.

- Edit a photo that you've selected on an image-selection screen by opening the menu and choosing Studio, followed by Photo Studio.

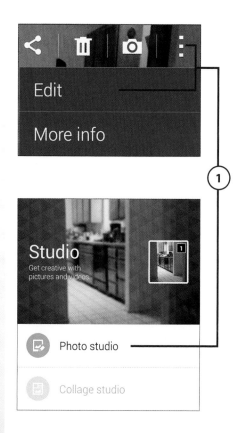

Make a Photo Collage

If you select *multiple* images and then choose the Studio command, you can select Collage Studio to create a collage from the photos.

2 Tool icons are displayed above and below the photo and are explained in the following steps. If the tools aren't visible, tap anywhere onscreen to reveal them.

3 *Enhance.* Enhance is similar to Photoshop's Auto Levels command, automatically adjusting tonal values in the photo. In some instances, tapping the Enhance button will be the only adjustment you'll need to make.

2 Undo Redo Discard Save Menu

Adjustment Tone Effect Portrait Decoration

4 **5** **6** **7** **8** **3**

4 *Adjustment.* Tap the Adjustment button to open the adjustment palette, enabling you to rotate, crop, or resize the image.

- Tap Rotate to rotate or flip the image. From left to right, the Rotate buttons enable you to rotate the image left or right in 90° increments, flip the image horizontally (left-to-right) or vertically (top-to-bottom), or split the image vertically to create a mirror image effect.

- Use a Crop tool to retain only a selected portion of the image, while discarding the rest. Tap the Free-form button if you don't want any restrictions on the cropping dimensions. To constrain the dimensions to a ratio, tap the 1:1, 4:3, or 16:9 button. To set the cropping area, drag the rectangle's edge and corner handles to change the size of the selection, and drag the center of the rectangle to reposition it. To create an irregular selection, select Lasso and use your fingertip to trace around the area you want to crop. In all cases, the bright area of the image will be retained; the dark areas will be discarded.

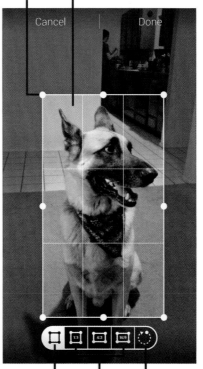

- Tap Resize to reduce the image size. You can tap a percentage button or resize manually by dragging a corner handle. The resulting size (in pixels) is shown above the image.

Size and Quality

Enlarging a photo results in some loss of resolution (clarity). However, the resolution loss correlates to a smaller file, which makes it easier to email.

Drag to resize   Percentage Handle Reduced
Marquee   reduction   size

(5) *Tone.* Tap the Tone button to adjust the contrast, brightness, saturation, temperature, and color attributes of the image. You can apply tone adjustments to the entire image or to a selected area. After selecting a Tone option in the scrolling list, do one of the following:

- To apply the Tone option to the entire image, drag your finger horizontally across the screen to increase or decrease the setting value.

- To apply a Tone option to a selection, tap the Marquee button, select a Marquee tool (Free-form, Rectangle, or Oval), use your fingertip to select the area that you want to affect, and tap Done. Then drag your finger horizontally across the screen to increase or decrease the setting value.

Before and After

To determine the impact of the new setting, press and hold anywhere onscreen to see the Before image. Release to see what it will look like if you tap Done.

Making Multiple Adjustments

If you want to make several tone adjustments, you must tap Done after each one. Otherwise, only the last adjustment is applied to the image. (Tapping a different icon is treated the same as if you tapped Cancel.)

(6) *Effect.* Tap the Effect button and select a special effect to apply from the scrolling list. To change the intensity of the effect, drag your finger horizontally across the screen. To compare the image with and without the effect, press and hold anywhere onscreen. Note that effects aren't cumulative; each one you apply replaces the current effect.

Selectively Applying an Effect

Like applying tone adjustments, effects can optionally be restricted to a selected area. Select any effect, tap the Marquee button that appears, use a Marquee tool to select the desired area, and tap Done. Then select the effect that you want to apply and, if you're satisfied, tap Done.

(7) *Portrait.* Tap the Portrait button to apply facial corrections (ideally to a head shot). To use the Remove Red-Eye tool, tap each eye that you want Studio to automatically correct. Out-of-Focus enables you to blur the background, making the person stand out. You can set the intensity of the active tool by dragging your finger horizontally across the screen.

No Zooming Allowed

You can't change the magnification when applying facial corrections. If you intend to crop the photo, do so *before* using the Portrait tools.

(8) *Decoration.* Select options from the Decoration button to apply decorative embellishments to a photo—adding a sticker, text label, frame, or freehand drawing. Note that many of these items can be resized, moved, and rotated.

Drawing with the Pen and Eraser

Use the Pen and Eraser tools together to do freehand drawing or write on the image. If you want to correct part of the Pen's drawing, you can remove it using the Eraser.

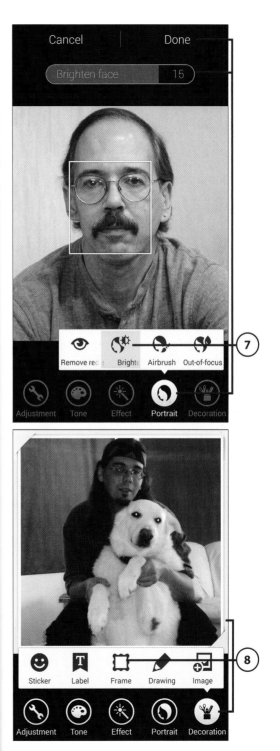

(9) When you finish editing, you can save your work. Tap Save, select a quality setting in the Save As dialog, and tap OK. The image is saved to a separate file in the Studio folder—not to the original file, which remains unaltered. The edited file is named with today's date and time. To rename the image, open it in Gallery, tap the menu icon, and choose Rename.

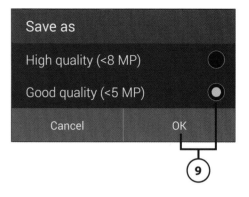

Running a Slideshow

You can create a slideshow with transition effects and music using all or selected images from one or multiple folders. The show plays in portrait or landscape mode, depending on the phone's orientation.

(1) In Gallery, select the folder(s) or images that you want to include in the show. (If you're reviewing a photo that you just took with Camera and request a slideshow, the Camera folder is automatically used as the basis for the show.) You can use any of the following file and folder selection techniques:

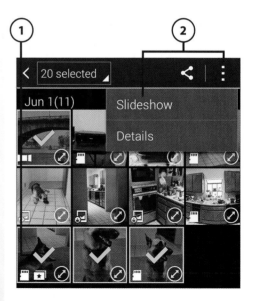

- On the main screen (in any view), select nothing to include all stored photos in the show, or select one or more folders in Album view to include all of their photos.

- If a folder is open, make no selection to use all of its photos or select the particular photos that you want to use.

2 Tap the menu icon and choose Slideshow.

3 Set options for the show in the dialog that appears:

- Select a transition effect to use when transitioning between slides.

- Select a filter to apply to each slide.

- Select a music track to accompany the show. To change the current track, tap its name. To run the show without music, set the track selection to None. Select a song in the Slideshow Music dialog box or—to use a track other than the listed ones—tap Add Music, select a song, and tap Done.

4 Tap the Start button to begin the show. To end the show, tap the screen or press the Back key.

Posting a Picture on Facebook

One major change in society in the last decade has been the ability to post pictures and videos in public photo-sharing websites, such as Facebook, Pinterest, and YouTube. Many grandparents get the first look at a grandchild when parents post a picture on Facebook. Many retailers post pictures of their products on Pinterest in order to create consumer demand. And many musical artists post videos with music on YouTube as the launch mechanism for their new releases.

For More Information

If you want a comprehensive look at posting pictures on Facebook, I recommend *My Facebook for Seniors* by Michael Miller (Que Publishing). This section only briefly covers the viewing and posting options.

View Pictures on Facebook

Pictures posted by friends automatically appear in your News Feed when you're logged into Facebook. You can also see pictures and albums posted by specific friends.

1. Open the Facebook app and tap the Favorites icon (the three horizontal bars) in the upper-right corner of the screen. Then tap Friends.

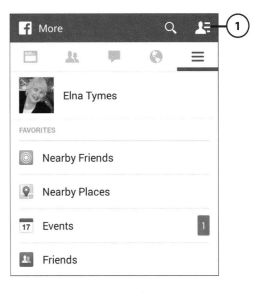

2 Scroll through the list; tap the name of a friend, and scroll down to find a picture.

Photo Albums

Some of your friends who particularly like photography might have created albums. To see the albums and scroll through them, find your friend's "wall," and tap the box labeled Photos. At the bottom of the page, tap Albums and then tap the name of the album you'd like to see so you can scroll through the pictures. To see a full-size picture, tap it.

Post Pictures to Facebook

Any photo that is currently in your Gallery is something that can be posted to Facebook.

1 To share one of your pictures on the Facebook News Feed page, tap the Photo icon at the bottom of the page.

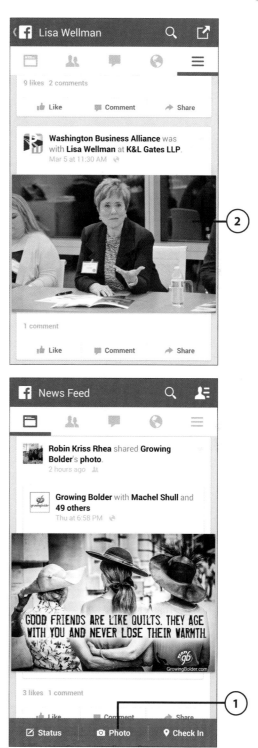

(2) Scroll through the pictures in the Gallery and select one or more to post. Selected photos are enclosed in a blue box. Tap the Use button on the top right.

(3) Write a caption and tap Post.

(4) Your photo appears on your News Feed.

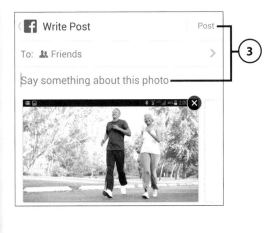

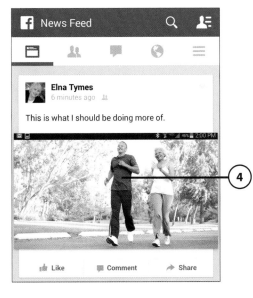

In this chapter, you learn how to use the Galaxy S5's built-in GPS app to help you navigate between points. Topics include the following:

→ Enabling and disabling GPS
→ Using Voice Search and S Voice to request directions to a destination
→ Exploring direction and navigation options in Google Maps
→ Configuring Location Settings

Travel and Driving Applications

You can use the phone's GPS chip in conjunction with Google Maps, the preinstalled location-based app, for viewing maps and getting directions between any pair of points.

Using the GPS

The Galaxy S5 has an embedded *GPS* (Global Positioning System) chip that enables the network to determine your phone's current location. When the GPS is active, the phone can use E911 emergency location services to transmit your location (see "Emergency Calling" in Chapter 4, "Using the Phone"). Some apps can use the GPS to provide information relevant to your current location, such as notifying you of nearby friends and businesses. The most common use of the GPS, however, is to run apps that display maps of your surroundings, provide turn-by-turn driving and walking directions, determine the distance to locations, and show you where you are in relation to your friends.

Enabling/Disabling GPS

As with Bluetooth and Wi-Fi, you can enable and disable the phone's GPS as needed. Because the regular polling of GPS drains the battery and consumes data, you can disable the feature when you aren't using it. Use any of the following methods to enable or disable GPS (Location):

- Pull down the Notification panel and tap the Location button to toggle its current state. Enabled Quick Setting buttons are bright green.

Notification panel

Enable/disable GPS

Settings

Quick Setting buttons

- Open Settings (switch to the Home screen and tap Apps, Settings or tap the Settings icon in the Notification panel). In the Personal section, tap Location. Tap the Location slider to toggle its state.

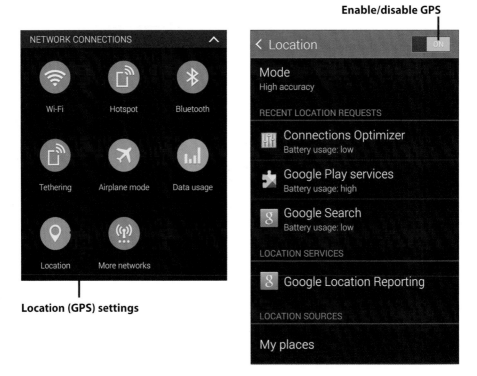

Enable/disable GPS

Location (GPS) settings

The Direct Route to Location Settings

The fastest way to go to the Location screen in Settings is to press and hold the Location Quick Setting button.

- If you perform an action in an app that requires GPS (such as requesting navigation instructions or tapping the AccuWeather widget for the detailed forecast) but GPS isn't enabled, you are usually asked to enable it in Location Services. Enable GPS by toggling the Location slider to On.

> Current location
>
> Location services is disabled. Go to Settings > Location services to enable Location services.
>
> | Cancel | Settings |

Open Location Services Settings

Getting Directions from Google Maps

The most common use of GPS is to get turn-by-turn driving, bicycling, or walking directions from your current location (determined by the GPS) to a destination. Turn-by-turn directions and detailed maps are provided by Google Maps. There are two ways to use Maps. First, if you know your destination, are in a hurry (already driving, for example), and don't care to set options, you can use a voice command to go directly to Maps' turn-by-turn voice navigation. Second, if you don't have a specific destination in mind (you might be searching for a gas station or pizza restaurant, for example), want to view a map, or want to set options, you can launch Maps and *then* specify the details.

Voice Search: Direct to Navigation

(1) If the Google Search widget is installed on a Home screen page, navigate to the page, and say "OK, Google" or tap the microphone icon. Alternatively, you can tap Apps, followed by Voice Search.

(2) Voice Search launches. Request directions by saying "Go to *destination*," "Drive to *destination*," or "Navigate to *destination*," where *destination* is a business name, street address, landmark, or city, for example.

Complete Action Using

If an app that provides similar functions to Google Maps is installed (such as Sprint's Scout) and you haven't specified a default app to automatically use, a Complete Action Using dialog box appears. Tap Maps and the Just Once button. To prevent this dialog box from interrupting *future* navigation requests, make Maps the default by selecting it and tapping the Always button.

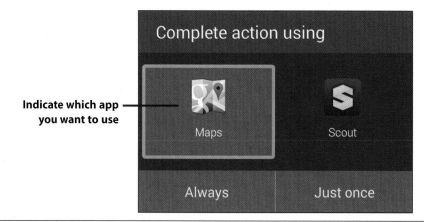

Indicate which app you want to use

(3) Assuming that Voice Search can identify an unambiguous destination, Maps launches, displays a route map beginning from your current location, and speaks the first direction. At each location change, Maps provides a new instruction.

Use S Voice to Fetch Navigation Instructions

You can also request navigation instructions using Samsung's S Voice. Quickly press the Home key twice to activate S Voice, or go to the Home screen and tap Apps, S Voice. When S Voice launches, follow Steps 2–3 from this task.

Launch Google Maps

Navigation and maps are provided by the Google Maps app. You can launch Maps using any method that's convenient, such as the following:

- On the Home screen, tap Apps, followed by Maps.

- If there's a Google folder on your Home screen, it contains shortcuts for every preinstalled Google app. Open the folder and tap Maps.

- If the Google Search widget is installed on a Home screen page, navigate to the page and activate it by saying "OK, Google." Then say "Open Maps."

- Quickly press the Home key twice to activate S Voice. When S Voice launches, say "Open Maps."

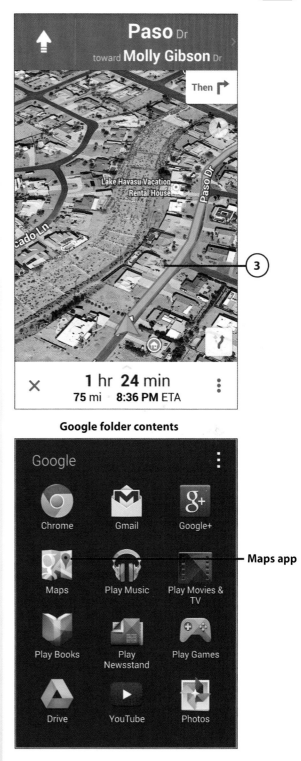

Google folder contents

Maps app

Set a Trip within Google Maps

Google Maps provides maps, text directions, and voice-guided navigation between any two points. When you want more control over options for your point-to-point trip, launch Maps (see "Launch Google Maps") and specify options within it.

The Order Is Up to You

The following task is presented in a *general* (rather than a specific) order. You'll find that you can perform most of the steps in any order that's convenient. In many instances, you can also step back to make changes by pressing the Back key.

1. Ensure that GPS (Location) is enabled (see "Enabling/Disabling GPS," earlier in the chapter) and launch Maps using any of the methods outlined in the previous section.

2. *Optional:* If your current location (represented by a blue dot) isn't visible on the map, tap the My Location button.

3. Tap the Directions icon to specify your starting point and destination.

④ Indicate your mode of travel (Driving, Public Transit, Bicycling, or Walking) by tapping an icon at the top of the screen.

⑤ *Optional:* To begin from somewhere other than your current location (as determined by the phone), tap My Location. Perform a search for the starting point or select it from the recently visited and searched locations.

⑥ Tap Choose Destination. Indicate your destination by typing, tapping the microphone icon and speaking, or tapping a history entry.

Try a General Search

In addition to searching for a particular business, you can search for a type of business by entering a search phrase, such as *gas station* or *dentist*.

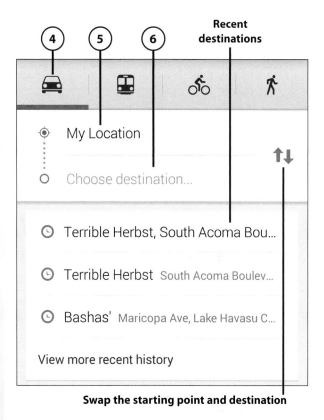

Recent destinations

Swap the starting point and destination

(7) Do one of the following:

- If the starting point is a location other than your current one, a list of routes appears. Tap a route to view it. (If desired, you can change routes when the map is shown.)

- If the starting point *is* your current location, tap a route to view it or tap Start Navigation to accept the proposed route in the miniature map and immediately begin navigation.

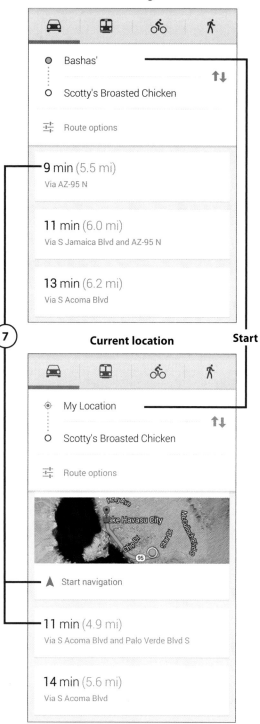

Different starting location

Bashas'

Scotty's Broasted Chicken

Route options

9 min (5.5 mi)
Via AZ-95 N

11 min (6.0 mi)
Via S Jamaica Blvd and AZ-95 N

13 min (6.2 mi)
Via S Acoma Blvd

Current location   **Start**

My Location

Scotty's Broasted Chicken

Route options

Start navigation

11 min (4.9 mi)
Via S Acoma Blvd and Palo Verde Blvd S

14 min (5.6 mi)
Via S Acoma Blvd

(8) A route map appears. Prior to beginning navigation, you can optionally do any of the following:

- Alternate routes are gray. To switch routes, tap one of the alternates.

- To view text-based directions for the selected route, tap the route description at the bottom of the screen or swipe it upward. When you're finished, press the Back key or swipe the text directions downward.

- To change the display, tap the menu icon and choose options, such as displaying a satellite view or a normal map view.

- To change the origin or destination, tap the box at the top of the screen. To *clear* the current trip, tap the X.

(9) Do one of the following:

- Tap the Start icon to begin turn-by-turn voice instructions. This option is only available if the trip begins from your current location.

- If you're starting from a different location, a Preview icon appears rather than a Start icon. Tap it to view the trip.

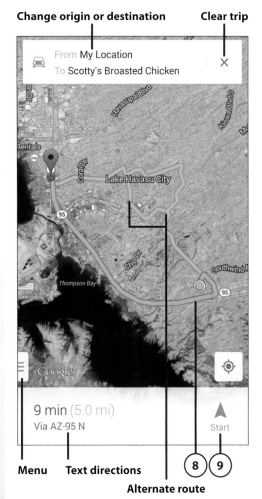

Change origin or destination **Clear trip**

Menu **Text directions** (8)(9)

Alternate route

Changing the Magnification

While viewing the map or navigating, you can change the magnification by double-tapping, spreading your thumb and forefinger apart, or pinching your thumb and forefinger together.

Configuring Location (GPS) Settings

There are several ways that your phone can determine your location. You can vary the Location mode, depending on your data plan and whether you're within Wi-Fi range.

(1) Open Settings and tap the Location icon. (Alternatively, you can open the Navigation panel and then press and hold the Location button.)

(2) Tap Mode.

(3) Select a Locating Method: High Accuracy, Power Saving, or GPS Only.

What Are the Advantages of Each Method?

High Accuracy combines information retrieved from GPS, Wi-Fi, and other mobile networks to give you the best possible estimate of your location. It also uses a lot of battery power. Power Saving only uses Wi-Fi and other mobile networks. GPS Only does not use Wi-Fi or other mobile networks. The latter two sacrifice accuracy, but they're better if you're concerned about how much battery power is being used.

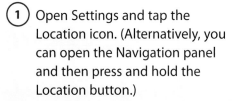

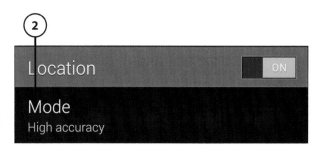

It's Not All Good

My Places

By tapping My Places at the bottom of the Location Settings screen, you can record some important locations (such as Home and Work) and add others, as well as specify a non-GPS method for determining these locations: Wi-Fi, Maps, or Bluetooth. Apps that require location information are supposed to be able to use entries in My Places in lieu of constantly pinging your GPS.

Unfortunately, *how* one gets the apps to use My Places is beyond me. For example, the Weather widget insists that Location be enabled to determine my current location—even though my Home entry clearly indicates my town. Even Maps doesn't appear to provide a way to set a Places entry as a trip origin or destination—other than Home, that is.

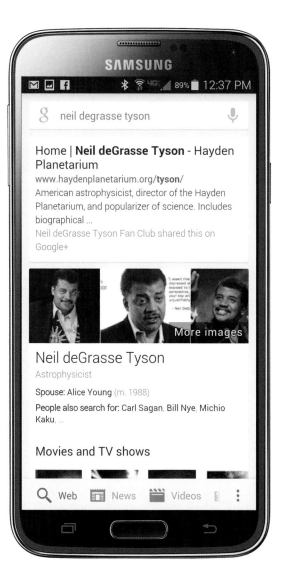

In this chapter, you become familiar with the mechanisms of searching for people. Topics include the following:

→ How to specify your search
→ Using free sites
→ When to use the Intelius sites

Searching for People, Places, and Things

Want to find what happened to your best friend in high school? How about that long-lost cousin? Even wondered how many towns are named "Podunk"? Or what "syzygy" means? One major benefit of the Internet is that you can look up anything and quickly find an answer. In fact, that's why search engines like Google were invented.

There are a number of search engines available, but the five most popular search engines are (in order) Google, Bing, Yahoo! Search, Ask, and Aol Search. Each operates in a similar way; how they differ is in how many searches they perform and where they look.

Your Galaxy S5 lets you use any search engine you choose, but the example in the next section uses Google Search.

Using Google Search

You can use Google Search to perform a text-based or voice search of the Web. The first time you use the Google app or the Google Search widget, you're asked to enable Google Now.

Enable Now, Disable Later

If you later decide that Google Now isn't for you, launch the Google app, tap the menu icon in its lower-right corner, and choose Settings from the menu that appears. Drag the Google Now slider to the Off position. Although Google Now is disabled, Google Search continues to function normally.

Perform a Text-Based Search

(**1**) Tap in the Google Search widget or tap Apps, Google.

(**2**) Type the search term or phrase in the text box that appears. As you type, potential matches are shown.

(**3**) If you see an appropriate suggestion, tap it to perform that search. Otherwise, continue typing the search term or phrase. Tap the search key when you're ready to perform the search.

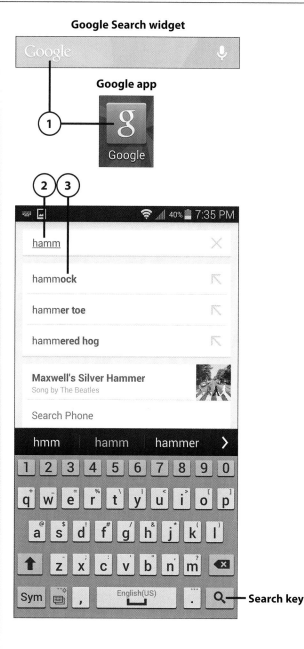

Google Search widget

Google app

Search key

Perform a Voice Search

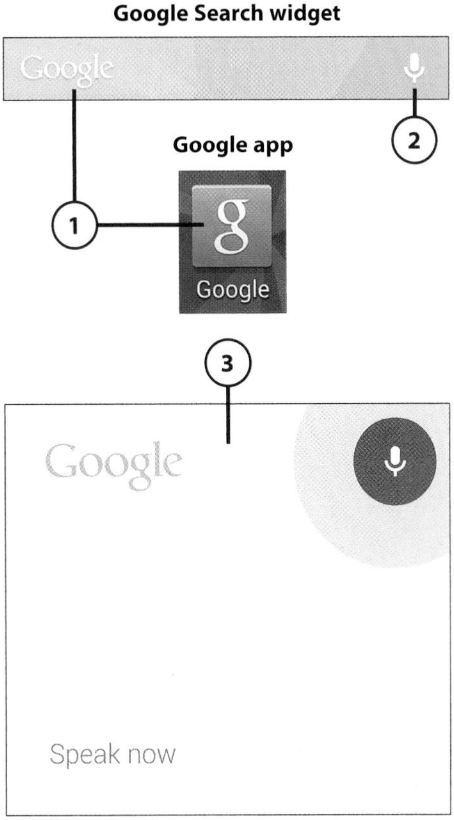

Google Search widget

1. Display the Home screen page that contains the Google Search widget, or switch to the main Home screen page and tap Apps, Google.

2. Initiate a voice search by tapping the microphone icon or by saying "OK, Google."

3. Speak the search term or phrase. The results are presented as a series of links.

Google app

Google

Google

Speak now

Specifying Your Search

If you're over 50, chances are you didn't learn about search terms when you were in high school or college, unless you took a Logic course.

(1) Search for someone by tapping the Google icon on your screen.

(2) Enter the person's name (for instance, Neil Diamond) in the blank bar. You can also tap the microphone and state who you're searching for.

(3) Scroll through the list to select the person you're looking for.

Searching for Places or Things

Use the same steps to search for places or things.

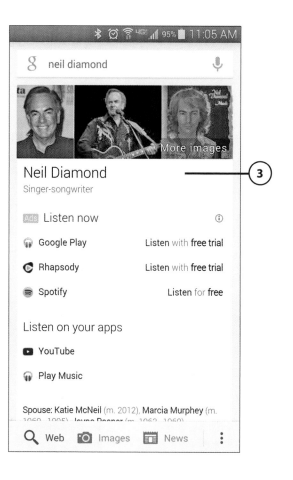

Search Techniques

You may want to modify your search using search operators or punctuation. Search operators are the words or symbols you can use to indicate the kind of query you have.

- When you search using an operator, don't add any spaces between the operator and your query. A search for **nytimes.com** will get you to the site for the New York Times, but **n y times.com** will give you different results.

- Use quotation marks to search for an exact word or phrase. This can be useful if you're looking for song lyrics or a line from a book. Use this only if you want an exact word or phrase, or you might exclude many helpful results.

- Put a dash (-) before a word to exclude all results that include that word.

- Get results only from certain sites or domains. For example, you can find all mentions of "olympics" on the NBC website by typing "Olympics NBC" or any .gov websites by typing *.gov for a government website.

- Find pages that link to a certain page by typing **link:** followed immediately by the page address. For example, you can find all the pages that link to google. com by typing **link:google.com**.

- Find sites that are similar to a URL you already know by typing **related:** immediately before you type an address. If you search for related sites to AARP.org, for instance, you can find other sites about people 50+ who you might be interested in by typing **related:AARP.org**.

- Add an asterisk within a search as a placeholder for any unknown or wildcard terms. Use an asterisk with quotation marks to find variations of that exact phrase or to remember words in the middle of a phrase. For instance, you could search for **"a * saved is a * earned."**

- Use OR (capitalized) between words if you are looking for pages that have just one of several words. Without the OR, your results will show only pages that match both terms. For instance, searching for **Super Bowl location 2015 2016** brings up results that include both 2015 and 2016, but searching for **Super Bowl location 2015 OR 2016** will show results that include only one of those years, as well as results that include both.

- For a range of numbers, such as dates, measurements, or prices, separate numbers by two periods with no spaces (..)—for instance, **flat screen TV $100..$200**.

When you search, most punctuation and special characters are ignored. However, there are some punctuation marks and symbols that work in searches, as shown in Table 20.1.

Table 20.1   Punctuation and Special Characters for Searches

Use This	To Do This
[+]	Search for blood type [A+] or for a Google+ page such as [+Chrome]
[@]	Find social tags like [@Google]
[&]	Find strongly connected ideas and phrases such as [peanut butter & jelly]
[%]	Find a percent value, such as [27% of 50]
[$]	Find a price, such as [Nike$100]
[#]	Search for trending topics by hashtags, such as [#funnycats]
[-]	Limit search to words that are strongly connected, such as [90-year-old-man]
[ ]	Connect two words like [quick_step]. Your search results will find this pair of words either linked together (quickstep) or connected by an underscore (quick_step).

Alternative Google Searches

In addition to the familiar search site, Google offers several other kinds of searches.

Do a Google Advanced Search

You can invoke a more detailed kind of search with Google by typing **www.google.com/advanced_search** in the space where you enter a URL. This enables you to narrow your search more specifically and is useful if you know your initial search will result in a lot of entries.

(1) Enter the advanced search URL, and Google displays the screen where you can enter how you want to narrow your search.

(2) Scroll down to see the second part of the screen, fill in as much relevant information to help Google find what you're seeking, and tap the Advanced Search button. Google displays the results of your search.

What Can I Do with an Advanced Search?

You can use an Advanced Search when you're looking up medical information, or if you're trying to find technical information about an engineering project. It's also good for finding historical information about a place or a person.

(1)

www.google.com/advanced_sea C 🗔 ⋮

Advanced Search

Find pages with...

all these words:

this exact word or phrase:

any of these words:

none of these words:

numbers ranging from: to

Then narrow your results by...

language:

any language   ▾

region:

any region   ▾

terms appearing:

anywhere in the page   ▾

SafeSearch:

Show most relevant results   ▾

file type:

any format   ▾

usage rights:

not filtered by license   ▾

Advanced Search   **(2)**

Do a Google Image Search

Google lets you search for images, too. Use a word or a picture as your search item to find related images from around the Web.

For instance, suppose you are writing a report about seniors and want to know if there are photos about seniors on the Web.

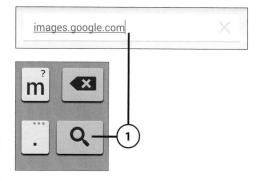

1. Enter **images.google.com** in the URL field and tap the search icon on the keyboard.

2. The standard Google search window appears, with the word **Images** under the Google logo.

3. Enter the word **seniors**. Tap seniors from the results list that appears and scroll through the pictures that appear.

4. Scroll through the images that appear and tap one you want to use to go the URL for that specific image.

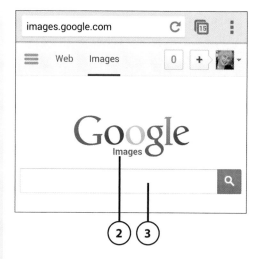

(5) Tap the menu icon in the upper-right corner and then tap Share.

(6) Tap Copy to Clipboard to save it to your Gallery, or choose one of the other options to post it elsewhere.

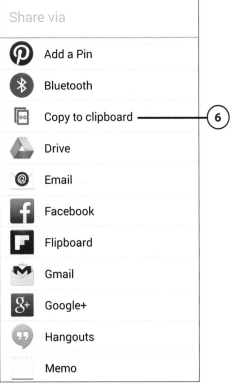

(7) Search by the image by tapping the menu icon in the bottom-right corner and then tapping Search by Image.

(8) Google shows you a list of sites that have similar pictures, as well as a set of pictures that are visually similar to the one you specified.

For Best Results

Google's Search by Image feature works best when the image is likely to show up in other places on the web. You'll get more results for famous landmarks than you will for personal images such as your latest family photo.

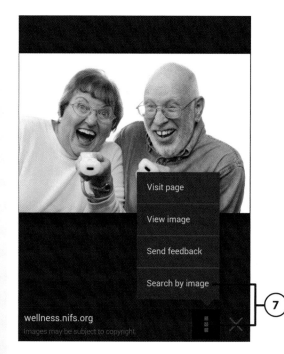

Do a Google Scholar Search

Google Scholar lets you search scholarly literature and find recent work in your area of research. It also shows you related works by citation, author, and publication.

Google Scholar is not for generic searches. That's what the Google icon is for.

1. Tap the Google icon and in the URL field type **Scholar.Google.com**. The Google Scholar search box appears.

2. Type your search term in the box, such as Alzheimer's, check the type of search you want (most of the time it will be Articles), and tap the search icon.

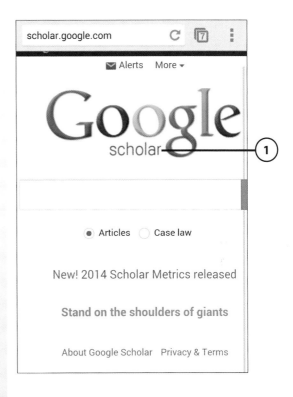

(3) You see a (long) list of articles referencing your search term.

alzheimer's	🔍

Scholar   Any time ▾   ▾

... of **Alzheimer's** disease Report of the NINCDS-ADRDA Work Group* under the auspices of Department of Health and Human Services Task Force on **Alzheimer's** ...

G McKhann, D Drachman, M Folstein, R Katzman... —————(3)
Neurology, 1984 - AAN Enterprises

Abstract Clinical criteria for the diagnosis of **Alzheimer's** disease include insidious onset and progressive impairment of memory and other cognitive functions. There are no motor, sensory, or coordination deficits early in the disease. The diagnosis cannot be determined ...

Cited by 20963   Related articles   More

Alzheimer's disease: initial report of the purification and characterization of a novel cerebrovascular amyloid protein

GG Glenner, CW Wong - Biochemical and biophysical research ..., 1984 - Elsevier

Summary A purified protein derived from the twisted β-pleated sheet fibrils in cerebrovascular amyloidosis associated with **Alzheimer's** disease has been isolated by Sephadex G-100 column chromatography with 5 M guanidine-HCl in 1 N acetic acid and ...

Using Free Search Sites

The most popular search sites are free, as are most specialized search sites.

(**1**) Do a Google search for Zabasearch, which is a good search site for name and address searches.

(**2**) Click Zabasearch and type the name of the individual you want to find, such as Neil Diamond, and tap Search.

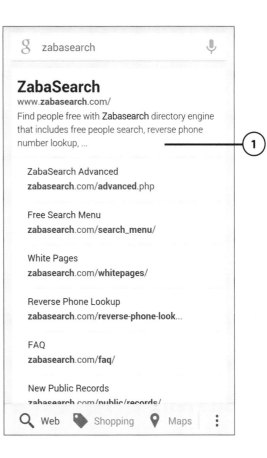

3 Scroll down to see more ways to find information about Neil Diamond.

4 Tap Background Check on Neil Diamond to see more information.

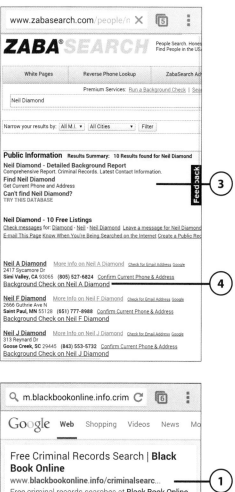

Check Public Records

You can use a search engine to check public records.

1 Use Google to search for **m.blackbookonline.info. criminalsearch**. When the Google search results appear, tap the first record.

2 Select the type of criminal record you want to see (for instance, the Sex Offender Public Web Site for an address in Seattle, WA). Tap the Search button.

3 For this example, tap the Sex Offender Public Web site, then tap the disclaimer at the bottom.

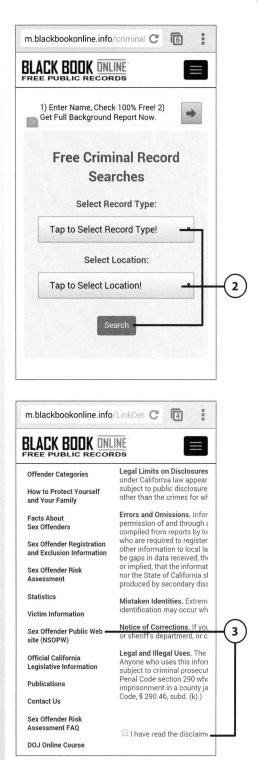

(**4**) After you enter an address, city, and state, the site produces a map showing where the sex offenders live within a mile of the specified address.

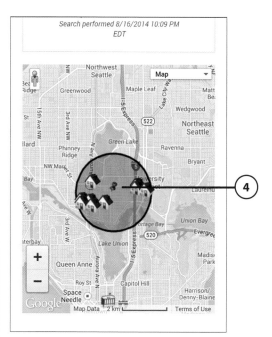

Search performed 8/16/2014 10:09 PM EDT

Finding Other Search Sites

You can enter **Free Search Sites** in the Google search bar to see a (long) list of free sites. Be aware that some of them offer limited searches for free, but charge for more detailed information, and some of them are known to carry viruses.

Be aware that some search sites charge for information, such as most of those owned by Intelius. Many of these sites access public information that you might be able to find by yourself after spending a lot of time searching; the paid sites can save you search time. You should weigh whether the information you want is worth the charge you'll pay.

In this chapter, you find out how to use your phone to view videos from a variety of sources, as well as to shoot and share your own videos. Topics include the following:

→ Streaming video over the Internet to your phone
→ Using the Video app to play videos
→ Converting DVD videos for playback on your phone
→ Recording videos with the rear and front cameras
→ Using dedicated video chat apps

Watching and Creating Videos

With the pair of cameras on the Galaxy S5, you can record videos of yourself, others, or anything that moves. The phone's high-resolution screen makes it ideal for viewing those videos, as well as movies and TV shows that you've extracted from DVDs, rented or purchased online, or streamed to the phone.

Streaming Video to the Phone

Streaming video is sent to your phone as a stream of data that plays as it's transmitted. Unlike material that you download, streaming requires an active Internet connection and doesn't result in a file that's permanently stored on your phone. If you want to watch the same video again, you need to stream it again. You can access streaming video through dedicated apps such as YouTube or by clicking web page links.

Streaming with a Dedicated App

The two common classes of streaming video apps are subscription-based and free. Examples of subscription-based apps include HBO Go, Max Go (for Cinemax), and Netflix. To access Netflix movies, you must be a Netflix streaming subscriber. To access HBO or Cinemax, you must currently receive HBO or Cinemax through a supported satellite or cable TV provider.

After installing and launching one of these apps, you sign in with the username and password that you use to log on to www.netflix.com, www.hbogo.com, or www.maxgo.com. (In the case of subscription TV services, your username and password are generally the ones you use for your cable or satellite provider's website.) The apps are designed to remember this login information, so future launches won't require you to reenter it.

Many other apps for streaming video don't require a subscription for basic access. Examples include Adult Swim, MTV News, and YouTube.

Depending on how the streaming app was designed, when you select a video to view, it plays in a dedicated player or in Video, an app that's preinstalled on the Galaxy S5. The controls most players provide are similar to the ones in Video.

Streaming from Web Pages

Video clips are embedded in many web pages. When viewed in the Internet or Chrome app, these clips play in a similar manner to what you'd see in a computer browser—although the controls might be different. For example, some embedded clips display only a progress bar. However, if you search carefully, you might find a Full Screen icon or a similarly worded link that enlarges the video and adds normal playback controls.

Full Screen

IT'S GONE!

The advantages of streaming are that the videos can be viewed on virtually any popular device (computer, tablet, phone, or iPod touch) that has Internet access. However, there's a downside to streaming. What happens if you want to watch a particular video or clip, but you don't have Internet access, don't want to rack up connection charges with your cellular service, or—if the unthinkable happens—the video is removed from the website or streaming provider's servers? The solution is to get a video capture application that can record a streamed video and convert it to a compatible format for playback on your computer, phone, or other device. Try a Google search for "streaming video recorder" to find an application that meets your needs.

Playing Videos with the Video App

Regardless of whether a video was downloaded, bundled with or converted from a DVD, sent by a friend, or rented or purchased online, all compatible videos stored on your phone play using the Video app.

Technically Speaking

The Video app is *not* the app that actually plays your videos; it's Video Player—a linked app, *but one that has no icon in Apps*. When you want to return from the Home screen or another app to continue viewing a paused video, press the Recent Apps key to see the list of active and recently run apps. You'll see that both Video and Video Player are listed. If you tap Video Player, playback resumes. Tapping Video takes you to the Video app launch screen rather than to your video.

(1) From the Home screen, tap Apps, followed by Video. (You are required to have a Samsung account to do this. You can sign up during this step.)

(2) To play a video that's stored on your phone, select the video by tapping its title or thumbnail.

Video Selection Assistance

To make it easier to find the video that you want to watch, your video collection can be displayed as live thumbnails, as a list, or organized by the folders in which videos are stored. Tap the menu icon, choose View As, and select an option. If you have many videos, you can specify a different sort order for the thumbnails or list by tapping the menu icon and choosing Sort By.

You can also open a video in Gallery, My Files, or another app. Doing this launches Video Player, enabling you to skip Steps 1 and 2. Tap the Play icon to play the selected movie or clip.

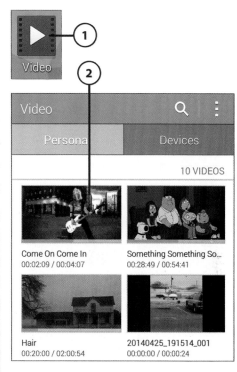

Sort options

(3) The controller appears and the video begins to play. Rotate the screen to the desired orientation: landscape or portrait.

(4) You can tap the screen while the video is playing to display the controller and then do any of the following:

- Start/restart or pause playback by tapping the Play/Pause button.

- Tap the Video Size icon to change the way the video is sized to fit the screen. Depending on how the video was encoded and the intended display type, some sizes may stretch the image in one direction, and others may clip the image horizontally or vertically to fit. Tap the icon repeatedly to see all display options.

- Jump forward or backward in the current video by dragging the position marker to the approximate spot.

- Tap the Rewind button to jump to the beginning of the current video or, if you're at the beginning, to the previous video in the list. Press and hold the Rewind button to scroll backward through the current video; the longer you hold the button, the faster it scrolls.

- Tap the Fast Forward button to jump to the next video. Press and hold the Fast Forward button to scroll forward through the current video; the longer you hold the button, the faster it scrolls.

- Adjust playback volume by tapping the Volume icon and dragging the slider that appears. (You can also change the volume by pressing the Volume control on the left side of the phone.)

- Leave the current video by pressing the Back key twice. To exit Video, press the Home key.

>>>Go Further

SMART PAUSE

If the Smart Pause system setting is enabled, you can pause the current video by turning your eyes away from the screen. When you're ready to resume, face the screen again. To enable or disable Smart Pause, open Settings and tap Motions and Gestures, Mute/Pause. Ensure that Mute/Pause is On, and then tap the Smart Pause check box. Smart Pause works best when you're not wearing glasses.

You might also want to enable the other Mute/Pause options, so you can pause a video by turning the phone over or covering the screen with your palm.

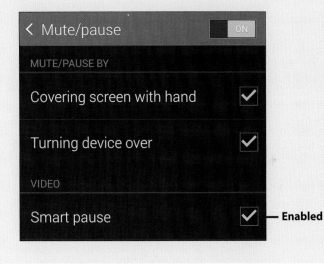

>>>Go Further
PICTURE IN PICTURE (POP-UP PLAY)

If you want to continue viewing a video while doing other things on your phone (reading email, for instance), tap the Picture in Picture icon. A miniature, movable version of the playing video appears on your Home screen. Use your fingertip to move the video to any part of the screen. If you switch to a different Home screen page or launch an app, the Picture in Picture video moves, too. (Note that this feature is only available for unprotected videos.)

To pause playback, tap the Picture in Picture video. Tap it again to continue, or tap the X icon to end playback. To resume playback in Video, double-tap the Picture in Picture video.

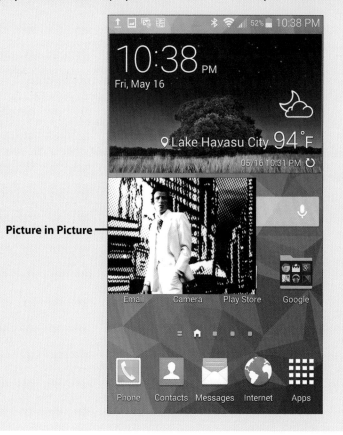

Picture in Picture

Using the Video Menus

On Video's main screen, you can tap the menu icon and choose from these commands:

Main screen menu

Select
Delete
View as
Sort by
Auto play next

- *Select, Delete.* Delete unwanted videos that are stored on the phone. Tap the check box of each video that you want to delete, tap the Delete icon or Done, respectively, and tap OK in the confirmation dialog box that appears.

- *View As, Sort By.* See "Video Selection Assistance," earlier in this section.

- *Auto Play Next.* When enabled, this option causes Video to automatically play the next video in sequence when the current one finishes.

While a video is playing, you can press and hold the Recent Apps key (or pause the video and tap the menu icon), and then choose from these menu commands:

Playback menu

Edit
Share via
Delete
Chapter preview
Listen via Bluetooth
Subtitles (CC)
Settings
Details

- *Edit.* Launch Video Trimmer to remove extraneous material from the beginning or end of the video, or launch Video Editor to create a video by combining photos and videos. You can add themes, music, voiceovers, and special effects. (If Video Editor isn't installed, choosing this command launches Samsung Apps so you can download and install the app.)

- *Share Via.* Transmit the video to others (Messaging, Email, and Gmail) or another device (Bluetooth and Wi-Fi Direct), or post it on a social networking or chat site (YouTube, ChatON, Google+, and Facebook). Note that many videos are too large to be shared via text messaging, email, or Gmail.

- *Delete.* Delete the current video, removing it from your phone. Tap OK in the confirmation dialog box.

- *Chapter Preview.* Displays thumbnails representing breakpoints in the video. When you tap a thumbnail, the video resumes at that point.

Chapter Preview thumbnails

- *Listen Via Bluetooth.* Transmit the audio to a paired Bluetooth headset.

- *Subtitles (CC).* If subtitles/close captioning are stored as part of the video file, you can elect to display them.

- *Settings.* Change playback settings for all videos, such as setting the brightness, switching to a mini controller, and adding an onscreen capture button to simplify the process of taking screenshots of favorite scenes.

- *Details.* Display information about the video, such as its file format, resolution, size, and storage location.

>>>Go Further

MORE VIDEO SOURCES

In addition to extracting videos from your personal DVD collection, there are other sources of ready-to-play videos for your Galaxy S5. You can rent or purchase videos in the Play Store, Play Movies and TV, Amazon Appstore, and carrier-provided online stores; some recent DVDs include a version for phones and other multimedia devices; and you can install software that can convert streaming video to MPEG-4 videos that you can play on the phone.

Recording Videos with the Phone

Using your phone's cameras, you can create movies that are suitable for posting on websites, emailing to friends, and playing on your phone or a flat-screen TV.

(1) Launch Camera by doing one of the following:

- Tap a Camera shortcut on the Home screen.

- On the Home screen, tap Apps and then Camera.

- On the lock screen, slide the Camera icon up (if present).

(2) Decide whether to shoot the video in portrait or landscape. Rotate the phone to the proper orientation.

(3) *Optional:* Switch between the rear-facing and front-facing cameras by tapping the Switch Camera icon. (Yes, you can make "selfie" videos.)

Settings Shortcuts

You can change the Settings shortcuts that appear at the top of the screen to ones that you use more often, as explained in "Configure and Use the Shortcuts" in Chapter 18, "Shooting, Editing, and Sharing Photos."

When You're in a Rush

You won't always have time to leisurely set options before you begin recording. If you're in a hurry to capture something that's happening right now, you can often make do by simply launching Camera, rotating the phone to the appropriate orientation, and tapping the Video button.

Settings shortcuts

3

Storage setting

(**4**) Tap the Settings icon to check the current settings in the scrolling Settings palette. Note that most settings are for photos and have no effect when shooting a video. However, you should pay close attention to these settings:

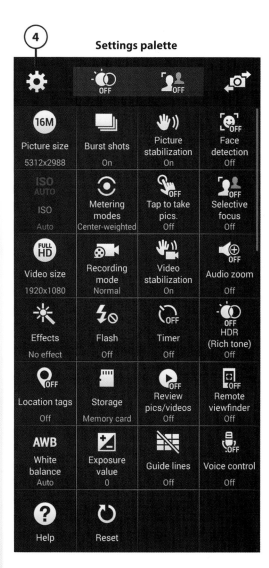

(**4**) **Settings palette**

- *Video Size.* Select a Video Size that's appropriate for the device on which the video will be played. Each setting specifies the horizontal by vertical dimensions (in pixels). For playback on a flat-screen TV in letterbox format (16:9), select any of the first three resolutions: 3840×2160, 1920×1080, or 1280×720, depending on whether the set or video monitor is capable of displaying UHD/4K videos (2160), full HD (1080), or only HD (720). Select 640×480 (4:3) for playback on the Web or for video that you intend to email. Note that the Galaxy S5 can play videos at any of these resolutions.

- *Recording Mode.* Tap the Recording Mode icon and select a setting. Use Normal for a standard recording and Limit for MMS for a video that you intend to attach to a multimedia (MMS) message. For a description of the other settings, tap the *i* (Information) button.

- *Video Stabilization.* Compensate for camera shake while recording. (Picture Stabilization, on the other hand, must be disabled while recording.)

- *Audio Zoom.* When enabled, zooming in on a person or object amplifies sound coming from that source.

- *Storage.* The video can be stored in the phone's internal memory (Device) or on a memory card, if one's installed.

- *White Balance, Exposure Value.* Adjust one or both of these settings to accommodate difficult lighting conditions.

When you finish making changes, dismiss the menu by tapping anywhere else onscreen, tapping the Settings icon, or pressing the Back key.

(5) Set the zoom level by placing two fingers on the screen and spreading them apart or squeezing them together. Note that you can change the zoom level as you record.

(6) Set the focal point for the recording by tapping the approximate spot or subject on the viewfinder screen.

(7) Tap the Video button to begin recording.

Information

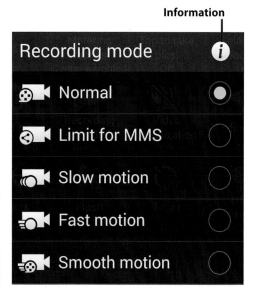

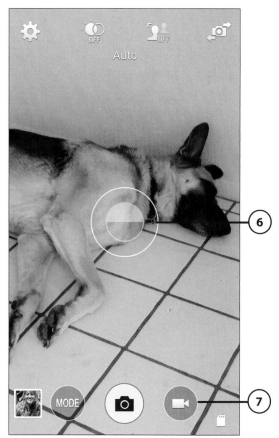

8 Temporarily pause during recording by tapping the Pause button. To resume recording, tap the button again. When you finish recording, tap the Stop button. The MPEG-4 video is automatically stored in the DCIM/Camera folder in the phone's built-in memory or on the memory card, depending on the Storage setting in Step 4.

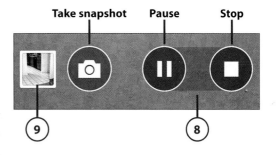

Take snapshot   Pause   Stop

9   8

Take a Quick Snapshot

While recording, you can also take photos by tapping the Camera button.

9 If you want to view the resulting video immediately, tap the thumbnail icon in the lower-left corner of the screen.

>>>Go Further

OTHER SETTINGS

Although you won't commonly use the following settings for recordings, there are situations when they can come in handy:

- With varying degrees of success, you can shoot in dim or even pitch black settings when Flash is forced On. Repeatedly tap the Flash icon to change its setting.

- You can apply an Effect (such as Grayscale or Moody) as you record. To download additional free or inexpensive camera and recording effects, tap the Download icon near the beginning of the Effects list. To remove a selected effect, tap the No Effects icon.

- Enable Guidelines if you have trouble framing your subject.
- When Voice Control is active, you can begin recording by saying "Record video."

Chapter 21

Participating in Video Chats

A final video-related use for your front (and, occasionally, rear) camera is participating in *video chats*—Internet-based conversations that combine voice and video. Not only can you hear each other, but you can also *see* the other person's expressions as he/she talks, as well as what's happening nearby. Because of the large amount of data exchanged during video chats, they're best conducted over Wi-Fi or between users who have steady, high-speed connections and unlimited data plans.

To get started with one-on-one or group video chats, launch Google Play (Play Store) and search for *video chat*. As you read the app descriptions, you'll note that many require you and your friends to use the same app and be on the same platform; that is, Android, not Apple's iOS. Some apps also let you chat with people who have a desktop or tablet version of the app. Regardless, to test any of the apps (other than those that permit uninvited chat requests from strangers), you need someone willing to download and try them with you. Skype is one such application that is well-known.

The Newsstand gives you access
to a variety of news sources

In this chapter, you learn how to use your Galaxy S5 to explore the news. Topics include the following:

→ Exploring online news sources
→ Subscribing to a news source

Getting the News

We briefly discussed in Chapter 16, "Adding, Removing, and Using Apps," how to use Play Newsstand to get the news you want, sorted by category. This chapter takes a more detailed look at finding the kinds of news you most want to read, how to subscribe, and how to recognize free content versus paid content that requires a subscription to access.

Using the Play Newsstand

The Google Play Newsstand is your home base for accessing all kinds of news on all kinds of topics. Customized based on your own usage and interests, it contains online editions of mainstream newspapers, magazines to which you can subscribe (some are available for free), and much more. Even among those who have retired, there isn't enough time in the day to read everything available to you through your trusty Galaxy S5.

Change how news is organized — (Read Now)

Search for news

Default news categories — HIGHLIGHTS   NEWS   BUSINESS   ENTERTAINMENT

News stories available to read — Great Design Plant: Anise Hyssop Delights Licorice Lovers

Houzz
1 hour ago   Plant

Tailored News

The Newsstand behaves a bit differently based on how you've used your phone in the past and if you have set up Google Now. Your screen will more closely resemble the screens used in this chapter if you've configured Google Now and have logged into your Google account.

Navigate the Play Newsstand

To access the Newsstand, you need to either locate its icon on your Home screen, or go to the Apps page, as shown here:

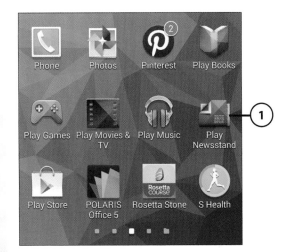

(1) Tap the Play Newsstand icon.

(2) Tap the Menu icon to change how news is organized.

Organization Options

You can organize your Newsstand homepage by Read Now, My Library, Bookmarks, or just Explore.

(3) Swipe left or right to change Categories.

(4) Swipe up or down to see more news stories on the page.

(5) Tap a new story to read it.

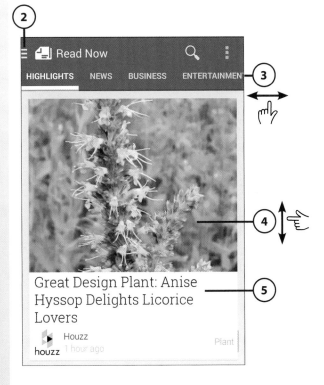

Explore the Play Newsstand

If you have a general idea of what kind of news you're looking for, but not the specific source, you can browse news sources using the Explore tool. To get started, open the Newsstand and follow these steps:

1. Tap the Menu icon and select Explore.

2. Select a Category.

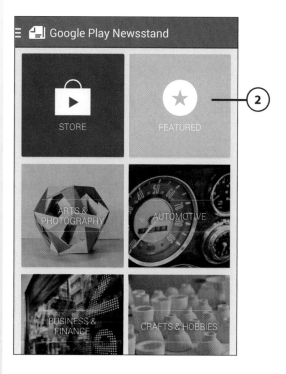

3 Choose a news source or magazine within that Category.

News versus Magazines

Sites with free content, like most newspapers and websites, open immediately and allow you to browse and read content, as described in the previous section. Paid magazines require you to purchase a specific issue or subscribe.

4 To purchase the current issue, tap Buy (the icon also lists the price).

5 To subscribe to the magazine, tap Subscribe.

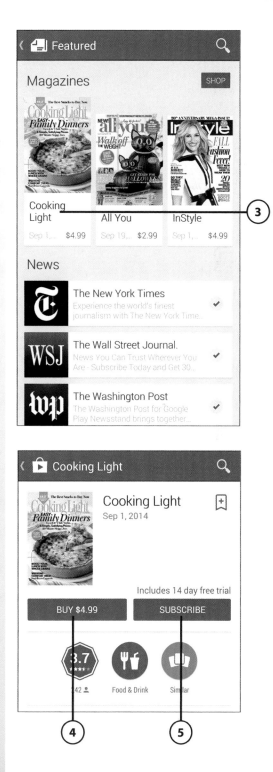

Subscribe to News

If you have some favorite news sites or magazines, you can subscribe to them and follow them from My Library. Open the Newsstand and follow these steps:

(1) Open the Menu icon and tap My Library. You'll see some sites already bookmarked, by default.

(2) Scroll to the bottom of the page.

Magazines

You can sort through your magazine subscriptions by choosing its category at the top of this screen.

(3) Select Add more.

Subscriptions

If you already subscribe to the print version of a magazine, very often this also gives you access to an electronic subscription at no extra cost. Some magazines don't support this feature, but many do.

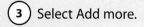

(4) Choose a category of site you want to find.

Searching

If you know the site you want to find, find it faster by tapping the Search icon and entering its name instead.

(5) Locate the site you want to bookmark and tap the + icon associated with it. The site is added to your My Library news page.

Adding Multiple Sites

You can add as many sites as you want from this page.

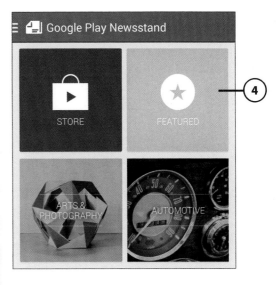

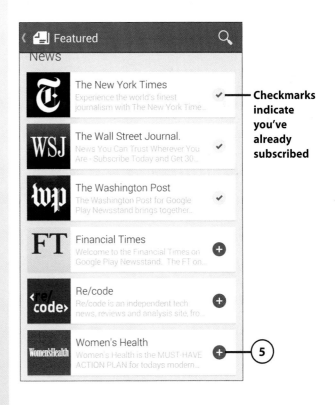

Checkmarks indicate you've already subscribed

(6) Tap the site in your library when you want to see its contents. (Refer to Step 1.)

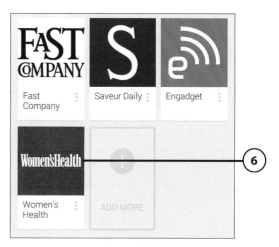

>>>*Go Further*

BOOKMARKING CATEGORIES

In addition to bookmarking sites to your library, you can also bookmark entire categories as well. Just open the Explore menu item, choose a category, and tap the + sign that appears next to it at the top of the page.

Bookmark an Article

If you find an article you want to save for later use, you can bookmark it. Just open the Newsstand and follow these steps:

(1) Locate an article you want to save and tap it.

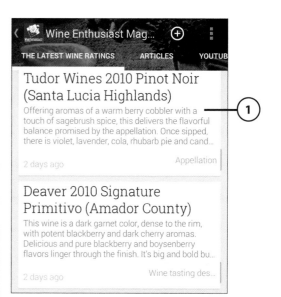

(2) Tap the + sign at the top of the article. This saves it at as a bookmark.

(3) Open the menu and select Bookmarks.

(4) Tap the bookmarked article to read it.

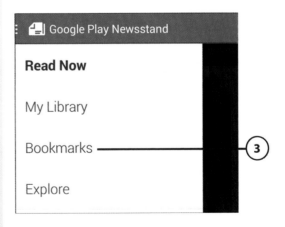

>>>Go Further
SHARING ARTICLES

In addition to bookmarking articles, you can share them in a variety of ways. Instead of pressing the Bookmark icon, as in Step 2, tap the Share icon immediately to its left. From here your Galaxy S5 shows you a list of apps you can use to share the article. This list will vary based on what apps you have installed, but it can include everything from emailing out a link to the article, to linking it on your Facebook wall, to pinning it to your Pinterest board.

Local weather information

In this chapter, you learn about the weather applications you can use on your Galaxy S5. Topics include the following:

→ Setting up your phone to localize weather reports
→ Setting up your phone to receive severe weather alerts
→ Using weather maps

Weather

As long as you carry your mobile phone with you wherever you go, you have immediate access to weather reports and forecasts. Ordinarily this wouldn't be a big thing, but if you live in an area where there are tornadoes or hurricanes, or if your area is prone to periods of intense rain and flooding, up-to-date weather information is important to you. And it's as close as your Galaxy S5.

Your Home screen shows you time and temperature and your location (by city). However, you can get more localized information by tapping the name of the city. This reveals another screen, which gives you more weather information:

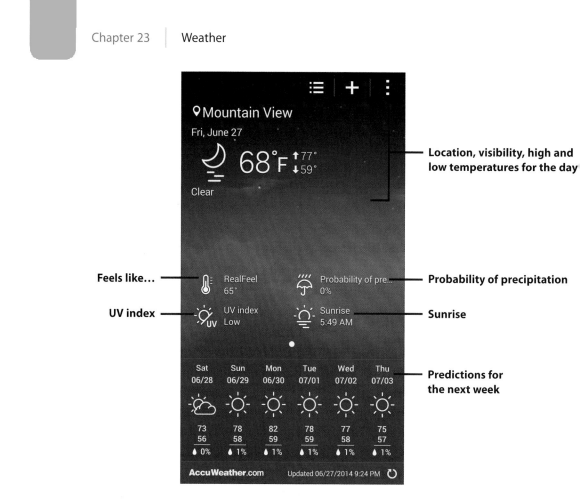

Location, visibility, high and low temperatures for the day

Feels like...

UV index

Probability of precipitation

Sunrise

Predictions for the next week

Setting Up Localized Weather Reports

The Home screen comes ready to report your local weather. However, first you have to tell it where you are before it can do so.

(1) Tap the Settings icon.

(2) Tap Location in the Personal section of the Settings menu.

(3) Make sure the Location button is turned On. When Location is On, most of the options on the page are enabled.

You Can Always Be Found

The Emergency 911 location can't be turned off. This means that your emergency locator is working, even if you just purchased your Galaxy S5 and haven't enabled your location yet.

(4) Tap Google Location Reporting to check the status of your phone and to see if a history log is being maintained about your location.

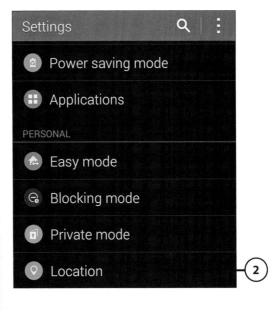

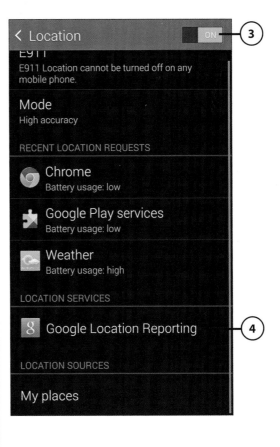

(5) You can turn off Location
Reporting and Location History
by tapping on each and then sliding the button to Off.

But I Want To Be Alone!

If you want to be sure you won't get
location-based email, or you really
want to hide your location from people
who want to find you, you can turn off
Google Location Reporting. The only
aspect of location reporting you cannot turn off is the kind of emergency
reporting that happens when you dial
911.

(6) To establish a list of locations
where your Galaxy S5 can
find you, tap My Places on the
Location screen.

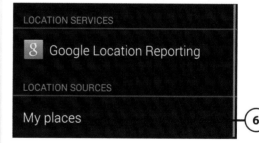

7 Tap Home.

8 Tap Select Method to tell your Galaxy S5 how to determine where you are, and then select the appropriate method:

- *Maps* tells your Galaxy S5 to look at Google Maps to determine your location.

- *Wi-Fi* tells your Galaxy S5 to look up the location of your current Wi-Fi connection and use that as your location. If, for instance, you're currently connected to Wi-Fi in your local Starbuck's, you can specify that as your Home or Office location. Or, if you're visiting another city, it will show you the weather there.

- *Bluetooth* tells your Galaxy S5 to take your location from wherever your Bluetooth receiver is located. If this is in your car, wherever your car moves will be taken as your current location.

- The *None* option sets your S5 so that location recognition is turned off for that specific location.

9 Tap OK to proceed or Cancel to back out without making any changes to the method.

10 Repeat the process for your Work and Car locations.

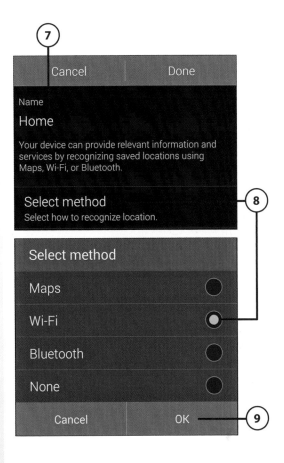

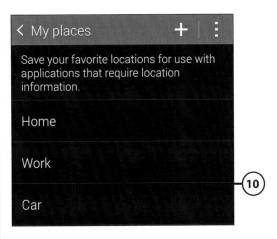

Receiving Severe Weather Alerts

If you live in a part of the country that's prone to tornados, hurricanes, or snowstorms, you know the importance for immediate, accurate weather information.

Before You Get Started

The first time you access Messages, you will see a warning asking if you want to change the messaging app from Messages+ to Messages. For now, answer No. You can go back later and change the app to Messages+ when you have finished setting up your other apps.

1 Tap the Apps icon and then tap the Emergency Alerts icon.

2 Tap the menu icon and select Settings.

(3) Tap Emergency Alert Tone to test the default emergency tone. (Warning: It's loud!)

(4) Tap Alert Types and select the kinds of alerts you want to hear about.

- *Presidential Alerts* are things like 911 alerts, assassinations, or other national emergencies. You don't get to choose to receive those.

- *Extreme Alerts* are situations where, for example, a fire or a tornado is headed for your home and your life and property are at peril.

- *Severe Alerts* are often weather alerts about hurricanes or severe thunderstorms or heavy rainfall that could lead to flooding.

- *Amber Alerts* are warnings about local child abductions.

‹ Settings

Alert types ──── **(4)**
Receiving all alert types.

Emergency alert tone ──── **(3)**
Play a sample emergency alert tone.

Vibrate ✓
Vibrate for emergency alerts.

Alert reminder
Off

Speak alert message ☐
Read emergency messages aloud with text-to-speech.

‹ Alert types

Presidential alerts
Presidential alerts are mandatory and always enabled.

Extreme alerts ✓ ──── **(4)**
Receive alerts for extreme threats to life and property.

Severe alerts ✓
Receive alerts for severe threats to life and property.

AMBER alerts ☐
Receive alerts for child abduction emergencies.

The Weather Source

Weather information for your Galaxy S5 is provided by a connection to AccuWeather.com, which has more information on its website at m.accuweather.com. This may be useful in seeing whether a source of tornadoes is headed your way, or if the snowstorm on its way to your home has an ice storm associated with it.

Using Weather Maps

You can see weather maps from AccuWeather on your Galaxy S5. The simplest one is local temperatures across the continental United States and parts of Central and South America. (However, you can scroll around the map in order to see other cities.)

(1) On the Home Screen tap the city to bring up the local weather.

(2) Tap the menu icon and tap Weather Map.

(3) The map takes a few minutes to load but then shows you the current temperature for your current location, as well as current temperatures in other major cities.

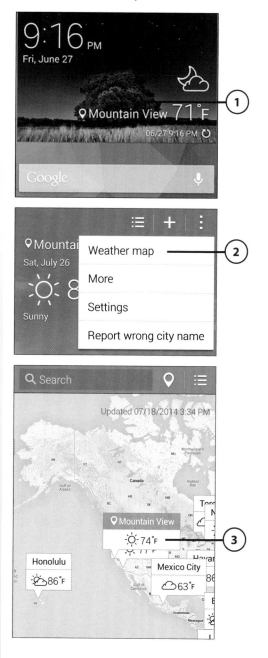

(4) Tap any city name to see a weather forecast for that city. For instance, if you're interested in going to Hawaii on vacation, slide the map around and tap on Honolulu.

(5) You see the local forecast for Honolulu.

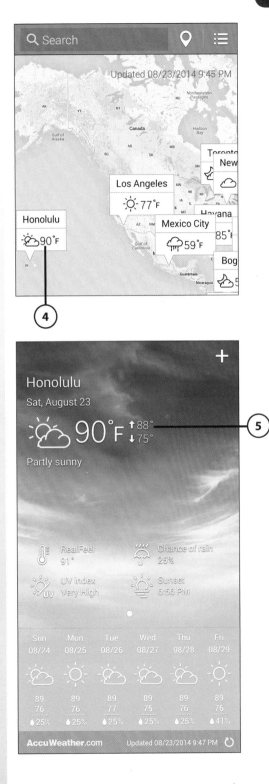

Number of steps taken   Number of calories burned   Number of calories eaten

Menu

Number of steps taken   Amount of exercise   Heart rate monitor   Other health apps you have installed

In this chapter, you learn about using the health-monitoring app on the Galaxy S5 and finding other health-related apps:

→ Setting up S Health
→ Using the Pedometer
→ Using the Exercise Record
→ Using the Heart Rate Monitor
→ Setting up your music
→ Working with health apps

24

Monitoring Your Health

You can use your Galaxy S5 to monitor your health and create a fitness program and goals. You can track your physical activity, calories, stress, and sleep patterns. You can also set up music to listen to while you exercise.

Using S Health

S Health is designed to work with either data you enter or data retrieved from a monitoring device plugged into your Galaxy S5. It has one built-in monitor: the heart rate monitor located on the back of your Galaxy S5.

Set Up S Health

1. Tap the Apps icon and then tap the S Health icon.

2. Tap the menu icon and select Settings.

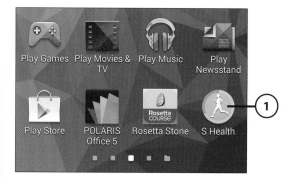

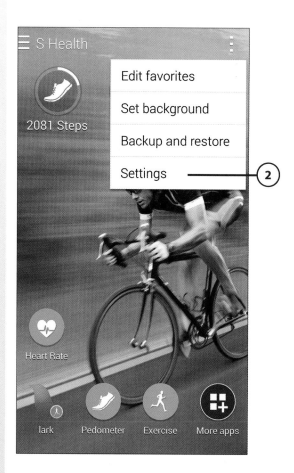

3 Tap Profile to view statistics, such as your height, weight, BMI, and normal amount of exercise. Metrics for amount of recommended exercise, heart rate, and other measurements are taken from this. Tap the left arrow to go back to the Settings screen when you're done.

Entering Your Statistics

To initially enter your height, weight, and so on, or to make adjustments when the data changes, tap the pencil icon in the upper-right corner of the screen.

4 Tap Accounts to back up and restore your health data to your Samsung account. You can also see where you rank compared to other Galaxy S5 users and other users in your age bracket. (Read Chapter 7, "Setting Up Accounts," for more information about getting a Samsung account.)

5 Tap Password to set a special password for your S Health data that's different from your Galaxy S5 password, your Samsung account, or any other passwords used with S5 apps.

6 Tap Unit Settings to directly change your height and weight from pounds to kilograms, and feet and inches to centimeters, rather than doing it on the Profile screen. In addition, if you're setting distance goals (for running or biking, for example), you can change it here.

Tap to go back to the Settings screen

Tap to make adjustments to the data

Owner of this profile

Birthdate

Height

Weight

BMI

Normal activity level

7 Tap Notification to toggle on or off your health notifications.

Turning Notifications On and Off

If you set goals for yourself, such as a certain number of steps a day with your pedometer or a distance or calories burned goal for bicycling, and you don't meet those goals, you can turn on Use notifications to remind yourself of the goals you set. You'll get a message every day that you don't do what you set out to do.

8 Tap My Accessories to identify any accessories, such as a pedometer, pulse indicator, or heart rate monitor, so that you have their measurements that can be used by S Health.

9 Tap Reset Data to reset data about your pedometer, exercise amount, heart rate, food intake, weight, amount of sleep, amount of stress, and your S Health "coach."

< Settings

GENERAL

Profile

Accounts

Password

Unit settings
Select the units to use in S Health.

Notification   ✓ — **7**
Receive notifications of new events.

ACCESSORIES

My accessories   — **8**

Compatible accessories

DATA

ACCESSORIES

My accessories

Compatible accessories

DATA

Reset data   — **9**

INFORMATION

Check for updates

>>>Go Further

HEY COACH!

Your Galaxy S5 comes with a personalized coach, ready to give you advice and activities to help your progress toward your exercise goals. Tap on the three bars in the upper left of the first S Health screen to pull up your profile. Tap Coach to see what your coach has to say today. If this is your first session with your coach, you'll need to answer some questions to help the coach tailor a program just for you. When you finish the session, your coach produces a set of suggestions such as the ones shown here.

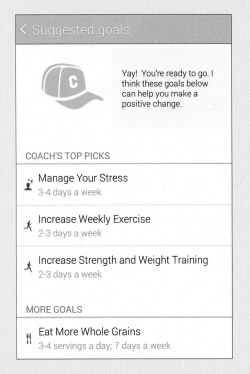

Based on goals you set for yourself, your coach may also send you daily or weekly reminders about things you can do to help you reach your goals.

Use the Pedometer

Your Galaxy S5 has a built-in pedometer to measure the number of steps you take during your exercise. You simply need to be carrying it as you exercise.

(**1**) To measure the number of steps, tap the Pedometer icon on the opening S Health screen.

(**2**) As long as you're moving, the Pedometer counts the number of steps you've taken.

(**3**) Tap the Pause button to take time out in your step counting (to stop for coffee, for instance). When you're ready to resume, tap the Pause button again.

(**4**) If you want to record your daily steps, press the trophy icon in the lower-right corner. You'll be prompted for your Samsung account information.

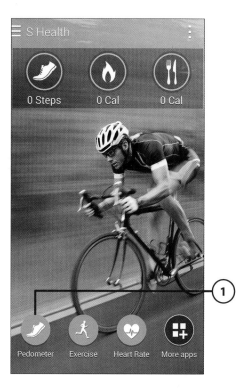

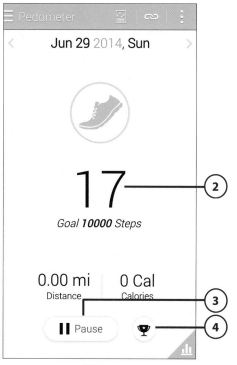

Use the Exercise Record

You can track the number of calories you burn based on the specific type of exercise you do.

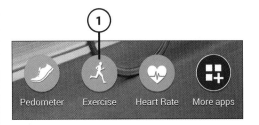

1. Tap the Exercise icon.
2. Tap the icon related to the type of exercise you'll be doing.
3. Tap the Basic Workout bar.

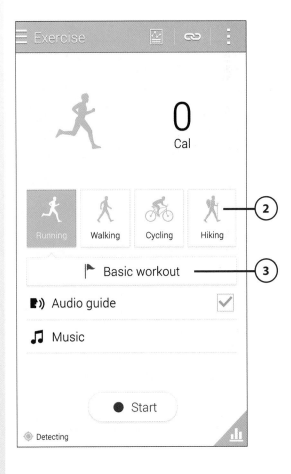

(4) Tap Distance Goal to set a goal based on the distance you want to go during your exercise.

(5) Slide the green bar along the ruler to set your goal for this exercise period.

(6) Tap Save.

Alternative Goals

You can also set goals for time, calories burned, and training effect if you prefer to track your workout using one of those methods.

(7) Tap the left arrow on the Set Workout Goal screen to go back to the general Exercise screen.

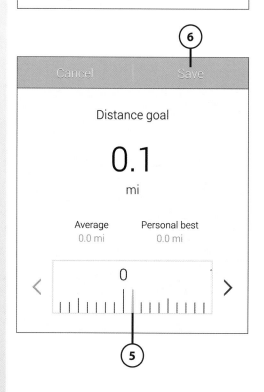

(7)

< Set workout goal

Basic workout
Set a workout with no goals.

Distance goal ——————————— **(4)**
Set how far you want to run/walk/cycle/hike.

Time goal
Set how long you want your workout to last.

Calorie goal
Set how many calories you want to burn.

Training effect goal
Set the effect you want your training to have. Connect a heart rate monitor to start your workout with this goal.

(6)

Cancel   Save

Distance goal

0.1

mi

Average   Personal best
0.0 mi   0.0 mi

< 0 >

(5)

8 Tap the box next to Audio Guide to turn it on and configure it to your preferences.

9 Tap the Start button. When you're finished with your exercise session, tap the Done button. This records your performance, the route you took, and other data if you want to use it again.

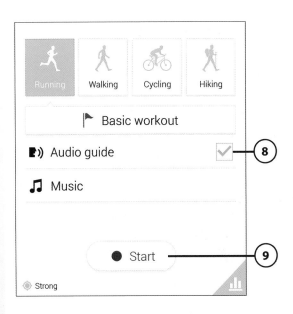

Use the Heart Rate Monitor

The only built-in health monitor on the Galaxy S5 is the heart rate monitor on the back of the device. It's located just below the camera, and when activated, it measures your number of heart beats per minute.

1 Tap the Heart Rate icon.

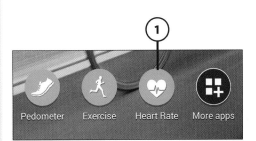

2 Follow the instructions on the screen. Check the Do not show again box and tap OK when you're ready to begin.

3 Place your finger over the sensor on the back of the Galaxy S5 and hold it there for 10 seconds. Try not to move during this time.

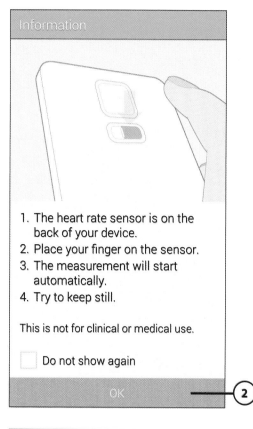

Information

1. The heart rate sensor is on the back of your device.
2. Place your finger on the sensor.
3. The measurement will start automatically.
4. Try to keep still.

This is not for clinical or medical use.

☐ Do not show again

OK ———— **2**

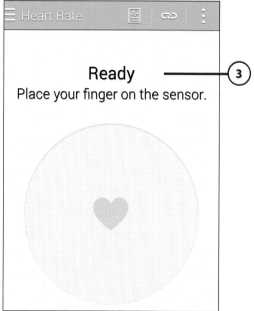

☰ Heart Rate

Ready ———— **3**
Place your finger on the sensor.

(**4**) When you remove your finger, the screen shows your heart beats per minute.

Try, Try Again

You might need to try several times to get a reading. If your first attempt doesn't succeed, try positioning your finger differently, or try using a different finger. The thumb seems to work very well.

(**5**) If the reading was successful, a message will appear on the front of the screen. The previous reading is at the bottom of the screen.

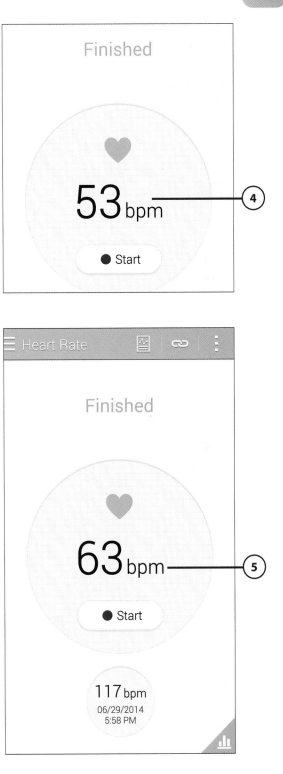

Setting Up Your Music

You can set up music to play through earbuds, or just play on the Galaxy S5, while you exercise.

(1) From any exercise screen, tap the Audio Guide bar to turn it on.

(2) Tap the Music bar.

(3) What appears on the Music screen depends on what's been loaded onto your Galaxy S5. The screen shown here shows what it looks like when your Galaxy S5 is brand new.

Loading the Playlist

Load your playlist with whatever you want to hear, press the Start button (the triangle in the middle at the bottom of the screen), and start your exercise. When you finish your exercise tap the double bars where the Start button was.

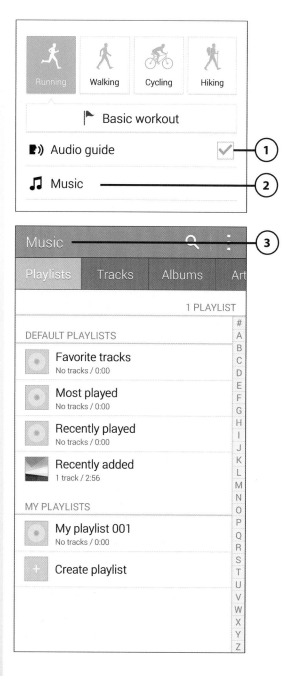

>>>Go Further

WORKING WITH HEALTH APPS

There are a number of health apps available on the market that work with your Galaxy S5. Some work only with monitoring devices; some are independent. Tap the More Apps icon on the S Health home screen to see the installed health apps.

- *Workout Trainer* is a subscription-based service that lets you choose from a menu of workouts. It comes with a free six-month trial period.

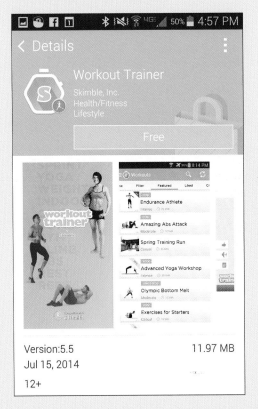

- *Lark Activity Tracker* is a free app that tracks your progress over a period of time, such as a month. You need only to carry your Galaxy S5 with you as you exercise to get the measurements.

You can also search the Play Store to find other apps that will help you make the most out of your exercise routine.

Index